DISCOVERING HAPPINESS

"HAPPINESS BEGINS ON THE INSIDE
AND FLOWS OUT, IT DOESN'T EXIST ON
THE OUTSIDE AND FLOW IN."
Dennis Wholey

"Happiness is having a sense of self—
not a feeling of being perfect
but of being good enough
and knowing that you are in a process of
growth,
of being, of achieving levels of joy . . ."
Leo Buscaglia

"An ongoing relationship with the same people
is the key to happiness . . .
A lot of people are getting the message
that happiness is not
the equivalent of a higher salary . . ."
Rabbi Harold S. Kushner

"One key to happiness is,
of course, that you're healthy.
Another key is to be appreciative
of the things you have.
You have to be grateful
and have a sense of appreciation
and not be one of those people who say,
'Is there anything else?' "
Willard Scott

"To be happy,
it's terribly important to find the kind of work
you really love to do."
Julia Child

"Happiness involves self-respect
and having some feeling of value.
It also means having an impact on the world,
whatever form that takes.
It may be the ability
to make very good bookcases
or it may be running the best diner in town."
Gloria Steinem

"It all goes back to the fourth grade,
the first time I was on the stage.
I was running for class secretary.
I did impersonations of the people in school,
and the waves of laughter came.
To me it was incredible.
I made up my mind right then and there.
This is it.
I don't care what I have to go through."
Carol Channing

"To say that there's any age
at which you shouldn't take a crack at
something is foolish."
Malcolm Forbes

"When many people are in the 'in between,'
where most living is done,
they feel they're in a kind of doldrum existence,
which they can't possibly equate
with happiness.
Actually, they're happy and don't know it."
Theodore Isaac Rubin, M.D.

DISCOVERING HAPPINESS

PERSONAL CONVERSATIONS ABOUT GETTING THE MOST OUT OF LIFE

DENNIS WHOLEY

Cleveland Amory
Jack Anderson
Joseph Arends, M.D.
Edward L. Bernays
Ivan Bloch
Julia Chang Bloch
Joyce Brothers, Ph.D.
Leo F. Buscaglia, Ph.D.

Joan C. Harvey, Ph.D.
Margo Howard
Robert K. Jarvik, M.D.
Ken Kragen
Rabbi Harold S. Kushner
Eda LeShan
Og Mandino
Ashley Montagu, Ph.D.

Pat Carroll
Carol Channing
Julia Child
Max Cleland
James Coco
Marva Collins
Charles W. Colson
Norman Cousins
Ruby Dee and Ossie Davis
Agnes de Mille
Shelley Duvall
Wayne Dyer, Ph.D.
Malcolm Forbes
The Reverend Peter A. Fraile, S.J.
Martha Friedman, Ed.D.
Dick Gregory

Pierre Mornell, M.D.
John Naisbitt
Tom Peters
The Reverend John Powell, S.J.
The Reverend Vaughan Quinn, O.M.I.
Daryl Race, M.D.
Theodore Isaac Rubin, M.D.
Carole Bayer Sager
and Burt Bacharach
May Sarton
Dr. Robert Schuller
Willard Scott
Ted Shackelford
Richard Simmons
Benjamin Spock, M.D.
Gloria Steinem

Jack Gregory, M.A.
Helen Thomas
Congressman Morris K. Udall

AVON BOOKS ▲ NEW YORK

Published in hardcover as *Are You Happy?*

The author is grateful for permission to quote from ''The Work of Happiness'' from *Selected Poems of May Sarton,* edited by Serena Sue Hilsinger and Lois Brynes. Reprinted by permission of W. W. Norton and Company, Inc. Copyright © 1978 by May Sarton.

AVON BOOKS
A division of
The Hearst Corporation
105 Madison Avenue
New York, New York 10016

First Avon Books Printing: May 1988

AVON TRADEMARK REG. U.S. PAT OFF. AND IN OTHER COUNTRIES, MARCA REGISTRADA, HECHO EN U.S.A.

Printed in the U.S.A.

K-R 10 9 8 7 6 5 4 3 2 1

Dedication

This book is for my nieces and nephews—
Kerry, Mark, Pat,
Megan, Jane, Kate, Skef, and Sarah.
And for Midge, Peter, Elsa, Jessica, and Maggie Dawn.

Contents

Acknowledgments

My sincere thanks go to the contributors to *Discovering Happiness* who gave so freely of themselves. It is their book as well—a collective effort.

I am especially grateful for all of the efforts of my researcher and good friend David Dodd. This is our second book together, and once again David has gone the extra miles to make this effort a reality. The book would not have come together were it not for David's personal encouragement and professional support. It has been exciting to watch his own growth as an excellent writer and reporter.

Robin (Stawowczyk) Thompson handled all my correspondence, the bulk of the transcription work, the final editing, and the completed manuscript. This is our second time around as well, and Robin's contribution has been outstanding. I am most thankful for her excellent and enthusiastic work. Robin and I received an important assist with the transcripts from a good friend, Yvette Mandell, Sandy Forsyth, and the wonderful group at Proficiency Plus in Warren, Michigan: Linda Smith, Susan Pritchard, Barbara Frankowski, Christine Walker, Juanita Smith, Sheryl Smith, Mary Ann Lahr, and Doris Louie.

I would like to thank all who worked with me to set up the meetings and interviews with the contributors: Manuel Viscasillas, Dolores Bartlett, Lynda Long, Larry Smith, Matt James, Lou Tracey, Angella Carroll, Carol Braxton, Marjorie Kelley, Barbara Hagler, Nancy Fields, Eve Brandstein, Eda LeShan, Jokichi Takamine, M.D., Maya Labos, Nelson Keener, Norma Peterson, Bill Cadafee, Jr., Stuart Bloch,

Charles Lowe, Denise Anderson, Don Garson, Stephen Miny, Barbara Gervais, Debbie Neubauer, Heidi Pokorny, Lillian Gregory, Terrell Greene, Linda Harned, Marion Probst, Melissa Manson, Gail Miller, Jayne Pearl, Michael Branch, Laurel Altman, Opal Ginn, Ken Wilson, Jane Abbott, Marc English, Terrie Osborn, Kitty Witwer, Annette Wolf, Steven Short, Gary Wagnild, and the added efforts of Mary Ryan, Bob Lescher, Marge Murphy, Glenn Triest, Philip Movius, the staff of Celebrity Service, the U.S. Postal Service, Joan Pheney, and the Monday Night Group. I sincerely thank and apologize to anyone whose name I may have omitted.

Many people at Houghton Mifflin contributed to *Are You Happy?** I especially thank Austin Olney for his continuing belief in my work and his support for me as an author. Larry Kessenich made excellent suggestions to improve my efforts, and manuscript editor Gerry Morse performed efficiently with her green pencil to help make the words flow. My thanks also go to Tira Nelson and Cary Wyman in Austin Olney's office, manuscript editing supervisor Sarah Flynn, Larry Cooper, Mary Troeger, Steve Lewers, Carolyn Amussen, Marly Rusoff, Susan O'Donnell, Louise Noble, Bob Overholtzer, Anne Chalmers, Steve Pekich, Diane Higgins, as well as to the typesetters, proofreaders, and members of the sales and publicity staffs—with an assist from Lisl Cade. They played a major role in the publication of this book.

My agents, Richard and Arthur Pine, have become very special to me, and I appreciate their friendship and professional expertise and the efforts of their assistants, Lori Andiman and Eleanor Levine.

On a personal note I offer a sincere thank-you to three late friends who played a very special role in my life, the Reverend Gilbert V. Hartke, O.P., of Catholic University's Drama Department, Steve McCoy of New York City, and Jon Shortino of Apalachin, New York, and San Juan, Puerto Rico.

Once again, I owe a special thank-you to Paul Kasper for his support and to the many others who have walked the journey with me, especially Nonie, Dottie and Steve, Margie and, of course, my dear mother.

*_Discovering Happiness_ was published in hardcover as _Are You Happy?_

Foreword

Norman Cousins is the former editor of Current History *and* Saturday Review. *He is the distinguished author of many books, including* Modern Man Is Obsolete, Who Speaks for Man?, The Celebration of Life, *and* Anatomy of an Illness. *Among his many awards and honors are the Eleanor Roosevelt peace award, the Family of Man award, and the U.N. Peace Medal. Norman Cousins is adjunct professor in the school of medicine at the University of California at Los Angeles.*

Happiness is probably the easiest emotion to feel, the most elusive to create deliberately, and the most difficult to define. It is experienced differently by different people. To some it is nothing more complicated than the absence of pain; to others enough money in the bank to cover outstanding checks; or babies who have stopped crying in the middle of the night; or having your bag come off first on the airport carousel; or sinking a thirty-foot putt on the first hole; or finding an Italian restaurant that really knows how to make a meat-free tomato sauce; or a chance to meet with your grown children on the basis of mutual respect; or a wife who is willing to put up with you; or being able to get words down on paper that say precisely what you want them to say; or being able to think sequentially about a problem, giving you confidence in the solution; or having a pretty young lady wink at you after you've reached the age of seventy—or any combination of the above. Whatever it is or isn't, just be glad you're around to think about it.

Norman Cousins

1 The Question

This book is about people and what makes us happy. It is also about all of us as human beings and where happiness fits into the life process.

No one finds happiness after a long search. Happiness comes to us as the direct result of positive self-worth, personal attitudes, specific actions, and the way in which we relate to other people.

Freedom to be ourselves, good feelings, satisfaction, contentment, peace of mind, joy, laughter, and happiness are the rewards of life. They are available to all of us for the doing—not for the wishing, asking, or demanding.

You may know me as the former host of the PBS television series *LateNight America* or the author of *The Courage to Change*, a book about alcoholism. I am an alcoholic. Once I realized that alcohol was the central problem in my life and I quit drinking, my life changed in a very positive way.

I was an unhappy adult for a long time, although I enjoyed some success along the way. When I finally set aside the alcohol (and Valium), I began to go about the business of growing up and becoming happy. As an unhappy person I looked outside myself for answers. Like most unhappy people, I blamed people and events and situations for my misery, depression, and sadness. I thought if I impressed everyone with my accomplishments, people would love me and that would make me feel good. I did that as a kid. I was the family comedian and magician, did shows in the living room, and got my applause. I'm sure that I became a television interviewer to continue the same act as an adult.

Unselfishness was not part of my personality earlier in my career as a television interviewer. Show business was a way to be noticed and get approval. For most of my adult life I pushed relentlessly toward my goal of hosting a national television talk show at the sacrifice of my personal life. I pushed at life with the same grim determination. As a patient in therapy over many years, I took more notes than the psychologists and psychiatrists did.

I thought as I struggled through life that if I were perfect everyone would respect me. I have come to learn that perfection is a horrible burden. Being a perfectionist takes its toll on those around us because we demand that perfection in others and they, of course, can't meet our expectations. In the end perfectionism drives people away. What I have learned in the past few years is that humanness is much more attractive to others.

In the past my life was ruled by insecurity and feelings of inferiority. I did many things to ingratiate myself with others to win their praise and love. My shyness was really self-centeredness, and my perfectionism kept me from trying many things. I am happy today in direct proportion to the lack of conflict in my life. I know now that most of the time when conflict arises, I have created it myself out of my own selfishness.

When I got out of my own way as a person and television performer, I did a better job. With the *LateNight* staff I became part of a successful team effort, and as an interviewer on the air I was able to get out of the limelight and help the guests shine. Five and ten years earlier, my motivation had always been to make Dennis look good. During the past few years on *LateNight*, critics, guests, and audiences, all seemed to agree that my work as an interviewer was at its best. I did my homework, cared a lot, let me be me, and stopped working at life so hard.

Until I left *LateNight* I kiddingly referred to myself as the second most visible nondrinking alcoholic in America. As far as I am concerned, anyone else can claim the top spot.

I was nervous the night I told the *LateNight* audience about my alcoholism. One of the rules of life I had learned backward was that to reveal myself would identify me as weak. I thought I would be considered less of a person. As it has turned out, my vulnerability is probably my greatest strength.

Some time ago I started considering the question "Are you happy?" on a personal level. I had the trappings of success but I questioned my own happiness. Several times after a *LateNight* interview, I asked the psychologists or psychiatrists who had been guests, "What percentage of American people do you think are happy?" The highest figure I ever got was 20 percent. The low figures surprised me because happiness seems to be everybody's number one goal.

Poet and writer May Sarton, whose thoughts on happiness appear in this book, believes that most nonfiction books are created because the author is confronted with a burning question. The writing of a book is an attempt by the author to bring some order from the chaos of reality. This idea was certainly true for me in putting together *Discovering Happiness.*

Personally and professionally I wanted to know what other people thought about happiness and the process of life. I was curious to discover what made happy people happy and learn their tricks of living. As with *The Courage to Change*, I thought, "Perhaps I can get a lot of happy people to talk about happiness, and maybe we can help a lot of unhappy people get happy."

During my career as a broadcaster I have interviewed thousands of guests, so I came up with a list of some of those I thought were happy. I also added some names of people who appeared to be happy, but whom I didn't know. From a distance, they seemed to me to have a certain spark. Some of the contributors in this book were suggested by others; one of the dividends of doing a book like this is meeting new people. Letters and proposals were sent out and the contributors to the book responded with enthusiasm. Little did we know the depth of the subject.

During the months I worked on this book, I had the

wonderful opportunity to travel across the country and talk
with the participants. They are all interesting people who
have made significant contributions to our lives. They are
human as well, and they have shared themselves willingly
and openly. We have laughed together and even cried together on a few occasions while talking about life and
happiness. The voices of the contributors are strong, so I
have edited out my questions. What they have to say needs
no intrusion from me. From them I have learned a lot.

There seem to be two kinds of people: positive or negative; happy or sad; participants or spectators. Happy people are optimistic and know that feeling good is the way
you are supposed to feel. They seem to operate on a philosophy of positive thoughts, positive expectations, positive action, positive results. They always look at a half-
full, not half-empty glass. Happy people accept life and
see it as an adventure.

Unhappy people always seem to want something different, while happy people like what they have. If happy
people don't like what they have they put in the extra effort
to change it. Happy people know that they must deal with
the world as it is and not necessarily as they would like it
to be. They understand that life brings some joy, some
frustration, some sadness, and some disappointment, but
they are confident they can handle everything life deals
them because of an inner sense of confidence and peace.
Happy people are involved with a variety of interests and
other people. They are the givers. They subscribe to the
philosophy of an old song—"Make someone happy, and
you'll be happy too"—and the saying—"Those who bring
sunshine into the lives of others cannot keep it from themselves."

Happy people are unselfish. They are not mired in the
bondage of self. They appreciate and respect themselves.
Happy people are outgoing, and they give of themselves
to others without expecting a payback. The net result is
that good things happen to good people. For them, happiness is an attitude; it's part of their being.

Unhappy people are consumed by anger and resentment. They are critical of others; they live in fear; they

worry and they procrastinate; they wallow in self-pity and depression; they try to change other people instead of themselves.

Abraham Lincoln said, ''Most folks are about as happy as they make up their minds to be.'' ''Easy for him to say,'' you may think. However, there is wisdom in Lincoln's statement.

There are as many varieties of happiness expressed in this book as there are viewpoints. It is possible that the value of what is here for you is between the lines and not even on the printed page. The spirit and the message are what is important. If faith can be belief in the experience of other people, there are lessons about happiness to be learned. You may find something that will work for you and bring more sunshine into your own life. I hope this book will cause you to examine your own life and your own happiness through the thoughts and feelings of the contributors. The ideas that introduce them are principles of living I have been learning for myself over the past few years and new insights I've gained while working on this book. Perhaps the questions asked will aid you in evaluating your own happiness.

Personally, I'm at my happiest when I contribute unselfishly to the lives of family, friends, and others. I do my best work when I'm more focused on bringing out the best in someone else. I like myself most when I'm fulfilling my own needs, my faith is strong, and I'm accepting and appreciating me. I enjoy others when I see their goodness and drop my own unreasonable expectations.

I feel good about this book. It caused me to take a hard look at my own happiness. In many ways it has already changed my life. There are some things I want to work on and I am putting in that effort. I know the best is yet to come because I now know how to be happier.

The writing of this book has helped me. I hope the reading of it will help you. So as we begin, the first question is, Are you happy?

2 Happiness

It is the people in our lives who bring us the most happiness. Family, friends, and co-workers who are part of our inner circle share our experiences, hopes and dreams, successes and failures, joys and pain. Too often many of us get on the fast track of life and take each other for granted. Many adults pursue success only to find themselves isolated and without friends. Loneliness in America is a national tragedy; it destroys lives. Since we were old enough to remember we have heard the old saying, "Money doesn't buy happiness." Yet we strive for the externals and pay a harsh price. The essence of happiness is the unconditional love we have for the people in our lives and their unconditional love for us. *Is my happiness tied to the important people in my life? How do I demonstrate my love for them?*

Rabbi Harold Kushner helps us to examine the quality of our relationships with friends and family.

Rabbi Harold S. Kushner, the senior rabbi of Temple Israel in Natick, Massachusetts, is the author of the bestselling books When Bad Things Happen to Good People *and* When All You've Ever Wanted Isn't Enough.

Rabbi Harold S. Kushner

Without any question, the key ingredient for happiness, in my mind, is an ongoing relationship with the same people in your life. When I could have left congregational work

and gone full-time into traveling, writing, and lecturing, I
would have made a lot more money in a much less emotionally demanding way. I couldn't do it because I'd be
living with strangers all the time. The importance of remaining in my job as a congregational rabbi is that I deal
with people I've known for twenty years. I see the same
people week after week, month after month.

The forty-one-year-old husband and father who walks
out on his family thinks it's his last chance at the brass
ring. He is so suffocated with responsibility, with mortgage payments, with being tied down; he wants freedom.
He thinks that's his breakout to happiness, so he leaves his
family, sells the station wagon, buys a two-seater sports
car, moves into a singles complex, and grows a beard. He
thinks he's going to gain happiness by shedding his responsibilities.

The real key to happiness is maintaining responsibility.
It's having an ongoing relationship with people who depend on you and whom you know you can depend on.
Having the same people in your life at a serious level is
essential. A friend moving out of your life is almost as
much of a loss as a death. The fact that such a person is
alive and functioning in Indiana means he hasn't died, but
he's still out of your life. There is a sense of loss, and
people don't know how to cope with that loss. People
don't understand. "Why am I feeling depressed because
my best friend got a promotion and moved?"

I have a sense, from my own congregational involvement, that there's less of this than there was a few years
ago. Maybe it's the economy changing or people changing or perhaps it's because more women are going back
to work. I find among my colleagues in the rabbinate a
lot less scrambling for promotion to a bigger congrega-
tion or a higher salary. A lot of my colleagues are saying,
"If I'm happy where I am, if I like these people, if my
kids are in good schools, if I can pay my bills, why do I
want twice as many members, which means twice as
many people in the hospital, twice as many people complaining to me, twice as many funerals to officiate at?"
A lot of men are saying, "If my wife has a $20,000 a

year job and I move for a $10,000 raise and she has to give up her job, I can't guarantee she'll find as good a job someplace else. What's the gain?'' More people are saying, ''I'm not going to pick my kids up out of their schools. I'm not going to pick my family up out of the good situation that it's in.'' I'm finding it's happening more in the early stages of a career. A lot of men in their forties are saying, ''I'll pass on that promotion. I'll stay here. I'll get my annual raise. I will move within the community in a job transfer that doesn't mean relocating my family.'' A lot of people are getting the message that happiness is not equivalent to a higher salary and more responsibility. A lot of people are looking at their bosses and saying, ''You know, I'm not sure I want to change places with him. He's exposed, he's hassled, he's got to take his work home.''

In a sermon about freedom and slavery, which is one of the themes of the Passover celebration, I said, ''Who are the slaves today and what's the definition of freedom today?'' In the time of Moses and the time of the Bible, slavery was a master who owned someone's body. In the 1980s, slavery is a master who owns someone's time. The person who does not control his or her own time is a slave. The person who has an income in six figures but cannot take off a morning to see a son pitch in the Little League or a daughter perform in a dance recital is a slave. That person may be a very well-paid slave, but that person doesn't own his or her own time.

The second ingredient for happiness, I think, is the sense of commitment to doing something hard. It's important to feel that your abilities are being challenged. In the same way that the body needs physical challenges, to get exercise, to push against something, I think our spirit needs challenges. We've got to do something strenuous from time to time. You have to measure yourself. You have to see how good you are. That's just every now and then. I found out when I was lecturing, for example, that I didn't need the high of a thousand people giving me a standing ovation three times a week. Once every other month was plenty.

If I found I needed it every day, I worried that I was getting addicted.

The third ingredient of happiness is not to be afraid of feeling. One of the things that keeps people from being happy in American society is that we are so afraid of pain that we armor ourselves. We anesthetize ourselves to make sure nothing hurts. We do it so well that we not only don't feel pain, we don't feel joy or hope or fear or love or anything else. We sleepwalk through much of our lives. We have deadened ourselves to our family, to our job, to our neighbors, to make sure that nobody can hurt us. The result is, we never know that we're alive. We have to go out and do something absolutely crazy to break through that numbness just to feel that we're alive again. When I say deaden ourselves or anesthetize ourselves, I mean we have taught ourselves to keep our distance emotionally. I have received many letters from women who told me that when they got sick or when they found out that they had a sick child, their husbands left them. A lot of men go into a marriage looking for happiness, and when they find out that marriage also brings pain and confusion and helplessness, that's not what they bargained for. I suspect these men didn't leave their families because they were cruel and unfeeling, but for the opposite reason—because they cared too much. It hurts so much to see somebody you love suffer. Men don't know how to handle that kind of hurt, so they run away. Whether through their fear of emotion or their fear of latent homosexuality, a lot of men get uncomfortable in a work relationship if somebody starts to get too close.

One of the things that really concerns me about the divorce rate in a community like mine is not the husbands and wives. They'll hurt, but they'll survive. People survive divorce. I'm really afraid that we are raising a generation of children who will be afraid to love. Because it hurts so much when it doesn't work out, they will look for intimacy without commitment and for reward without risk.

A couple came to see me in preparation for their marriage at the temple, and we were going over the ceremony. The young man said to me, "Rabbi, would you mind making one change in the wedding ceremony? Instead of our saying, 'As husband and wife till death do us part,' would you pronounce us husband and wife for as long as our love lasts? We've talked it over and we've decided that if we ever get to the point where we don't love each other, we don't think it's right for us to be stuck with each other." What they were saying to me, I think, is that if the marriage becomes painful, they want a painless way out of it. They want to shake hands and go their separate ways with no hard feelings. In order to do that, you have to have an undercapitalized marriage. In that situation they are not really investing all of themselves, so if the marriage doesn't work out, they will have minimized the downside risk. They're just afraid that if they care too much about somebody and it doesn't work out, they'll be hurt. The message of society is "Don't let yourself get hurt."

There are bound to be disappointments in relationships. There is bound to be anger when you're close to somebody. The only way you can avoid the anger and the hurt is not to get close. The philosopher Schopenhauer has an image of two hedgehogs on a cold night. They want to get close to warm each other up, but because they're hedgehogs they stick each other every time they get close. So they come close and move away and they come close and they move away. I think that's what a human relationship has to be. You need the warmth and you need the closeness so you put up with the risk that at times you're going to get stuck.

· To be happy, I would also add the necessity of feeling you are making a difference. Erik Erickson, writing about the stages of man, says that when you get to middle age, the choice you have to make is either to pass on what you have or to stagnate. This is what happens to us in our forties. We want to make sure we've left something behind. We do it as parents, we do it as teachers, we do it as bosses in a company. A secretary shows the tricks of the trade to a new secretary. A factory assembly-line worker becomes a Little League coach or a soccer coach as a way of mentoring. The sense that comes to us in middle age, that we're going to leave some impact behind, is another one of the sources of contentment.

You become happy by doing the right things, and then you realize that you have become happy in the process. Caring about others, running the risk of feeling, and leaving an impact on people—bring happiness. In the same way that certain kinds of food are nourishing and certain kinds of food are toxic, I'm convinced that certain kinds of behavior are nourishing spiritually and certain kinds of behavior are toxic. You literally feel better when you've gone out of your way to help somebody; and unless you're a complete psychopath, you feel bad when you've taken advantage of somebody, told a lie, or been cowardly in a difficult situation. It's as if you've eaten the wrong thing, and it's not doing your body any good.

I think one of the paths to happiness is just to find out how the world works and how to live in harmony with it. There is randomness in life. All you can do is accept it. Accept the unfairness, the unevenness of life, and find meaning not in what happens, but in your abilities to transcend and respond to what happens.

In 1966, when we learned that our three-year-old son had progeria, would not have a normal life, and would die in his early teens, as he did; the first thing I tried to do was make sense of it. I felt guilty. What did I do that I'm being punished for? I felt angry at God. Why did he do this to a family that deserved better? I didn't like feeling guilty and I didn't like feeling estranged from God. The key to saving me from that was the sense that life doesn't make sense. Bad things happen to good people—tragic deaths, accidents, fires, shootings, even hijackings. Real human life does not fit geometric schemes. The longer you insist on perfection, the longer you insist on happy endings, the longer you insist on things coming out even, the more you are going to go crazy. The key to living in a world of unfairness is to admit that life is unfair, and to find the hand of God not solely in the precision and evenness and the goodness of life but in the resiliency of the human spirit—the ability of people to go on living when they find out how unfair the world is. I had a teacher who used to say "Expecting the world to treat you fairly because you are a good person is like expecting the bull not to attack you because you're a vegetarian." It's fair. It's right. But the world doesn't work that way.

I've been doing a lot of traveling and lecturing about how to cope with grief and tragedy. One of the things I say at the end of my lectures is that the real question about good people suffering is not "Why does it happen?" That's a futile question; it focuses on the past. The real question, now that it has happened, is "What are you going to do about it? How will you respond?" I tell people that suffering leaves you uniquely qualified to help other people because you know what's in their hearts. You know what are the right things to say and what are the wrong things. You know how important it is to reach out and not to hold back. You have the right to say things to other people that the guy next door doesn't have the right to say because he hasn't lived through it. The circumstances of your life have uniquely qualified you to make a contribution. And if you don't make that contribution, nobody else can make it.

The Talmud says, "When a human government stamps out coins in the emperor's image, every one is exactly the same; when God stamps out human beings in his image, every one of them is unique." One reason that people are not able to realize their uniqueness is that there are so many of us. We get treated as masses. There are 240 million Americans and 5 billion people in the world. Go out to see the crowds at the airport on the day before Thanksgiving or travel to India or Mexico. It's easy to see us all as the crowd, the masses. The other reason is that society tends to see us functionally in terms of what we can do and not in terms of who we are. In terms of what we can do, we are interchangeable parts. If a bookstore clerk comes down with multiple sclerosis and can't do her job, we find somebody else to sell books. If a taxi driver decides to go back to college, we find another taxi driver. We don't see people in terms of who they are. We see them in terms of their function.

The single indispensable element I insist on for happiness is that you have people in your life to whom you come across as a whole person and not only as your function. The philosopher Martin Buber said, "When two people relate to each other authentically and humanly, God is the electricity that surges between them." I agree with Buber that God exists in a relationship. In order to be alive and human you have to be in contact with other people.

To live life only for ourselves will bring us nothing but sadness and misery. A self-centered life is an unhappy life. Selfishness is a major stumbling block to happiness. Our feelings of insecurity and low self-esteem cause us to be "takers" rather than "givers." Our selfishness is often a mask for fear. If we don't think much about ourselves, we have a lot of work to do in order to enhance our self-worth. Dramatic action is called for so that we can begin to feel good about ourselves. We must live life for something greater than ourselves. To be happy, we must get out of ourselves. We must place ourselves in situations with others who feed us a message, as the result of our actions, that we are good and lovable. An unhappy person must turn outward, not inward, to find happiness. *What am I living life for? What have I done for others today?*

Educator Marva Collins tells us how loving others pays her the dividends we all seek—happiness and love.

Marva Collins is the founder and director of the Westside Preparatory School in Chicago, a school which has been studied by educators around the world. Her success has been profiled in countless magazines, newspapers, and national television programs; The Marva Collins Story, a television movie, starred Cicely Tyson. In 1980 Marva was offered a cabinet post as Secretary of Education by President Ronald Reagan, an offer she declined.

Marva Collins

My happiness is really what I do for other people. Some people are happy if they have a second home in Rome or in Florida or in New York. Even if you have fifty thousand homes, you can sleep in only one bed.

I am unhappy when I know that people who are important to me are unhappy. When I see children who are going to fail, when I see a sixteen-year-old kid who can't read, or when I see people on the street eating from garbage pails and sleeping in cold places, those things make me unhappy. I'm not really in this life to buy a lot of things for myself. I ask the children, "If you died, what would you like the newspapers to say?"

Do you want to live just for assets to leave to your own children and family? Or do you want the world to know that you've lived here, and you've done something for somebody besides yourself? I could care less about my balance in the bank, about what society says, and about getting thanks for what I do. I know I've done it.

I can't do a thing about what's going on at City Hall in Chicago. I can't do a thing about the drugs in the public schools. I can't change those things. But I can change and influence the children who are here at the school. I do what I can. I see life as a challenge. People say to me, "I don't know how you do what you do. I couldn't do it." I don't know how I could *not* do what I do.

I define my own life because I'm the one who has to live with Marva. Every child here says, "Will you teach me?" Yet I expect so much from them. They hardly have time to breathe when they're with me. I'm constantly telling them, "This is your life I'm working on. You can't afford to blow it. You can't afford to throw it away." Children know when you really care about them.

I have a wonderful marriage. It's the best of times; it's the worst of times, to paraphrase Dickens. Nobody is happy ever after. My husband, Clarence, and I argue; we disagree. There are moments when I give 100 percent and he gives nothing. There are days when he gives 100 percent and I give nothing. There are times I love him, and there are times I hate him momentarily. There are times I say, "Why on earth did I ever marry you?" I'm sure he feels the same way. We have three wonderful children, no drugs, no alcohol. But we've had our problems about money, about clothing, about taking care of the house, about mowing the lawn, about cleaning their rooms, about bringing the car in on time. That's life. I tell my children, "When you were born, God forgot to send me directions. I've made a lot of mistakes, but to the best of my ability, I have done the best I could. I've taken you as an imperfect child; why can't you take me as an imperfect parent?"

Everybody expects perfection from you, but they fail to see their own imperfections. One day I had some crumbs on my mouth, and one of the children told me about them. "I know," I said, 'but let them stay there. I'm not going to let you all make the perfect Marva Collins, because I'm not perfect." I do things that are stupid. Some days I don't like me very much. Most of the time I like me.

I think whites feel that blacks are happy because they've learned to smile through their tears. Many times I have been teaching my heart out in the school and I have wanted to cry. The tears are dropping inside. But you go on doing what you have to do. O. Henry said that life is made of sobs, sniffles, and smiles, but that sniffles predominate. Kahlil Gibran said that when happiness is with us, sadness is waiting on the bed.

If you really want to feel sorry for yourself, you can. People are going to use you. People are going to be unkind. People are going to be unpleasant. You have to ask God for strength every day as you're getting up, especially when your whole world is pulled apart. You have to say "God, give me the strength to put it together again." That's the attitude I leave home with every day. It took me all this time to halfway find out who I am. I'll be dogged if I want to go back to those years of trying to figure out who I was or where I was going. I can admit things now that I would not have admitted twenty years ago. If someone had called me a fool, I would have been highly insulted. Now it's fun to me. Things that used to irritate and upset me don't bother me anymore. You either become a bit battle fatigued or you become wiser.

You've got to be awfully strong to keep up with everything that society wants you to be. They're not going to make me an issue-a-week person. I'm sorry. I can't go through that many lifestyles. We're constantly responding to what we think people want us to be. One day, as we were getting ready for a teacher-training session, a woman said, 'If I had known you were going to be here, I would have dressed differently.'' I said, "When I get dressed, I dress for me. You dress for yourself, not for me, because I do not matter; you do.''

We need love, and I get it from the children here at school. I know that they love me. When I walk in the door they all say, "Hello, Mrs. Collins." They kiss and they hug me. The boys and girls follow me. I have to sneak away from love. I get too much. Some days I just can't take another hug. I feel adequate because I am lucky. I have to be who I am. I'm not perfect and I'm not an angel. I have no monopoly on goodness. But I'm not all bad, either.

Happiness involves an understanding and appreciation of the way life works. Life is composed of a variety of people, relationships, events, and situations. Some of these are rewarding, some are routine, and some are painful. To experience what life has to offer is to know the mystery, the challenge, and the opportunity of life. To accept the concept that we have little or no control over life is not to roll over and passively let life run us. The opposite is called for. We must seize life and make it happen for us.

If life were a game, the happy people would be the players, the unhappy people the spectators. If life were a parade, the happy people would be marching and the unhappy people would be standing on the sidewalk watching the parade go by. Happy people are active and involved. It is necessary to continually risk new activities, experiences, and people in order to be happy. *Am I waiting for the phone to ring? Am I living life or is life living me?*

According to Leo Buscaglia, "Part of my work is encouraging people to experience joy—not only to know they're capable of it, but also to know they have a right to it."

Leo F. Buscaglia, Ph.D., is probably the best-known educator in America. He has gained national recognition through his lectures on public television and his best-selling books, Love, Loving Each Other, *and* Living, Loving, and Learning. *His latest book,* Bus 9 to Paradise, *was number one on the New York Times* best-seller list a week before its official publication date.

Leo F. Buscaglia, Ph.D.

I truly believe that the happiest people are those who love many things with a passion. The key is loving intensely and loving many, many things. Genius often comes from focusing on one thing, but geniuses are often unhappy people. Happy people have a wider focus. They love children and family and trees and cooking and eating and celebrating. They love sunrises and sunsets and snow and spring and winter and fall. They love life. They have even learned to love pain and despair, recognizing that we must not dichotomize. We must not set up things like joy as being the opposite of despair. It's just the other side of despair. These things are really one and the same thing and one often grows out of the other. Some of the greatest wisdom I've ever gained was from a despairing situation.

It's often been said that if women who have borne children could remember the pain of childbirth, they would never have another child. But the joy so overwhelms the pain that they almost instantaneously forget the pain when it's over and are ready to go through it again. If we ever thought of how painful it is to say good-bye to somebody we love, we would never become involved again, but we choose to become involved again because we forget. The joy of our involvement and the joy of birth are so overwhelming that they overwhelm the despair. Joy is a more powerful force than despair.

Happiness is having a sense of self—not a feeling of being perfect but of being good enough and knowing that you are in the process of growth, of being, of achieving levels of joy. It's a wonderful contentment and acceptance of who and what you are and a knowledge that the world and life are full of wondrous adventures and possibilities, and you are part of the center. It's an awareness that no matter what happens you will somehow be able to deal with it, knowing that everything does pass and even your deepest despair will vanish.

Happiness is not the direct result of external forces. They may help, but if somebody thinks that when he or she makes a million dollars he or she will be happy, that person is a very great fool. The money will get the nicer car and it will make it easier to go back and forth to work, or it will pay a chauffeur, which means less strain, but you're still carrying *you* in that car. It isn't going to change you, it's just going to change the circumstances that may temporarily affect you. It always amazes me that people think they will find happiness on a mountaintop in Nepal or on the French Riviera or in Rome or in the Scandinavian countries. They go there, changing the environment and having all kinds of newness fed in. For a while it's like a placebo and you believe it's making a difference. Then you begin to emerge. It goes right back to you. Happiness is within you, just as despair is.

There's no such thing as happiness outside of ourselves; that's ridiculous. You can't put store in thinking that things will make you happy; that time will make you happy; that other people will make you happy; that getting things your own way will make you happy; those are all externals.

They will not make the difference. Happiness is intrinsic, it's an internal thing. When you build it into yourself, no external circumstances can take it away. That kind of happiness is a twenty-four-hour thing.

Everything else is in transition, but the happiness you create within yourself is permanent. We have to concentrate on the happiness that we build into us. Happiness is a choice and as we reinforce that choice, happiness becomes a deeper and deeper part of us until we are Happiness. Then as we move through life being Happiness, we create it everyplace we go. We dissolve conflicts. We come into tense situations and people feel relaxed. People feel very open with a happy person and think, "My goodness, I can be me." People aren't threatened because we bring into every situation the joy that's ours. Being Happiness requires no intensity; it just is. It's an ever-present element, so you go to bed joyfully, you dream joyfully, you wake up joyfully, you go through the day joyfully. It is literally a learning process and a volitional process. You simply have to select joy. The converse is true as well. There are people who select despair. Everything is hopeless, and as they go through the world they emanate despair. They lay their despair on everybody. They make the choice, but they don't have to choose despair. Anything that is an option can be changed.

We are actually most productive in our moments of happiness when we are at peace with ourselves. Despair may help temporarily to do away with pain, but those who remain in despair are impotent. They can't function at maximum. All we have to do is remember what happens to many of us when we sit down for a test or an interview. We're often so afraid that we're unable to express even our most basic knowledge or our most basic feelings. When the fear is removed and we feel joy, we are not afraid to reveal ourselves. Some people say you learn best through pain; I say you learn best through happiness, though you can indeed learn through pain. To dichotomize pain and pleasure is wrong because they interweave. All at once maybe pleasure can become painful or pain can become pleasureful. We should see everything as a continuum.

There are no ends to those continuums; they just seem to go on and on and on.

If you think about it, all the big questions about life are unanswerable. Is there a purpose in life? Is there an after-life? What happens in death? Is there a God? It seems as though we're all required to deal with what is really essential through faith. The knowledge that happiness is there for you must begin as an act of faith. You must believe that it is. If you start by saying, "Happiness is not for me; there's no such thing, and it's an illusion," you're not going to find it. Some people want to exclude themselves from the possibilities of joy and joyous people because if they could truly believe that it was possible for anybody to be happy, then it would become a challenge to them to be the same and they are fearful of accepting that challenge. To be happy you must have faith. You must have the hope. You must have the will. Then you must make it happen.

Many of us are afraid of happiness. We are brought up in an ethic that says if we're too happy we're going to be punished. It's almost a sin to be too happy. I remember being brought up learning that we are here to suffer, we are not here to enjoy, we are here to go through a life of drudgery in order to then face God in another life and have eternal joy and happiness. It's very difficult for me to subscribe to that. I think the world is so beautiful and so full of exciting and wondrous things that we were meant to enjoy them. To me the natural state is the state of joy.

I've written seven books, but not one is a "How to" book because there are as many ways to joy as there are people. I have only my way, and my way could fail for you. Only your way is going to work for you.

Life is a joyous struggle. Beautiful moments do not linger; they pass. No magical moment will stay forever. We have memories, positive moments, and that's wonderful. They give us the courage to meet the next conflict. But simply by walking down the street, we're likely to encounter another conflict. To deny that and become unhappy because that's the way of the world is to succumb to frustration. You have to accept the whole package, the good and the bad. There's a peacefulness that comes from the moment of acceptance, the saying to life, ''Whatever you give me I will accept. I will meet it in the best way I can. I'll meet it as a challenge, I'll meet it with joy, or I'll meet it with despair, but I will take it.'' In this case we really don't have any choice, do we? The only other choice is to end life. Nothing could ever cause me to do that. Life is too wondrous a process. Even tears and despair and loneliness are incredible processes and I want to experience them.

I would never expect to live always in contentment and peace and happiness. The despairing situations challenge me to continue to seek and grow. To live constantly in joy and peace and self-centeredness would become very boring after a while. Unless we are growing, unless we are changing, unless we are becoming more, there would be very little excitement in life. I accept the struggle as joyfully as I do what the struggle produces.

If you're now in despair, wishing that you could be happy, you are wasting time. You must make the decision that you are going to be happy and you must manifest it in action. Then you must take the next move, which is the search for happiness, recognizing that the search is internal, not external. There are many external forces that will reinforce your happiness, reinforce your growth, reinforce your goal and guide you on to it.

Many people never see anything. I say see everything. See the evil but also take the time to see the good. Will you stop long enough to really observe the faces of your children before they grow up and you forget that they were ever children? It happens so fast. Will you take a moment to look at the tree that is going through its wonderful cycle of spring and autumn? Will you stop long enough to talk to people and find out that their fears are yours and their joys are yours? Will you realize that perhaps you should stop defining a beautiful day as a day in which everything went your way and begin to define a beautiful day as one in which everything you did helped others to achieve a more beautiful day?

The happy person is the one who sees all things as possibilities, not dead ends, and lives with great élan, fully, embracing everything. When you cry, cry; when you laugh, laugh; when you love, love; when you feel passionate, be passionate. Don't be ashamed of human feelings and the exposure of them. That's the way we connect.

Some people see life as an adventure. Some see it as a struggle. Happy people have a positive attitude about themselves and about life. Since our attitudes originate inside of us, they are really ours. We can choose our attitudes. As humans we are all going to experience problems. However, even with problems, we are free to choose our reactions. The choice of our attitude will have a profound impact on every facet of our lives. *What is my attitude toward life? Is my attitude positive or negative?*

Jimmy Coco's early years had a major effect on his life. He recalls, "Our family was always laughing. We all had a great sense of humor about ourselves. I always saw the humor in things. I still do."

James Coco received an Emmy Award for his performance in the television series St. Elsewhere *and an Academy Award nomination for* Only When I laugh. *His Broadway appearances include starring roles in* Last of the Red Hot Lovers, Little Me, *and* You Can't Take It with You. *Jimmy appeared on all the television talk shows, and his diet book,* If I Can, You Can *is in its seventeenth printing.*

James Coco

I could be truly happy if a loved one was never ill or in pain or dying. That's when I'm most desperate and feel so helpless. It seems selfish somehow; but yet, I'm talking about my own individual happiness.

I was thirteen when my mother died. I loved her desperately. There's a whole five-year period in my life, after her death, that I barely remember.

I have a wonderful sister who really became my mother, I guess. I can remember feeling happy, finally, when it all passed. Nowadays, when I hear that somebody else is ill, I'm at my worst. I'm a collector; I collect friends and loved ones. I have friends who have been my friends for many, many years. I'm possessive; I don't want to lose them. I don't want them to be in pain and I don't want them to be hurt in any way because I get hurt then. I have to be the mother to all of them. I have to be strong, and put everyone in a good mood, and reassure everybody. I'm sure that my friends would go through the same thing if I were ill.

I recently lost a woman friend whom I was crazy about. We were friends for thirty-five years; I couldn't believe it. Her dying lasted two years. Sure, I worry about becoming ill. Naturally, nobody wants to be in pain, but I don't think about that too much. I just want to go on.

Happiness is never having to think about being happy because you are. You just go out with a grin on your face all the time 'cause you're happy. You just know it's happening to you. There's a bubble that's going on. I sometimes find myself talking to myself in such an up fashion. "Ain't it swell? Ain't it great? Isn't it wonderful? I can't wait." You'd think I'm crazy; no, I'm just being happy. I also find myself talking to myself when I'm not happy. "Do I have to go through this again?" or "Who do you have to pay to get out of this world?" I'm a person who probably has done everything or, if I haven't, I'm furious. I'll end up doing everything at one time or another.

I really love life. I love all the martyrdom that goes with it. You open a show and you think it's going to be great. It gets terrible reviews and you're miserable. You go on to the next one and you have a triumph. You win awards, you meet new people, and then you go into another flop and it's topsy-turvy.

Discovering something in an antique store or finding a new food can bring a lot of joy to me. I'm doing another cookbook and I'm gaining a lot of weight because we had to test four hundred recipes. I'm in a new play, and it's going very well. I enjoy the rehearsal process. That's when you're being most creative. You're creating a role nobody else has in a new play, and I wonder if I dare to do it, how it will work with an audience.

My friends are all wonderful. They put up with a lot and I put up with a lot, but we are there, truly there, for each other. That's a terrific feeling. There isn't one really good friend that I have that I wouldn't tell anything to. We don't judge each other. I think maybe that's special to the theater. I trust people.

My mother and I used to go to the movies all the time. Tweedle Dee and Tweedle Dum going to the Pilgrim Theatre and seeing matinees; I thought, "I just want to make people happy; I want to make them laugh. I want to be up there someday." I couldn't think of anything else I'd rather be than an actor. How marvelous it is to say "I'm an actor."

I had a wonderful time struggling. I sold toys at Macy's. I played Santa Claus. I was a messenger. I worked in restaurants. I was a switchboard operator in a hotel. That was kind of fun, watching all the hookers going in and out. I was always being fired.

I made my Broadway debut in *Hotel Paradiso* with Bert Lahr. I was an understudy, and I graduated, and I got the part. I used to stand in the wings and watch Bert Lahr, who was so unhappy off the stage, but what a genius. My first movie was *Ensign Pulver,* a sequel to *Mr. Roberts,* and I was in Mexico. The bit players were Larry Hagman, Peter Marshall, Jimmy Farentino, Jack Nicholson, and I. We were all sailors in this terrifyingly bad movie. We were all stuck in 110-degree heat in the middle of the ocean eating black bean sandwiches.

Everybody should have their five minutes in the sun. Opening on Broadway in Neil Simon's *Last of the Red Hot Lovers* was mine. Opening night on Broadway, I had my hand on a doorknob, waiting to make my entrance. I remember an usherette saying, "They're all out there. The world is out there." I thought I was going to faint. "I will now die before I get on that stage," I thought, but I survived, and it was wonderful, and it was exciting, and it ran for something like two years.

I'm recognized a lot. I've been on *Who's the Boss?* The next day it seemed the whole world had seen me. I've done the Carson show over a hundred times. People constantly stop me to talk about my appearance on *St. Elsewhere* because that show was rerun about four times. They may also have seen me in *Murder by Death.*

My diet book was an enormous success. It broke Bantam's hardcover sales record. That makes me happy. Success always makes you happy. My whole weight problem has always been up and down. But now it doesn't frighten me anymore. Even when I gain weight I know exactly how I will take it all off.

I grew up with a great deal of love, but of course, when you lose your mother at thirteen, you feel that you're being cheated, terribly cheated. That has a great deal to do with my life, I'm sure, and how I feel when a loved one is in pain or is going to die. It's as though something's going to be snatched away. It's probably responsible for my great love of life too, because I want to get it all in. I want to try it all. I don't want to be left out. Life is not dress rehearsal. This is it. We go around only once. Damn it, smell the daisies before they pop out of the ground. I'm sure there is a God because I've been so well taken care of. For me to get to the point where I am today and to have had so many good times proves I can't be a bad person. I love the mystery of life. I love to be teased, and life is a tease.

(James Coco died February 25, 1987.)

Some of us don't know how to play. We take life and ourselves too seriously. Perhaps we grew up in families in which there wasn't much fun and happiness. Perhaps we believe that being an adult is deadly serious business and that fun and games are for little children and teenagers. Perhaps it is the work ethic and the American cultural influence which suggest that once we reach adulthood, it's all work and no play. Happy people seem to enjoy all that life has to offer, and that includes the lighter side of life. There is balance in their lives, and that includes the ability to have fun. *Do I know how to play? When was the last time I had some fun?*

Eda LeShan says, "Being playful is being happy."

Eda LeShan has been an educator and family counselor for more than forty years. A member of the American Psychological Association, she is the author of eighteen books, including When Your Child Drives You Crazy *and* Oh, To Be Fifty Again. *A frequent guest on television and radio programs, Eda is a contributing editor to* Woman's Day, *for which she writes a monthly column,* "Talking It Over."

Eda LeShan

I've been riding the carousel in Central Park since I was five years old. Back then there were silver and gold rings. You had to get five silver rings or one gold ring to get a free ride. I spent my childhood in Central Park because I went to school on Central Park West. If I'm very depressed or if something's bothering me today, my husband, Larry, and I go back to the park. We get on the carousel horses and we start riding, and I start singing at the top of my lungs. It is pure and absolute joy and happiness. If I analyze it, I say that I'm being my child—the child is what's coming out. The childlike part of us, the playful part, gets lost. That's why there's this terrible, terrible hunger. When people say they're not happy it's because they have lost the child and the playfulness. The pushing of kids, the academic exploitation of children, is the way we lose it. We don't hold on to that inner child, the playfulness. Playfulness is really the basis of all discovery, and discovery is the adventure of living. If you lose that, you become crippled forever. The teenagers who are committing suicide, the kids suffering from anorexia, the kids who are taking drugs, are doing what they're doing because we've crushed them; we've crushed what was childlike.

When I was a kid, I went to the Ethical Culture School, which is a private, progressive school. Recently I was asked to do an alumni article for the school newspaper, and I began reminiscing about the things that had happened. I was thinking of the kinds of experiences that helped me to hold on to the inner child. In second grade we were studying the cavemen; we went across the street to Central Park and got big rocks, which we brought back into school. We heated the rocks in the oven. We put asbestos sheets on the floor under the tables in the kitchen, which was the cave. We put the hot rocks on the asbestos, and we put pieces of meat on the rocks. We made papyrus in the third or fourth grade. We made stained glass windows. It was really learning by doing and learning through playfulness. I never lost the sense of that miracle.

If, when I'm sitting at my desk in New Jersey and writing and I look out and see a cardinal on a tree stump, I go crazy, the way I did on the carousel. I'll stare at it for minutes, having no sense of time at all, and I feel utterly refreshed after it flies away. I have a feeling of discovery and playfulness.

Play is the basis for a lot of happiness. Every mammal in the world starts its life by playing. That's the way they learn about themselves and about life. I was lucky enough to have that experience in the first years of my school life and to have my parents encourage it. Most people don't allow the childlike playful part of themselves to continue.

Maurice Sendak does magnificent, wonderful drawings for children's books, which librarians think are terrible and children adore. Someone once asked him, "How do you think up these things?" He said, "I just talk to the child in me." Pablo Picasso was a perfect example of a childlike man. Most geniuses have known that playfulness was the source of their genius. Albert Einstein played with numbers and he played with concepts. He was a playful person. All the great artists and sculptors and scientists and philosophers were playful people. They managed to hold on to the capacity to know that whatever they wanted to discover and whatever adventures they were going to have were going to come through play.

Dancing is being playful in a different sense, but you are focusing as a child does. When you get to the point where you're dancing and you no longer even know you're dancing, that's meditation. You have then recaptured what every child has—the ability to concentrate totally on one thing at a time. We stop this in children. We give them computers in classrooms. We give them words to memorize. We treat them as if they're computers. When they grow up, they will go to all kinds of groups all over the country to learn how to meditate to learn body awareness. What are they doing? They're undoing all the garbage that happened to them when they were children. It seems kind of silly. If you watch children playing, doing anything, even though they might have a short attention span when they're very young, they are totally focused on one thing and nothing else is in their minds. That's really playful.

We should have a deep and lasting respect for all kinds of play and adventure. Go to a park with a child in the fall; pick up some leaves and really look at them. Collect some snow in the wintertime; put it under a microscope and let the child see what snowflakes look like. The most important thing is the spontaneity. The unexpected is the real play.

One hot-as-hell day in the middle of summer Larry and I were out walking. We came upon a fountain where little kids were in the water. Larry looked at me and I looked at him; we took off our watches and our shoes and we went into the fountain too. We arrived back at our apartment soaking wet, but it was wonderful. It was totally refreshing because it was so unexpected. We just looked at each other and did it.

Adults should ask themselves a few questions. Do I ever have moments when I'm doing only one thing at a time? Am I ever so totally absorbed I don't even know that time passes? Are the things I do free and natural physically?

Do I use my imagination? Do I ever do things with no strings attached?

You might decide it would be fun to paint with water-colors. You have no idea whether you can make anything or not, and it doesn't matter. If it ends up absolute garbage and mush on the paper, you had fun experimenting. That's playful. It is having absolutely no rules. It's supposed to be playful—fun and creative. It's doing something in which you don't care one damn whether you're any good at it or not. You want to take violin lessons and your music sounds like hell but you're having a ball. You go right on taking violin lessons only because you're enjoying them, for no other reason. That's playfulness.

Playfulness can also occur in relation to other people. You can have fun doing something with somebody else, such as taking a hike or walking. Lovemaking can be playful too. People take that so seriously. So many manuals make it technical, with fifty-seven different positions. It's like school again, like making art and music for which you get an A or a B or a C. It's supposed to be an inner creativity. It's the same thing with sex. When it's a technology, you lose the spontaneity.

Larry and I bought a rubber raft, which we named *Privasea*—"privacy." It was a stupid little rubber boat with little oars and we would take it through the marshes on the Jersey shore to look at the birds through our field glasses. Along would come fancy million-dollar boats that have a special place to hang fishing rods and a top deck on which to stand. The people aboard them would laugh and wave to us and make jokes about what we were doing. Larry and I felt that they would rather have been in our silly little raft than on a great big boat.

A lot of people have forgotten how to play. It's "I play tennis every morning at six o'clock." "I run through the park at five o'clock." "I'm going to be healthy." It's done with grim determination. It's not playful, it's not fun. Competition has become unbelievable in this society. From Little League to professional football games, it becomes mechanical; it becomes money. Playfulness in baseball has been gone since the days of Ebbets Field. There are so few places where you really see people playing. I was walking across Central Park yesterday. I stopped at a playground where two young mothers were racing around with their little kids. I thought, ''Thank God they are really enjoying this kind of thing; it's doing them more good than it's doing the children.'' Fred Rogers once said, ''When you have a child, you have another chance at yourself.'' What he meant is that you have another chance to become a child and play.

There's a wonderful cartoon of a father and his little child walking along on the street; there's a mud puddle next to the gutter and the father is wading in it and shouting, ''Hey, listen, you know, this is fun.'' We need children to help us play, which is crazy. We should be able to do it ourselves.

Larry and I have been married for forty-one years. The reason we have stayed married is that we don't know what's going to happen next. We've kept our sense of playfulness; we're constantly surprising each other. I don't think we've been bored for one moment in all those years. We've had a hunger to go on changing, and we have really done it through our entire married life.

In 1968, just before he died, the great writer and Trappist monk Thomas Merton gave a talk on the life process to a distinguished group of religious leaders from around the world. He spoke on our mission in life. Rather than offering some esoteric theological principle, he suggested that the journey of life was to discover the essence of ourselves and the purity of God's spirit within us in order to stand on our own two feet. *What do I think life is all about? Am I standing on my own two feet?*

Father John Powell writes, ''Happiness cannot be directly pursued. Like the elusive butterfly, if you set your hand and heart on some other accomplishment—like the ten elements which I believe are the essence of happiness—the butterfly will come and land on your shoulder.''

* * *

*The Reverend John Powell, S.J., is professor of theology
at Loyola University in Chicago. He has published over a
dozen books on theological and psychological themes, including* Why Am I Afraid to Love?, Why Am I Afraid to
Tell You Who I Am?, *and* Fully Human and Fully Alive.
*Father Powell is the second best-selling Christian author
(C. S. Lewis is first) in the history of the United States.
His new book is* On Becoming a Happy Person, *which
further develops his ten points.*

The Reverend John Powell, S.J.

As a priest with a doctorate in theology, I naturally have
made some theological assumptions about human life and
the human condition. I am subjectively certain that God
intended us to be happy. The kind of happiness that God
wants us to experience, however, is obviously not one
continuous euphoria. It is rather a deep sense of peace and
inner satisfaction that sustains us even in times of failure
and grief. It is something like the deeper waters of the
ocean, which remain tranquil even when the surface waters are churning and restless.

I have been involved with people all of my priestly
life. Many people have shared with me the agonies and
the ecstasies of their lives. Over the years I have made
many mental notes about the "less traveled" road to
happiness. There are certain dead ends that look attractive but lead nowhere. There are some hills that have to
be climbed one step at a time. There are ravines into
which we can so easily fall. Besides the experience
gleaned from the sharing of others, I am myself a human being in search of that destiny for which God created us: to be happy with him in this world and forever
in the next. I have had to try out these assumptions in
the laboratory of my own life.

The ten points I have listed here are, in a sense, my
own psychological-theological "Beatitudes" or steps to
human happiness. There are some hills to climb, some
dead ends to avoid, and some ravines to beware of. Still,
I am convinced that if a person were to take these beati-

tudes seriously and make a daily effort to live them, the payoff of peace and a sense of satisfaction would not be far away. Once you become a true believer that this is the road you have been looking for, very few things, if any, will ever seduce you to turn away.

1. We must accept ourselves as we are.
2. We must accept responsibility for our actions and reactions.
3. We must try to fulfill our human needs for relaxation, exercise, and nourishment.
4. We must make our lives acts of love by loving ourselves, others, and God.
5. We must stretch by stepping outside our "comfort zones."
6. We must learn to be "good finders," looking for what is good in ourselves, in others, and in the various situations of life.
7. We must seek growth, not perfection.
8. We must learn to communicate effectively.
9. We must learn to enjoy the good things of life.
10. We must make prayer a part of our daily lives.

3   The Search

Success—reaching a desired goal—should make us happy. However, many of us believe that material success means happiness. We have been sold a bill of goods that says happiness is found in the American Dream. Twenty years ago the American Dream translated into "a house in the suburbs and two cars in every garage." Nowadays, success, money, fame, and happiness have all been rolled into one goal, relentlessly pursued by many Americans.

To "make it" becomes not only the goal, but a way of life and the need to get ahead is often a primary cause of unhappiness. *What is my definition of success? Is success more important to me than people?*

Dr. Ashley Montagu points out, "We have become alienated and disengaged from each other rather than being involved and integrated with each other's welfare. We have become dispassionately disinterested in our fellow human beings, and you can't be happy that way."

Ashley Montagu, Ph.D., is one of the best-known anthropologists in the world and one of the leading social scientists in America. His areas of expertise include anatomy, genetics, paleontology, biology, sociology, and ethnology. Dr. Montagu has taught at many colleges and universities throughout the United States, including Harvard, Rutgers, and Princeton. He is the author or co-author of scores of books, including Man's Most Dangerous Myth: The Fallacy of Race; On Being Human;

Sex, Man, and Society; *and* How to Find Happiness and Keep It.

Ashley Montagu, Ph.D.

Most Americans lead a rather selfish existence, narcissistically developed by their own self-interest, which eventually leaves them out in the cold. Self-interest is not the important thing. The important thing is cooperativeness, reciprocal interest, and behavior designed and calculated in such a way as to confer benefits upon others in a creatively enlarging manner so they are a great deal better off than they would have been had it not been for you—not only enabling them to live, but to become more fulfilled than they otherwise would be.

We are a culture of success. The great god Success is the deity before whom we are taught to worship. We must have the right car, live in the right kind of house, marry the right kind of spouse, have the right kind of orthodontic appliances on our children's teeth, and go to the right kind of psychoanalyst in the hope of finding happiness, in the hope of finding the cure for what is making us miserable and unhappy. I'm afraid this is very rarely achieved in the psychotherapeutic or psychoanalytic situation. The truth is that we can only do something for ourselves. What we find in America is that people are out to be a success—specifically, a success measured by external validations.

There are no games or sports in America; big business is what there is, that's all. You play in order to win. I heard the president of the San Francisco Catholic University say, "The whole purpose of the game is to win." The great cultural hero of America, football coach Vince Lombardi, said, "Winning is not everything, it's the only thing."

You should never play a game for that reason. You should play because it's fun and you should do your best, hoping your opposite numbers will do their best. If you're playing tennis and your opponent is doing his best, he'll bring out the best in you. You will rejoice no matter who wins. It doesn't mean that you don't like to win. Of course, you'd like to show that you have great skill, but only for the sake of the pleasure you take in the skill.

I remember seeing an Indian tennis player in a match with an Australian champion. The Australian made a wonderful shot, which caused the Indian to stop, place his tennis racquet under his arm, and clap and laugh with pleasure at the marvelous performance of the other man. I've rarely seen this done in America. In England, where I was born, we played games just that way, for fun. I was an athlete: a boxer, a runner, and a high jumper. When I was playing tennis with a friend, he slipped in returning a shot and it went into my court. I could have returned it easily, and he would have missed it; my job was to hit it into the net, on the principle that you never take advantage of anyone else's disadvantage.

When I first came to Columbia University, in 1928, the captain of the football team told me that one of the first things they were going to do in the game against Yale was to get the quarterback out of the game by sitting on his knee. They knew he had an injured knee. I asked, "But why do you do that? You should give him every possible chance." He looked at me as if I were a lunatic. That's not the way you play the game.

Today, if you're a seven-foot-four high school student, you can get an $8 million contract for two years. This is the degradation. It is the corruption of the idea of success and sports and games. It affects our whole society. It affects every human being in this society.

No one ever tells you that the formula for success in terms of the American credo is also the formula for gastric ulcers or ulcers of the mind or dermatological eruptions all over your skin or weeping through your various other organs. Of course, no American man ever weeps because that is unmanly. A little boy is told this when he's young. You can't be a success if you go around weeping, because you'll be taken for a sissy.

The victor who belongs to the spoils is possessed by his possessions. He is a success and everyone marvels and worships him because he is. One man I knew, a very unhappy man, had almost a billion dollars at his disposal. He gave each of his children $28 million on his or her twenty-first birthday. It ruined their lives. The worst thing you can do to young people is to take away from them the necessity of making something of themselves. Making something of yourself means making yourself happy, too. It is within your power to make yourself happy or unhappy by setting yourself such goals as are within your range, and that you will enjoy achieving.

It is extremely important for us to remember that we're all born social creatures. None of us can ever live alone and like it. There's something not quite right about someone who lives alone and likes it. The price we pay for individualism is very high. It causes us to regard other individuals as tools for manipulation as we strive for success. This exploitive relationship, in which you use other human beings as instruments to achieve your own success, is, of course, a pathological condition. We are actually designed to be involved in each other's welfare and reciprocally to minister to each other's needs. Love is the most important of all needs of a human being, as it is of any other animal. We human beings are dependent on others for our growth and development. The first three years are crucial. It's enormously important for a child to receive a great deal of love; but love has to be supplied throughout a human being's life. It is always necessary; it doesn't stop at the age of three. You communicate to others by demonstrative acts your profound interest in their welfare. It's not enough to say "I love you." People can tell the difference between "Let's make love" and "I really love you." It's by what you do that you communicate to others that you're deeply involved in their well-being. Ultimately what you believe is not what you say. The only measure of what you believe is what you do. If you want to know what people believe, don't read what they write, don't ask them what they believe, but just observe what they do.

Interdependency with others is necessary. It's not merely conferring benefits in a creatively enlarging manner that enables others to live more fully. It's an interdependent relationship. While you're conferring benefits upon the other, the other is gaining and reciprocally conferring benefits on you. That's the origin of social life—the interaction between two or more organisms.

Loneliness in America is an endemic disorder. Believe it or not, the principal contributor to loneliness in America is television. What happens is that the family "gets together" alone. They're not communicating with each other; they're not even communicating with the television set. If you put an encephalometer on their heads you wouldn't find any brain waves. That's why it's called the lobotomy box. The loneliness which Americans feel so often is consolidated in the family, watching television alone and then saying Goodnight. Television, which could be the best educational medium ever developed, does not contribute toward the health of those who watch. Mental health is the ability to love, the ability to work, the ability to play, and the ability to use your mind soundly.

No matter who or what made you what you have become, that doesn't release you from the responsibility of making yourself over into what you ought to be. What ought you to be? You ought to be a warm, loving human being who lives as if to live and love were one. Unless you are that, no matter what else you are, you are a failure. You can be successful only if you are a warm, loving, relating human being who takes the whole world into his or her orbit. You can't do everything, obviously, but you can do something. Whenever you can do something cooperative with love, you should.

I have lived eighty-one years and have had a great deal of experience with this sort of conduct toward others. I had to learn to be this way. I was brought up as a stiff, stuffed-shirt Englishman who considered that any exhibition of emotion was low class. To be very cutting in one's wit no matter how unpleasant it was, how denigrating it was to another person, was correct behavior. I had to unlearn all this from experience, and I had the very good fortune to have the kind of experiences which forced me to unlearn. No matter how unloving a person you have become, that is not the end of the story; you can change, because we humans are the most educable of all the creatures in the world. We remain educable all the days of our lives. All this nonsense about aging is a myth. For most human beings I would not any longer speak of aging, I would speak of growing. You should grow because you have it in you to grow and part of this growing is modifying your behavior even though it has become habitual. If you've become a nasty, hostile, aggressive creature, that doesn't mean you can't change into a warm, loving human being. How do you do it? Simply by acting as if you *were* a loving human being.

I will spell out in plain English what a loving human being is and what love is. It's the demonstrative act toward others in which you communicate to them your profound involvement in their welfare, so that they can depend on you to stand by and minister to their needs. You will give them all the support, all the stimulation, all the encouragement for growth and development of their ability to be the kind of human being that you're being to them. That's love, and if you can communicate that to others, you can be said to love them.

If you're not yet a loving human being, what you have to do in order to change is begin to act "as if" you were by demonstrative acts, by communicating to others, by throwing your arms around them, by taking them by the hand, by putting an arm around their shoulders. It's enormously important to remember that "as if." You behave "as if" you were a loving human being.

If you go on behaving as if you were a loving human being, one day you'll wake up and find you've become what you've been doing. When you go to heaven you may say to God, "Oh God, I'm nothing but a fraud and I don't belong up here at all because I'm really a nasty, ornery character who has just been pretending, living 'as if.' I once read what Dr. Ashley Montagu thought about this and I started to behave like a warm human being, but I'm really not." God will say, "My dear chap, what do you think *I've* been trying to do all of these years?" That's what you have to do. That's the way I did it.

I regard myself as certainly one of the happiest men on earth because I've been doing what I like all my life.

Most people call it work, but for me it's play. I decided very early in life that one of the chief sources of happiness is to find something you enjoy doing and to make that not only your avocation, but your vocation. I enjoy the loving drudgery that goes with what other people call work, but which I call play. I find that many other scientists have much the same feeling about happiness, whether they are engineers or physicists or chemists. The difference between children and grown-ups is the price of their toys. They're just continuing to play with the same toys that they played with when they were young. This was well expressed by Bertrand Russell in his book *The Conquest of Happiness*. He wrote, ''The secret of happiness is this: Let your interests be as wide as possible and let your reactions to the things and persons that interest you be as far as possible friendly rather than hostile.''

Most people think that one of the important things in life is happiness, but their way of going about securing it is up a tree. If you go out and look for happiness you won't find it. Happiness is something that comes by the way of some pleasant experience when you have done something that has been very helpful to someone else, has given someone else a great deal of pleasure. You've done something that has increased the welfare of the other person and you rejoice in that. You may also find yourself walking on some sunny day out in a field somewhere and suddenly you stop, taking it all in, and say, ''Now I am happy.'' If you go out to look for these experiences you seldom will find them. Ask yourself whether you're happy, and you've ceased to be so. Happiness is a by-product of a satisfying experience. For that you don't need a cent. All you need is yourself.

Our roots play a major role in our happiness. Family, close friends, and knowing the territory give us a sense of security and comfort. It is not only our love and responsibility to others, but the reciprocal love and responsibility from others to us, which makes us feel good. It's important to take a hard look at our personal cost as we seek better jobs, fancier titles, and more money. We may gain, but we also lose. *What price have I paid for my success? What is the level of my involvement with my family—the family of my childhood?*

Dr. Benjamin Spock questions what we have achieved by "getting ahead." He says, "Happiness is mostly a by-product of doing what makes us feel fulfilled. Certainly that definition applies to me. Happiness is not something that we get by deliberately grabbing for it."

Benjamin Spock, M.D., is a distinguished pediatrician and social activist. In 1924 he rowed on the Yale crew, which won gold medals at the Olympics in Paris. He wrote Baby and Child Care *over a period of three years in the evenings. Published in 1946, the book has sold thirty-two million copies and been translated into thirty-one languages. Dr. Spock joined the National Committee for a Sane Nuclear Policy in the early 1960s, spoke at eight hundred universities and colleges during the Vietnam War at the invitation of undergraduates, and was the presidential candidate of the People's Party in 1972.*

Benjamin Spock, M.D.

I don't think America is very happy. Americans cultivate cheerfulness and optimism but my impression is that, quite to the contrary, America is probably the tensest country in the world, with the possible exception of Japan. We have much more violence than any other industrial country and we have very high rates of divorce, wife abuse, child abuse, suicide, and crime. In no European country are there as many as forty murders by hand guns per year. For a recent year in Great Britain the figure was eight; in the United States the number was 11,550. Along with this high number goes the fact that a great majority of murders are committed not by strangers but by family members against other family members. That gives you some idea of the stress in our country.

One of the causes of diminished happiness in the United States is that we have gotten rid of the extended family in most parts of the country, and we are getting rid of the community as well. In some sections of Los Angeles, people move on the average of every eighteen months. How can people have roots and draw comfort and security from the community and feel a responsible part of it if they are moving around at that rate? Of course, Americans in general move because they hear that there is a better job, better pay, or a better future in another job. We have substituted getting ahead for all the other values.

Ours is a social species and a family species. Family ties remain much more powerful in our species than any other. Also in our species, a person needs to feel that he or she is part of something bigger, more important than himself or herself. Throughout history people have been dedicated to their families. In many parts of the world they continue to work in families cooperatively. In America we don't value the family.

What is our species designed for? How did our species evolve? It seems clear to me that the relationship to family, neighborhood, and beyond that the nation and its gods, are what guide most people. (The majority of people are more comfortable if they can personalize their relationship to the Creation.)

Our species likes to be helpful. Children by the age of two start out wanting to help set the table and wash the dishes. In the right atmosphere, that helpfulness can continue and spread to service to the neighborhood, to the nation, and to the world. That's the natural unfolding of the sense of service to others. Under the influence of the pioneers, the Calvinists, and the industrialists, we emphasize rugged individualism too much and the service not enough. The majority of American kids are brought up with the simple ideal of getting ahead. But service doesn't mean sacrifice or depriving yourself. Actually, one of the greatest pleasures of life is cooperating and helping others.

I grew up in a tightly knit family, but it was also full

of tensions. My mother was very dominating and a fiercely moralistic person. She made all of us feel guilty throughout childhood, and we had trouble overcoming that sense of guilt. Human beings need some sense of guilt to keep them in line, but I think when it's overdone it can cause more trouble than good. We certainly were taught very strenuously that we owed a lot to other people, but instead of that being thought of as a joy, it was thought of as simply a deprivation. Obviously my mother was the most formative influence because she was with us all day and she was the one who applied pressure. My father was in the background. When I went into psychoanalysis I complained bitterly for the first three months about my mother, her oppressiveness and puritanicalness. It turned out that the person I was really afraid of was my father, who was actually a very calm and just sort of a person. This often happens, especially with boys. They load all their reproaches on their mothers because they're so much in awe of their fathers, especially a father who's so fair that it is hard to make an obvious criticism of him. I was brought up a very critical person. It's very hard for me not to be critical, judging other people from a moralistic point of view. Conscience and morality are very important, but I'd prefer that they not take such a scolding form.

I think that my political activity has largely been trying to shame the government. A few of my friends have suggested that I might be more effective if I were more positive rather than so critical.

I strike many people as hesitant and underassertive. That certainly is part of my manner, but way underneath I am unusually determined. I am proud and pleased with my accomplishments, but I have never become an easy person within myself. Although I felt I was awfully slow to be accepted, I knew that somehow or other I'd battle through.

As human beings we are equal. Each of us deserves to be accepted, respected, and loved just for being. To use our talents and abilities in positive ways and have our contributions recognized make us feel worthwhile and happy. Unfortunately, because of such prejudices as sexism and racism, society imposes on many of us barriers to happiness. Feeling good is the way we are supposed to feel. Too many have struggled too hard, too long. *Do I accept and respect others for who they are? Do I accept and respect myself for who I am?*

Gloria Steinem looks at women and their happiness in America. In looking at her own life she believes, "My happiness comes in part from the sense of being useful and of having an impact."

Gloria Steinem, co-founder, editor, and writer for Ms. *magazine, is a leading spokesperson for the women's movement. She has been chosen six times as one of "America's 25 Most Influential Women" by* The World Almanac *co-sponsoring newspapers. Gloria's writing appears in "Feminist Notes," her monthly column in* Ms. Outrageous Acts and Everyday Rebellions *is an anthology of her writing.*

Gloria Steinem

For many women there's been one big step forward—a willingness to admit that we are not happy. In the past happiness was imposed on us. Women were supposed to be happy under certain conditions. If we had a husband and children and weren't starving, that was happiness. "I have a nice house, I have nice children, why am I not happy?" was the question. Because we didn't have the self-confidence or the support to consider ourselves full human beings, we would say that we were happy externally and be mystified and feel guilty about not being happy internally. I think we've moved past that hypocrisy, so that now when individual women say they're happy, they're much more likely to really mean it and not just be conforming.

Happiness involves self-respect and having some feeling

of value. It also means being with people you feel close to. With them you can share what you're thinking and feeling, knowing you'll be understood. Happiness also means having an impact on the world, whatever form that takes for an individual. It may be the ability to make very good bookcases or it may be running the very best diner in town. It varies for each individual.

The way we know we are alive is by having some impact on the world around us. It's pride of work, pride of contribution. It isn't so much how many people you influence, it's that you feel that you're doing your best and you're being recognized for doing it. If people aren't allowed to feel that they can make a positive impact on the world, they will make a negative one. You see this phenomenon with young people who don't have jobs, who get angry and are so destructive. You also see it with women who are leading lives at home that they don't want to lead. They are not being honored as individuals, so they take it out on their husbands. There's the familiar phenomenon of the ex-wife who has no way to be positive, so she spends her life trying to destroy her ex-husband. Women want to have an impact on the world and if it can't be positive it will be negative. If you are not making an impact, how do you know you're alive? You feel you have no existence.

It wouldn't even be necessary for either women or men to work outside the home if the work inside the home was rewarded, if society said, "This is important work." Unfortunately, society doesn't say that often. Raising kids is more interesting than much of what goes on in factories or offices, but it isn't rewarded. We're really talking about a societal value versus an inner value. If people felt good about the contributions they were making in the home and were rewarded for them so they received all the social and financial rewards of any other kind of work, then it would be different.

Single parents who work and take care of children have a very tough time because they have two jobs. But a component of happiness seems to be the feeling that you have some control over your life. Even though it's physically harder, the idea that you can choose what you wish to do and do it is positive. That you're not being dictated to, you're not just *responding* but that you're *acting* seems to be very important.

I think patterns will change. In the past, in reply to some "Are you happy or not?" surveys, single women and married men reported themselves to be the happiest, and married women were the least happy. That will begin to change as marriage gets to be a more equal partnership, so it's not such an imposition on women and they can have more sense that they are in control of their lives.

An old adage says that to a man the most attractive thing about a woman is her capacity to be happy. While that could be positive, I think it's often negative. Women have felt the need to pretend to be happy in order to be feminine or to please their husband's or boyfriend's ego or to be entertaining. People on the street say, "Why don't you smile, honey?" That's a way in which the façade of happiness has been imposed.

Women have to admit their anger and work through their unhappiness in order to be truly happy. We have to pass through a kind of barrier and be willing to consider the happiness that comes from within. It's not designed to please others, and that takes a while. Women should keep repeating, "I'm not crazy; the system is crazy." A deeper way of saying it would be, "I'm a unique, worthwhile human being."

Our brains and our emotions are bombarded by millions of messages from the media that affect our happiness. It is difficult to be positive and happy in a world that appears so negative and unhappy. Television especially, which can be a positive, informative, and entertaining medium, is seen by many behaviorists as having a profoundly negative influence on our lives. The average American watches seven and a half hours of television each day. Watching television places us in a passive state, and its effect on our happiness through its content cannot be ignored. *How much television do I watch? Why do I watch? Does television make me feel good about myself and the world?*

Dr. Theodore Isaac Rubin warns, "Television deprives children of their imagination. We will eventually have a generation of people who are incapable of any kind of creativity because we spoon-feed them passively while they lie on their bellies watching one vision after another."

Theodore Isaac Rubin, M.D., a former president of the American Institute for Psychoanalysis, is a practicing psychiatrist in New York City. Ted is the author of more than twenty-five books, including Compassion and Self-Hate, Overcoming Indecisiveness: The Eight States of Effective Decision Making, *and the novel* Lisa and David, *which became the film* David and Lisa.

Theodore Isaac Rubin, M.D.

Happiness consists of feeling good. It's being relatively free of anxiety. Happiness is not exhilaration or highs of any kind. It's a relative state of equilibrium. If you're feeling pretty good, almost everything that you encounter has some pleasurable aspects. Going out on the street, new sights, new people, friends, conversations, food, a sunny day, and children all contribute to pleasure. If you're unhappy and not in a state of equilibrium, then all this eludes you and almost nothing is pleasurable. There are a great many people in our society who are happy, but since they don't know they're happy, they're not happy. That is the real problem. The major reason these happy people are unhappy is because their state of well-being is measured against a Shangri-la existence that they have in their minds. What they have in real life comes off as improverished compared to that.

If you ask unhappy people what would make them happy, they really can't tell you. Anything that is compared to what goes on in the imagination usually comes off poorly, because the imagination can do things that can't be done in reality. On top of that, what goes on in the imagination is so amorphous, so poorly delineated, that it doesn't really exist as an entity even in the imagination. People who are unhappy and very depressed lead an enormous life of the imagination. They have an idealized version of themselves and what their world ought to be, and they're constantly insulted by reality. They are frustrated by the limitations they find exist in themselves and the world they live in. People who imagine a life that may exist in heaven, which they can't possibly attain here on earth, can't know happiness relative to that.

I often say to patients, "What you've got now is probably as good as it's ever going to be." They are shocked, so I'm quick to add that it doesn't mean their lives can't change and that there won't be other nuances of quality and new experiences. It doesn't preclude change and growth. But since you have almost certainly been in a state of change and growth during the last few years, and since you have had all kinds of shades of quality in your life, some of which are very good, and since you have almost all of the basic necessities of life and a good deal more, and since you have experienced a certain degree of self-realization, we could say that you have had as much as the planet has to offer, and you can't expect more than that. There will be different permutations, but all still within the confines and limits of the human condition on this planet. If a person from a less prosperous country and culture could assume the roles we are living, that person would almost certainly be happy. What we have provides all the possibilities for happiness.

If happiness is to come it will not come from anything additional, from the outside; it must come from a rearrangement of how one perceives oneself vis-à-vis the world one lives in. If you're a stimulation addict, "This is it" is horrendous news because it no longer provides an adrenaline high. The adrenaline high is almost invariably based on always having to make new adaptations. It's the struggle, a little bit of suffering, and then the conquest.

We live in a manic-depressive society, and a lot of it

has been promoted by the media. The stimuli have become enormous. Whether it's the violence or tremendous success or tremendous failure or whether it's celebrities who come on as experts and project the aura of an ideal existence in which they appear to live, it makes for, or contributes to, a life that is viewed as being either very low or very high. When many people are in the "in between," where most living is done, they feel they're in a kind of doldrum existence, which they can't possibly equate with happiness. Actually, they're happy and don't know it.

They know when they get depressed. Then they begin to realize that what they had was pretty good. But as soon as they feel good, they want much more. What they want much more of, there is no more of. What they want is something in the imagination that will make for the high. The high is seen as something to attain.

We ought to be tickled with the life we have in these United States. We live in the lap of luxury. But we always want more. We want a little bit of embroidery, a little bit of whipped cream; but we've got so much cake. I'm not preaching "Be happy with what you've got"; but we have to redefine what it is we call happiness, what it is we want, and where it's at.

Probably the biggest health problem that exists in the United States is emotional depression. One of the main causes of depression is that people can't sustain these highs and successes, and our expectations are so exorbitant that we simply can't keep up with them.

The media have a terribly important impact on people and their happiness. Unfortunately, they really set the rules. For one thing, we're a youth-oriented culture. Therefore, the process of getting older, which is inevitable, already detracts from the happiness of individuals who really believe that there's something terrible about getting older and who feel that acceptance will not be there as they get older. They have to lie about their age, professionally, socially, and sexually. The media message is that you become a lesser person as you get older. How can that contribute to happiness?

In a culture that venerates the experience and wisdom of age, or at least accepts aging on some kind of equitable basis, getting older is not a cause of self-hate. It's not a cause for depression. It's a cause for celebration. It means we have lived another day. To live another day again comes down to living and enjoying the process. The excitement of life really lies in living to such an extent that it's wonderful to breathe a little fresh air, to see the rain, to have a good meal, to dunk a doughnut in some skimmed milk, and to live with everything that there is.

The media tell us that notoriety is more relevant than expertise. Being famous is what counts at all costs, and it pays off in dollars, cents, and happiness. We accept this, despite the fact that well-known people kill themselves all the time. The belief is that notoriety opens a door to a special world in which common mortals never live. The goal is to become famous, however you do it.

Another message from the media is that being beautiful is of extreme importance. Looks will do it. This promotes terrible self-hate and self-prejudice because not all of us are good-looking. In addition to the self-hate promoted, it promotes a terrible superficiality in that good looks become more important than almost any other value. This makes for a narcissistic, empty existence that precludes the possibility of the happiness of tapping inner resources. You can't stay on the surface and concern yourself with narcissistic things day and night and at the same time develop and evolve into a person who really gives a damn about anything else or anybody else.

High stimulation at any cost is also promoted by the media, and high stimulation on television often takes the form of aggression. The worst aggression is not that of guns and killing. This, of course, promotes all kinds of false values about heroics and really demeans life so that you feel cowardly if you want to preserve and save your own life. Television also broadcasts all kinds of mixed and silly messages about masculinity and macho images. What's even crazier and more insidious than that are the soap operas. If you watch television during the day you will find that members of soap opera families almost never give a straight message to one another. Their messages are always delivered in an adolescent, fighting, competitive, undercutting, hostile way, full of one-up-manship. This is aggression and hostility. What the soap operas portray is a paranoid world, and this really destroys trust.

The heroes and heroines of *Dynasty* and *Dallas* are really slimy people. They're duplicitous, they're hypocritical, they're self-serving, and they're narcissistic. What we learn from these shows is not about process living. What we learn is that you have to get what you want as quickly as you can. Expertise doesn't count; fooling other people does. Going through the struggle of becoming an expert, becoming well educated, learning a craft well, understanding it thoroughly, making a contribution—training, work, energy, time with other people—are really what life ought to be about, but that's not what's glorified in TV dramas. The fast deal is where it's at. Real effort in terms of self-growth or contribution are looked upon as foolishness. Manipulation is much better and much more important and makes you a much wiser guy than what accrues to you through hard work. The sucker is the hard-working guy.

The media also distort the news terribly. Only a few people present it with any objectivity or analysis. They sensationalize the news, contributing to a panic society, which is not a society made for happiness. The news has become a show—we all know about that—and it makes for a high-stimulation society, which is not a society geared for happiness. It's even more than go, go, go. It's go, go, go with poor judgment, with enormous highs, with chaos, with great anxiety, with fragmentation. We have created a society that takes a manic-depressive approach to living. People live either resigned and feeling hopeless or in the expectation that there's a deal to be offered and a high will be forthcoming. The disappointments become so painful that we can easily see why people even without any physiological predisposition could become alcoholic or addicted to almost anything because they need the protection of something or at least think they do, to numb the disappointments of the real world.

Success, of course, promises happiness, but it doesn't deliver. In our country success comes largely in two ways: either through enormous wealth or enormous notoriety. In the last few years—and television is largely responsible—notoriety beat out money. Television is a curse, and the shame of it is that television could be so productive. The possibilities are really great.

People in the United States are drowning in the media. The media are not happiness-oriented. They're high/low-oriented. If you use the right deodorant you will get one big high that will provide heaven on earth.

What we expect from ourselves is outrageous. We want everybody to love us. You'd be amazed at how many people believe that. They spend hours and hours being hurt and feeling abused because everybody doesn't love them. They expect never to be rejected. In a healthy state of being we want to tackle all kinds of people, things, and events. We want to participate in life to its fullest. Young men who want to date women know that they will be rejected a considerable number of times. So why not embrace rejection? Why not say, "Sometimes I'll be accepted and sometimes I'll be rejected." In that case, one is no longer paralyzed by fear of rejection. If you have to avoid rejection you are unable to tackle many things. With a rigid attitude, if you are rejected you have to rationalize. With a more flexible attitude, you can say, "I was rejected and who am I not to be rejected?" If you have to be successful in everything you undertake, you set yourself up for not being happy, because every time you are unsuccessful, you will be unhappy.

Unfortunately, we expect almost constant success in all areas of life. We expect no difficulties with our children or with our mates. The divorce rate in this country is largely due to the fact that people aren't willing to struggle one bit. They can't confront their differences and iron them out on any kind of equitable basis. They expect that if they're in love, it should be all honey and gold, twenty-four hours a day. At the first bump in the road, it's over.

In unhappy relationships the difficulty is usually the expectations we have of each other. "You should do it for me. You should provide the happiness. You should provide the high." If there's happiness in living with another person on a sustained basis, it's really in helping the other person.

When we do something for somebody else, when we are involved with another human being's self-realization we tap our assets as in no other activity, and when we tap our assets and use them, that's when we are happiest. That, to me, is happiness personified—the use of our inner resources. Whether we're using them to enjoy everyday things or whether we're using them to have a new thought or a new feeling, using ourselves well is the essence of happiness; and when we use ourselves well for the benefit of another human being there is no greater satisfaction. If we don't get satisfaction out of that then something is radically wrong. We're cut off. We have become too encapsulated and narcissistic. Then we need help.

Part of what destroys our appreciation of happiness and happiness itself is that we have become product-oriented rather than process-oriented. If you're doing something you enjoy, which gives you satisfaction, the doing is more important than the accomplishment. For me, the process of writing a book is really exciting. When the book is finished, that is another kind of satisfaction. However, if the end result is my only satisfaction, and the process is looked upon with disdain and contempt and is arduous, then I'm missing all the time and energy I put into writing that book waiting for the product. The result of the product is infinitesimal. The joy and happiness from the process lasts much longer and is more involving and more satisfying over an extended period of time in your life.

If you are totally goal-oriented in a success-oriented culture, and if the product is the goal, you have destroyed much of the possibility for happiness in your life, since almost all of your life has to be the process and not the product. You can't even get to the goal without participating in the process for a considerable length of time. If you are attempting to jump from goal to goal to goal to goal, then you are producing an incredibly stressed position for yourself, one which has to destroy happiness. If you can't live in peace with the process of living itself, there goes your happiness. If you get nothing out of the doing, because you are looking for the high that will come at the end, you're in serious trouble. But if you have indeed been nourished by the whole process, and it's given you great happiness, that result at the end of the road, positive or negative, isn't terribly significant. You just go on to the next process. I try to get my patients to appreciate process living, because the process is what life is all about. I'd say we're in the process 98 percent of the time. If you're living just for that final 2 percent, you're in trouble. The truth is that most of the population is in trouble.

There are some basic elements necessary for happiness, and the most basic element is an assessment of your perception of the whole issue. You have to ask, "Where have I been? Where am I? Where do I really want to go? Are my time and energy worth anything to me? If my time and energy are worth something to me, is now worth anything to me? What is the quality of the *now* in my life? How am I using my time and energy? Do I feel fairly comfortable with what I am doing? Do I feel that I'm enjoying my life? If I'm not, is it because the externals really are wrong, and if they're wrong, why don't I do something about them? The externals are the place I live and the work I do. If they are not really wrong, then is my perception wrong? Are my expectations wrong? Are my criteria wrong? Does something internal have to change? Does my perception have to change?

You have to analyze the situation. Keep in mind that nobody has everything; therefore you must have a hierarchy of priorities. As long as you continue to harbor the belief that you can have it all, you're going to have nothing, and in having nothing, you're going to be unhappy. Not only do the priorities have to be straightened out but you have to accept the fact that prices must be paid in life.

The human condition is very complex. Two ideas in that complexity that have to be reconciled are: you must not demean the here and now, and you must realize that nothing worthwhile will ever come without the postponement of gratification. If you are unwilling to grow up sufficiently to pay a price, then happiness is going to elude you. You are always going to be yearning for the impossible.

You also have to keep in mind that anything you do relative to what exists in your imagination will come off very poorly. You have to begin to realize that you've been sold a bad bill of goods. If your total happiness is achievement-oriented you're going to be in trouble, because you simply can't go from one achievement to another constantly. Nobody ever has. Life has to go along the lines of *being*, and happiness has to be process-oriented. You have to be happy with what you are involved in on a day-to-day basis.

4 Self-worth

If you don't like yourself, you can't be happy. Positive self-worth is the essential requirement for happiness. Unless we accept ourselves as we are, we will spend our lives trying to prove to ourselves that we are worthwhile by actions that will leave us feeling empty and relationships that are doomed to failure.

Self-worth is the ability to say to ourselves "I am a good person." We must believe this with all our heart. In accepting ourselves, we set aside any need to impress ourselves or others. We live at a level of comfort in which we can really be ourselves. The greatest luxury in life is the freedom to be ourselves, and to know we are wonderful just the way we are.

We must see our own goodness, appreciate our assets and abilities, and celebrate our humanness. We must acknowledge our differences and uniqueness from other people. We are one of a kind. We are special. *What do I really think about me? Am I a good person?*

Shelley Duvall reflects: "A healthy ego is one that doesn't have to concentrate on itself all the time. It's one that can perform unselfish acts so that it's not always *I, me, mine.*"

Shelley Duvall was twenty years old, studying in Houston, Texas, to be a research scientist, when she was discovered by director Robert Altman and producer Lou Adler. She appeared in several Altman films, including Brewster McCloud, McCabe and Mrs. Miller, Nashville, *and* Three Women, *for which she won the best actress award at the*

Cannes Film Festival. She has also been recognized for her film work in Popeye, Annie Hall, *and* The Shining. *Shelley is the creator and executive producer of* Faerie Tale Theatre *and* Shelley Duvall's Tall Tales and Legends, *which air on Showtime cable television.*

Shelley Duvall

I'm basically a happy person. I'm more on the optimistic side than pessimistic. I've always thought that everything you do comes back to you, so why not do good things. It does come back one way or another. It might not come back immediately or even when you want it, but then you can't go around expecting things to happen to you. The best things in life come to you when you're not expecting or looking for them.

I don't think this philosophy was learned. I had a very tough childhood. I had a very strict father. As a child I didn't know what was going on in his adult mind. I caught the brunt of it. I was the oldest child and I always was sort of a wide-eyed optimist even in the face of not being allowed to go out and play much. I turned a bit inward during childhood. I was very sweet and shy and was a bookworm.

I believe that people make their own beds. You make your own life what it is. I don't think it's a conscious effort as much as it has to do with attitude. I always thought that if you were nice to somebody, that person would be nice back to you. Well, I found out early in life that that wasn't the case, but I still thought it was the right thing to do, to be kind to all living things. I had an affinity for creatures great and small, for humans and ants in the grass. I didn't grow up on a ranch or farm, although I would have loved that, I think. I grew up in Space City, which is what Houston was nicknamed with the advent of NASA in the early sixties. My parents didn't have much money. My father was going to law school at night and he was everything from an insurance salesman to an auctioneer. He finally became a criminal lawyer. My mother started a real estate company when I was thirteen. When I was twenty-five, my parents got divorced and my mother was remarried about a year later to a man who has since died of cancer.

I was very close with my three younger brothers. Somebody would have a fight and I'd be the one to break it up and say, ''Are you kidding? Your parents will be home in a few minutes and if we don't have this spaghetti mess cleaned up you're really going to get it.'' We would join together in an effort to have everything cleaned up by the time they got home so none of us would get in trouble. There was a camaraderie formed by the little people versus the big people in the house.

I always thought there must be something better in life. There always had to be something better, and in the fourth grade I thought I wanted to be a scientist. I wanted to make a contribution. I wanted to be an Einstein. I wanted to be enlightened. Enlightened meant someone who saw life with wisdom and compassion and never stopped learning from mistakes in life or from living and observing. I observed a lot. That's probably what gave me the ability to be an actress. I did grow up in a very colorful place. There are a lot of eccentrics in Texas, a lot of characters.

I was an A student up until about the eleventh grade, when I discovered boys. I sort of rebelled around the age of seventeen, when I graduated from high school, and I spent a year or so just being wild, going out all the time. I had only one boyfriend for four years, so I wasn't wild in the way of going out and dating everybody. When it came time to go to college I didn't go in with a degree in mind. I wanted to find a cure for cancer because it was such a sad thing. Then I realized that I wasn't Einstein, and I got discouraged by the fact that there were twelve-year-olds in college, and I felt that surely by the time I was twenty-six or twenty-seven somebody else would have discovered a cure for cancer. That is a lesson I've learned in life: never assume that someone else will do it. When I got the idea to do *Faerie Tale Theatre,* my first assumption was that someone else was surely doing it because it's such a good idea. It's something that I would like to see. I remembered that old lesson about wanting to discover the cure for cancer and thought, ''Wait a minute, if you

want something done right, you've got to do it yourself.''
So I looked around and nobody else was doing it and I
found out why. People didn't believe that children's pro-
gramming would bring in any money. The industry said,
''Nice little girl, fairy tales, right, good-bye.'' I happened
to have been very lucky and I do believe in luck. It has to
do with attitude and how you approach life. If you believe
in something and you persevere and you know it's a good
idea in your own mind and other people have reinforced
that belief, then go with it, pursue it. If you really want
to do something in life you'll pursue it and you'll do it.
Some people go through life thinking, ''I really wanted to
do that but it wasn't successful or I wasn't able to do it.''
In their minds they didn't really want to do it or doubt
crept in. It's amazing what the response has been to *Faerie
Tale Theatre.*

People stop themselves from succeeding. Fear and self-
doubt often get in the way. They actually will throw a
stone into their path. Why? It's just a matter of studying
yourself and realizing the patterns that you repeat. Most
adults are still dealing with the problems they had as children. I really believe in self-analysis and going to see a
psychiatrist. I went to get help. I had a lot to deal with. I
wanted to dump my childhood garbage and not dump it
on other people. I wanted to study and see why I repeated
certain patterns. Most of us are prisoners of our childhood. It's pretty much accepted now that if a parent abused
you, you in turn will repeat those patterns unless you recognize them. With recognition comes understanding, and
with understanding comes forgiveness, and with forgiveness comes peace. It's self-forgiveness and forgiveness of
your parent. One of the things I had to learn was that all
men are not going to treat me the way my father did. Many
women have this problem. Many men have a similar problem with their mothers and with women.

Learning and growing is what life is. The more you
understand about yourself, the more you're going to understand about other people and the more you understand
about everyone and yourself, the more forgiving of everyone you're going to be, for their mistakes as well as your

own. Everybody has problems, no matter how good their lives look. If you piled up all your problems and then someone you thought had a wonderful life or a better life than yours piled up all her problems, you'd still pick your own pile. You wouldn't want to take anybody else's pile. It's not necessarily greener on the other side of the hill. You're only seeing perhaps one or two facets of a person's life. You're not seeing a whole picture.

I think that life is an adventure. You're just going down a river and you do have control as to where the boat goes along that river. Through your dreams you can make that boat fly or go on land. But it's nice to be enjoying the ride, not just be thinking about your destination. There are new problems that arise everyday. You're never going to be completely problem-free. In life you're always going to be working on something, trying to overcome something, trying to learn something or achieve something. You might as well just enjoy the process of life.

I've had lots of failures. I've had relationships fail, a lot because of my own doing. I've had failures in business. There have been times when I wanted an acting role and didn't get it, but I have to accept that, and that's the key right there. The keys are acceptance, being optimistic, and seeing life with a positive point of view. Everything happens as it should.

I was sitting on a plane next to a very old man. I like to talk to people, so I said, "Tell me, how'd you get to be as old as you are?" He said, "I'm ninety-two. Let me tell you, there are three things in life you can't live without— money and health and a good sense of humor. Now which one of those three do you think is the only one that you really can't live without?" I said, "I think I know. It's a sense of humor." And he said, "You're right. Many people are in poor health. They have a lot of pain to deal with in life, physical and emotional pain, but if they have a sense of humor they'll survive it and they'll have a good attitude. The money you can live without. There are lots of poor people who barely get by, but some of the poorest people are some of the happiest people because they can laugh and they appreciate things." We went into a discussion after this about attitudes and how important it was to have acceptance, to be able to accept whatever happens and to have a good attitude about it and look at the humorous things in life.

The members of Alcoholics Anonymous have adopted a wonderful philosophy: "God grant me the serenity to accept the things I cannot change, the courage to change the things that I can, and the wisdom to know the difference." That's brilliance; that's a wonderful prayer; that's a very good, positive way of looking at life.

We may not be responsible for our initial thoughts and emotions, but we are responsible for our actions. If we please others to win their approval, if we do things we really don't want to do, if we go against our gut feelings or conscience, the actions and outcomes will leave us feeling negative about ourselves and unhappy. Our actions are who we are, so "to thine own self be true." *Do I accept responsibility for what I do? Am I running my own life?*

John Naisbitt forecasts: "The more high tech in the society, the more the humanness of people is going to be important. One of the best-kept secrets in America is that people are dying to make a commitment."

John Naisbitt is the author of Megatrends, *an international best seller in seventeen countries, and co-author with his wife, Patricia Aburdene, of* Reinventing the Corporation. *John is chairman of the Naisbitt Group, which does social forecasting, advises businesses and institutions, and publishes "John Naisbitt's Trend Letter" and "The Bellwether Report."*

John Naisbitt

A sense of personal worth has to do with your realizing your full potential and not just being satisfied with some of your potential. People who work for a sense of personal worth keep working at it. They want to push and stretch.

They want to experience their potential. They want to get right out there to the edge, and that's what they keep pushing for. How can you know what your full potential is unless you put it at risk? You have to put it at risk. The only universal either/or is either you grow or you die. That's true of you and me and a tree or a city or a country. It is either growing or it's dying. There are a lot of human beings who are dying because they're not growing. They're not stretching. They're not risking. They're not trying to regroup at a higher level. They're saying, "This is good enough" or "I'm settling for this," though they don't articulate it. That has a lot to do with happiness and unhappiness. I think happiness is a journey. I don't think it's a goal. How can it be a goal? If it were a goal we'd find out what it was and everyone would rush to it. If it is a process, that means you have to be growing or you're dying, and if you're dying, you're not very happy. Happiness has to do with growth and defining a sense of personal worth. Growth takes more risk than effort. For most people risk is tougher than extra effort. It has to do with vulnerability. You might fail.

I've had a couple of businesses which have failed. Somebody said to me, "You counsel business and you've had some businesses fail." I said, "My God, you mean you only learn from successes? You can't learn from failures? You learn a hell of a lot more from failure than you do from success." Risk goes back to vulnerability, and people don't want to expose themselves that way. It shows weakness to ask someone else to help. You're supposed to take care of everything yourself.

A sense of personal worth doesn't mean some big swell accomplishment. It's a feeling. Mothers get it a lot. They get a sense of real personal worth because they truly understand that they're contributing to a human being, a baby, bringing it along. Personal worth involves your contributing something that's beyond yourself, whether it's a baby or an institution. It can be a very small thing. It doesn't have to be a big thing. It has to be your own sense of it, not someone else's sense of it. People get into big trouble when they allow those judgments to be made by other people. They react to the world around them. They react to what other people do and say instead of just doing what they're doing and letting other people react to them.

Don't let the world inform you as to whether or not you're happy, for heaven's sakes, or whether you're of any personal worth. You get in big trouble that way, letting the world decide. You decide.

If you asked me how many people in this country are realizing their potential, how many people in this country are really experiencing a strong sense of personal worth, I would say not many. I would say it's a small percentage. Happiness has to do with a developed sense of personal worth.

I'm a very optimistic, happy person. I have a very well-developed sense of personal worth and I try to acknowledge that in everybody. The most unhappy people seem to have no sense of any personal worth or value. It's not to be confused with egotism. It has to do with experiencing your own humanity. Of course, you have to get feedback from the larger environment and some people need more than others. There are some who don't need much at all. Having a sense of personal worth is absolutely connected with a sense of personal responsibility for whatever happens to you. The day I realized that I was personally 100 percent responsible for what happened to me was a breakthrough.

It was a bad time in my life, only eight years ago. I was pretty low. I had just been divorced. I'd filed for bankruptcy. I lived in a one-room apartment in a basement. I wasn't feeling sorry for myself because I'd started over before. I don't mind starting over. I wouldn't mind starting over tomorrow. But I was thinking about things. I thought through my predicament. I realized that whatever had happened to me, I had created. My actions had led to this situation. No one else in the world was responsible. I was responsible. The other side of it was that I could make anything happen. It's the same coin. A lot of people say, "Someone's doing this to me" or "If someone hadn't done that" or "What are they going to do about it?" Those are the most unhappy people because they think they're getting jerked around by the world. They don't realize that they're doing it themselves. The world's not ganging up on them; they're ganging up on themselves.

Right after my divorce I got into an unfortunate relationship with a woman. I walked away from that situation but it caused me some trouble. I found myself wanting to blame her. I realized that whatever happened was my responsibility, not hers. She was responsible for what she did. I was responsible for what I did. I stopped blaming her. It was so clear. Then I said, "Put that behind you. If you're responsible for some negative things that have happened, you can be responsible for some positive things that can happen." So I said, "Let's get moving." And I did.

Everywhere you go, there you are. Many of us spend incredible amounts of time and enormous amounts of energy attempting to win the approval of others—trying to control their behavior and feelings so we will be happy. We have been taught one of the major lessons in life backward. Happiness begins on the inside and flows out. It doesn't exist on the outside and flow in. People, places, and things are pretty much the same for all of us. It is futile to spend so much time and energy trying to fix everything on the outside with the hope of feeling good on the inside. The only person I can change is myself. Our energy and time would be best spent looking at ourselves, changing our actions and attitudes, and responding to people and life more positively. *Am I trying to change others for my benefit? Do I need to change myself?*

Dick Gregory has found the answer. He says, "One of the things I keep learning is that the secret of being happy is doing things for other people."

Dick Gregory, a high school and college track star, gained fame as a television, nightclub, and concert comedian. Using humor as a way of getting people's attention, Dick has used his success as an entertainer to assist causes in which he passionately believes. His participation in the civil rights movement and his efforts toward bringing about world peace, eliminating hunger, gaining the rights of the American Indian, and passage of the ERA amendment— and his fasts to call attention to these causes—are legendary. He is a self-taught authority on nutrition. His nine books include his acclaimed autobiography, Nigger.

Dick Gregory

I was exposed to things that a child shouldn't be exposed to. I heard people cussin'. I was exposed to pimps and whores and hustlers when I was shining shoes. I saw people kick one another in the mouth. I saw stabbings. I was bitten by dogs fourteen times. My hands don't work right now because they got so cold and frozen out there hustling. Then I found out the more jingle I had in my pocket, the better I was liked, even at home.

If I had it to do over again, I wouldn't take that route. Something is destroyed—a purity, a niceness, a kindness. That kind of life sets up a suspicion, and if you're really not able to flush it out it makes you overreact with your own children, by protecting them from something they don't have to be protected from anyway. That's not what the universe meant for us.

When my mother walked into the house she'd smile, and it was positive. But how do you change a seven-year-old child who just saw somebody stabbed to death? My mother died at forty-six, so maybe there was a sadness that we didn't know about. Maybe there was something down there and a little bit of her was dying. Maybe that was a game that she was putting on.

When I look back over my track days I realize that it was a stimulation by means of aggravation. I had to beat your son, I had to beat you, and I didn't beat you nicely. Every time I did, it wasn't a feeling that God was blessing me; there was more devil in me. It was power. I used that as an escape.

We see black gladiators do it now. Black athletes instead of bucking the system, saying, "I'm not going to tolerate it,'' get into athletic games where they are accepted, where ''I'm not black anymore, where I'm not poor anymore, where I'm not a hoodlum and a thug anymore. I'm none of those things that society said I am.''

Anytime happiness is based on being liked and not based on a likable self—in which you have no choice but to like me—I totally bypass my contribution. When you see a pleasant human being who totally loves himself in a healthy way, you have no recourse but to feel the same way. But when you believe that being liked is the type of ride you have, and the type of outfit you have, or following the follower, you're building up for sadness.

I got into comedy because I was missing the Saturday cheers I got when I was on that track. I walked into a nightclub and I heard a comic. Then I did my thing and it was to be liked. That feeling I could feel when I was running track and winning, I could really feel when I was tops in show business. What changed my life was the civil rights movement. I would go into Alabama and three hundred cops would meet me at the airport. God, man. I ain't never been able to whup nobody, ain't nobody ever been scared of me, but all at once I could terrorize whole towns. U.S. marshals were calling me and the president was calling me, saying, ''Don't go. We don't know if we can protect you.'' Nobody ever told John Wayne that. I had a new feeling inside of me. For the first time it wasn't me. For the first time it was doing something that affected something bigger than me, something that couldn't be turned back. It was the first time I was getting a stimulation that wasn't an aggravation. It was aggravating a corrupt system, but it was moving to a change.

You talk about a feeling. My life will never be the same. My life moved into another path, because once you feel it, you start seeing real power. You stop being afraid of nuclear bombs. You see it as a bunch of silly men who are playing with an extension of their sex organs. When you get up in the morning and see the sun come out, it's like nighttime cleaned out the sky. When you hear people talk about high tech, you say high tech is the nipple on a mother's breast. No scientists, no military industrial com-

plex have ever been able to reproduce it. That's high tech.
Real power is so beautiful.

The people who are happy are the people who are doing
something. The Ralph Naders, the Mother Theresas, the
Coretta Scott Kings, the heads of civil rights organizations, the heads of human rights organizations. I look at
Jack Healy, the executive director of Amnesty International; I met with the head of UNESCO. They are sitting
there so thrilled and so happy because what they are doing
is built on sharing and caring, not on getting. It's built on
''I give to you in a way that I make you think you're doing
me a favor by taking it.'' That's happiness.

Because of the society we're in we have to say that there
are two definitions of happiness. There's the one of happiness which you learn as a child. Then there's real universal happiness. It is something that's down in the gut; it
transcends all culture. That can be pushed aside because
real power will always move over for chumps. Fear and
God do not occupy the same space. The happiness you
find after a bill is paid, the happiness you find behind
drugs, behind alcohol, behind a love affair, those aren't
true happiness. In universal happiness you're so elated your
racism disappears. Your sexism disappears. Your ''isms''
and ''osms'' disappear. Your church background disappears. You become a total universal human being. Everybody you see you love; all the hang-ups are erased. I
believe there is a joy that we human beings were meant to
always have.

If I bring you a pocketful of horse manure, whose
pocket stank the whole trip, yours or mine? If horse manure in my pocket makes my pocket stink, then what does
hatred in my brain and racism and viciousness do to my
mind? Just as the horse manure in my pocket makes my
pocket stink, segregation, prejudice, and hatred in my
brain make my mind stink. If I had a choice between a
stinky mind or a stinky coat, I'd throw away my coat. You
can also cleanse out your mind. But so many people get
so groovy with that feeling of hate. It destroys you in the
long run.

I cannot be vicious to you without being vicious to my

family. Show me a black who believes that white folks are all no good and I'll show you a black who hates his old lady. Show me a white who believes every nigger on the planet should be dead and I'll show you one whose children are afraid of him. It isn't something you turn on and turn off. When you turn this heat on it cannot be for certain people, it's for everybody. However, once I unveil and drop my evilness and my viciousness, and accept you, that's universal happiness. You don't say, "I can't loan you money because the last person I loaned some money to didn't pay me." It is not my job as a beautiful human being to worry about payback. It's my job to give. People giving money for Ethiopia say, "You think it's getting there?" The one thing they can't steal is when you reach your hand out and drop it in the bucket. There's a vibration there that eliminates hunger. There's a universal order that's inside and that says thanks.

There is a legend that when you go from this to that other order, you won't be asked your color, what books you read, or what school you went to, but how much service did you give to your brothers as human beings when you were on this planet. You can't give service without joy. You can't give service without happiness. Real service is the planting, the planting of the seed.

When I tune in to my beautiful self, I get happiness. Everything in the universe belongs to me. If I really believe there's one God that's mother and father and I'm God's child, I've inherited the universe. You might put a fence around those oranges but those are my oranges. It's the same thing as if you're my father and I'm in jail. They might tell you you can't see me but that doesn't negate the fact that I'm your son and you're my daddy. Every Rolls-Royce out there is mine and I don't have to drive them all to prove that they're mine. In this whole universe I am the heir.

I learned a long time ago that God never needed leaders. If I'm willing to serve God—and who but a clown would mind being a servant in his parents' kingdom—I inherit this kingdom. I'm the hippest servant going because I'm the servant for the man and the woman who controls it all. I'm their child and I love it.

If our attitude toward life is negative, we are going to experience an unhappy world. There will always be too much traffic on the freeway, the service in the restaurant will always be too slow, our children's rooms will never be clean enough, the weather will never be nice enough, and we'll feel that family and friends should have done things better or differently. A positive attitude toward life and others is a requirement for a life of happiness. When negative situations do arise, the ability to see problems as challenges presenting opportunities for creative solutions is the difference between failure and success, unhappiness and happiness. *Do I criticize? Is my attitude positive or negative? Do my problems defeat me? Do I know that the solutions to my problems are within me?*

Julia Chang Bloch says with pride, "To have come from being a refugee to being a presidential appointee is what America is all about."

Julia Chang Bloch is the assistant administrator of the Bureau of Food for Peace and Voluntary Assistance at the Agency for International Development. After serving in the Peace Corps she received an M.A. at Harvard University on a fellowship. In Washington she has worked for the Peace Corps, the United States Senate, and the United States Information Agency. Julia is the sister-in-law of Ivan Bloch, who appears later in this book.

Julia Chang Bloch

I've been to the poorest countries in the world and the poor people in America live like many middle-class people in poor countries. The fact is, America is a democracy, and we have so many options here to make what we want out of our lives. This country provides a free education and, if we work hard and apply ourselves, we can achieve a great deal. If a family like mine can do what we've done, then I don't see how the opportunities here are overlooked.

I came to the United States from China in 1951. I was nine years old. I didn't speak English. My mother spoke broken English. She had to work three jobs to support the family. At one time she had a grocery store. She also sold materials. She also worked as a waitress. She scraped up enough money to buy her first restaurant. My father, who was considerably older, worked at the Asia Foundation for a while and then he retired.

My first summer here, I was put in a class for the mentally retarded because, in those days, some educators didn't distinguish between the fact that you didn't speak English because you were a foreigner and the lack of mental facility. After a day or two, the teacher realized something wasn't right. I spent the summer playing hopscotch and learned English very quickly.

My father told me that I had to learn to speak English. In fact, he used to try to put chop sticks or stones in my mouth to improve my diction. He said, "You're going to have a hard enough time as it is as a minority in this country. Do better than the Americans so that you can compete." It's something I've always remembered.

I went through the public school system in San Francisco. After high school I got a B.A. in communication and public policy at Berkeley, and then I joined the Peace Corps. I said on my application that I would only go to Asia and I was sent to Malaysia. It was a wonderful experience. I learned there that I can do anything if I put my mind to it.

I did a lot of traveling, but because you couldn't get into China in those days, I did the next best thing. I went to Taiwan and to Hong Kong and took a look. I met lots of people and associated with a lot of Chinese. I came to the conclusion that I am an American. An American woman has the best of many worlds. We have independence, options, self-reliance, and the chance to do whatever we put our mind to. The opportunities are here if we take advantage of them.

I have always loved what I do. My work is very satisfying. When I go out on trips I can see that my program saves lives, and that's very satisfying. I can have an impact on public policy. That is also very rewarding. It is a very demanding job, but I do not like to be bored. After five years in this job, I'm still finding new challenges. Every day there are new horizons to meet and that's exciting. At the same time, my husband, Stuart, and I have a very good relationship. We enjoy each other. We have a nice life.

If I had to make a choice, I would choose work. That is what makes life meaningful. A famous actress who was being interviewed on television was asked about her children and her husbands. She said, "Work, that's the only thing there is, really. It's all me and nobody can take it away from me." I would have to say, on the other hand, that without Stuart it wouldn't be as nice.

I didn't ever really care about getting married. It was not the thing that I desired most in my life. My career was what I was interested in. I thought that you really couldn't combine both very well. Remember, I got married almost twenty years ago. In those days the idea was that when you got married you would have children and you would have a family. Then when your children were grown, maybe you would go back to work. That wasn't what turned me on. So I thought, "Well, I just won't get married." I was going off merrily on that track until I met Stuart. A week or two before we were to get married, I got sick and I'm not a hypochondriac. It was probably the only psychosomatic illness I've had in my life. I literally could not speak and I didn't want to do anything. I couldn't get the invitations out. Stuart did everything. He even dragged me to New York and got me my wedding gown. I just broke down because I was so petrified about getting married, thinking that marriage was going to become the traditional prison. But it didn't turn out that way. We've been growing together on different tracks because we're different people. We have different interests, but our growth is in the same direction and at the same pace.

I think that our society socializes women to live their lives through their mates. You have to have a mate. To get a mate, you have to be attractive. You do things to please not yourself, but your mate. Once you get married, you live your life through your husband and your children. You put yourself second. Maybe you have to be selfish to be happy. I know pretty much what I like, what I don't like, what I enjoy, what I don't, and what I want and what I don't want. I don't let society, prohibitions, or rules pin me down.

Most women may mouth that they are pleased or happy with their lives. But because we're all individual human beings, we want to have some feelings of self-worth and a sense of accomplishment. I was involved with a lot of women when I was working in the Senate on the displaced homeworkers legislation. It was very sad to see women bereft at age fifty. Their husbands had dumped them for somebody younger and their children had gone. These women had no professional experience and they had to change their lifestyles considerably. Some of my friends who are successful career women and who are not married are unhappy because they feel they've failed in terms of society's concept of a successful woman. They still feel that they should be seeking somebody to marry. I also know some very happy women who have happy careers and happy marriages with children.

A lot of times women will say, "I'm just a housewife." I always ask, "Why do you say *just?*" It's as honorable to be a housewife as it is to be a working woman. A housewife works at home. Do what you do and be happy with what you do; don't denigrate yourself. The women who I think are happy live well-rounded lives.

I'm an optimist. I always believe that if you really put your mind to it, you can either overcome or you can make things change. Some people live in a dream world. They keep lying to themselves, and they don't do anything about certain aspects of their lives that may be cramping their happiness. You can't just be a pure optimist. A lot of people blame everybody else but themselves. Maybe that's their way of finding happiness. They can delude themselves by saying, "It's somebody else's fault." They don't have to face the fact that maybe they're a failure. If they took all the time spent worrying, pitying themselves, and blaming other people, they could accomplish something. To me, happiness is a state of mind. It's something that you either have or you haven't. You have to decide what makes you happy and then do it.

I like interesting people, interesting conversation, interesting food, interesting places and environments, interesting books. Friends are important, but I'm basically a private person. I don't know that I have to have friends to be happy. They make life nicer, but they're not absolutely critical. I like to read. I also like to do pots. I am a potter. I enjoy work. If I didn't work I probably would drive Stuart crazy. I have a lot of energy in me; it's productive energy. I want to do something meaningful with my life.

Stuart has taught me to relax. I used to be a very highstrung person. If I wasn't moving every minute, I felt that I was wasting time. I had to do things. We used to kid each other about who was going to take whose vacation next. My idea of vacation is to go to a place I've never been—the more exotic, the better. I will have read every interesting guidebook there is, and I will have picked out every place that I want to see. Every moment of the day is planned. I want to see everything. I don't want to miss anything. Stuart wants to go to the beach and lie in the sun.

You should live your life to the fullest. I have a thirst for learning and doing new and different things, but I think, as I'm getting older, I get more and more relaxed. Sometimes I think, "It would be nice to have a week when I can just putter around the house."

The American dream is to achieve your full potential. There are very few societies where you can do that. I don't think I've achieved my full potential yet. I'm still at it.

Harmony and balance are very Chinese. I think Stuart and I have a balanced relationship, a harmonious personal relationship. We never argue about anything major. If we ever have a fight it's over little things that don't matter. We've achieved a balance in our life in a sense that we're each other's best friend. It's just very natural. Our personal life is very harmonious. Stuart is my best friend.

In the Asian culture there is a goal of achieving inner peace. Everybody has a different state of inner peace. I think Americans go around psychoanalyzing themselves too much. Americans want to probe every ounce of their mental being. If there's not a problem then you find a problem. If you think long enough or talk about it long enough you're going to find something.

Living life—it's experiences.

We have two primary missions in life—to appreciate our uniqueness and to affirm the uniqueness of others. To validate, support, and sanction our own goodness and the goodness, talents, and dreams of others will bring us happiness. One of the most decisive factors in determining positive self-worth is approval. *Do I affirm others? Do I criticize and find fault?*

Ruby Dee contrasts herself with her brother and other black men in America.

Ruby Dee's acting credits include Go Tell It on the Mountain *and* I Know Why the Caged Bird Sings *on television;* The Taming of the Shrew *and* King Lear *for the American Shakespeare Festival; and* Buck and the Preacher *and* A Raisin in the Sun *in films.*

Ruby Dee

Happiness is a feeling of fulfillment. It's achieving a specific goal that you set out to achieve. It's a fleeting state, not a permanent one. When I wanted to achieve something and I achieved it, and it's been appreciated and accepted, that's a good feeling. It's also nice seeing others achieve something that they tried so hard to do. Your contentment is tied up with theirs. You feel happy when they reach their goal. It's like watching somebody come up a hill and finally getting there. Whether you are standing at the top of the hill or along the side, you are happy when they reach the top. You can feel happy for yourself or for your children, husband, friends, and neighbors.

One of the attributes of happiness is that you forget what it was that made you happy the last time you were happy. You can't repeat it. You are not happy again the same way. Every happy is a different happy. Happy results from so many things. It's nebulous, will-o'-the-wisp. It's the pure enjoyment of a moment.

When as a child you get the correct sanction in some way, it follows you all of your life. It's a happy turn of events when your parents, teachers, and friends recognize and support something in you that you enjoy doing and you're awfully good at. They help define you in a way. They give you confidence to pursue something because they recognize that what you like to do is what you should do. You don't have to doubt yourself and think, ''Oh, I shouldn't be doing this,'' or ''I wonder if I should try something else.'' One attribute of happiness is a sanctioning of who you are and what you want. My girlfriend's mother and father told me that I should go on the stage and that I would be a very good actress. In a sense they sanctioned; they gave me a kind of moral support.

My brother, on the other hand, didn't read very well, but the truth is he was really an electronic genius. When he was about ten or eleven he made a telephone system across a wide avenue between his friend's house and our house. He also built a radio. A policeman even came to our house because my brother's radio was interfering with the police circuit. We were very shocked that he had built it. My brother's friends in the Army said he could fix anything. Had he been sanctioned, another approach could have been offered him. He wasn't like his sisters who could read. There are different ways to be brilliant. My brother was affected because he wasn't sanctioned. That's a big, big unhappy. He might have been something really special had somebody paid attention to his particular kind of genius.

My mother had wanted to be an actress at one time, and many black people were accepted for singing and dancing and boxing and ball. These were the traditional ways that black people have made it out of poverty. Parents don't want you to be poor. They want you to be successful. They can't afford to send you to medical school and you don't get a scholarship. So if you can sing or dance, those are the ways that white folks approve of your advancing. In that kind of a racist context, no matter how subliminal it may be, your values are very much affected. Unless you come from the stock that says, "We fight here." There are those kinds of people. My mother came from people who wanted to be doctors and lawyers. Those were other kinds of professions, but you were sort of let in to those professions.

The unions came. Blacks were excluded. This was a very damaging thing, because being accepted for what you can do is to be happy. Not being able to get into a union because of being black has happened to countless blacks. The effects are still with us. To be accepted by one's fellow creatures and recognized for your worth is a happy.

What a tremendous job has to be done to make black men happy today. The threat is economic. The basis of slavery was economics. As Martin Luther King, Jr., so clearly pointed out, if slavery had not been profitable, there would have been no slavery. A black man has so many strengths internally that were he to have the economic power, it might be more than the white population, especially the white males, would think they could stand. There has been an effective heel in the groin of the black man. I hope it's not fatal. I hope that the strengths inherent will grow roots and mush through this blind spot. Black men and black people in general have lived for so long with so much unhappiness.

I don't know where the impetus will come from, but we are going to live on this earth as brothers and sisters and we are going to embrace each other. We're going to do a lot of things that right now might not seem apparent.

Racism tends to gut confidence. It almost happened to me. To have some essence about you discovered, recognized, and appreciated is to be happy.

* * *

If you had a happy childhood, the chances are you will be a happy adult. People who have grown up in a family with love, support, encouragement, and self-acceptance adjust to life. Adults who come from happy childhoods have learned lessons about optimism, self-worth, the necessity for effort, and a variety of values such as honesty, self-confidence, and integrity. They experienced love, feel secure about themselves—"I am lovable"—and are free to give love to others.

No single job is more important for parents than to help their children feel positive self-worth. We begin to feel positive (or negative) about ourselves as children. As adults, if we choose positive actions, people, and experiences, more positive messages come our way. Those messages are that we are good and worthwhile. When we contribute to the lives of others unselfishly, we reap the love, admiration, and respect of others, which in turn bring about a personal sense of self-worth, satisfaction, contentment, and happiness. *What is the purpose of my accomplishments? Am I doing them for others? Am I doing them for me?*

Congressman Morris K. Udall of Arizona's Second District has served with distinction in the Congress since 1961. In 1976, at the urging of fifty House colleagues, Congressman Udall sought the Democratic presidential nomination, an effort that won him a national reputation and following. As chairman of the Interior and Insular Affairs Committee, Mo Udall is deeply involved with legislation affecting nuclear energy, public lands, national parks, and Indian affairs. He led the fight for the Alaska Lands Bill, considered by many to be the most significant conservation measure of this century.

Congressman Morris K. Udall

With all my shortcomings I feel comfortable with who I am and what I'm doing. I don't yearn to be different. Whatever I am and whatever success I've had is owing in large part to being raised in a religious family in a small

Mormon town. The emphasis in the Mormon church has always been on family and honesty and all the good qualities and virtues.

My parents were optimistic, and the lessons we learned were that work is good, people should share, people should help, be fair to other people, be tolerant, enjoy life a little bit, and don't be too dull and sour about things. The Mormons have a concept of free agency. Things are not predestined. You can change the world, you can improve yourself, you can achieve. That's been a part of my underlying philosophy.

I lost an eye in an accident when I was six years old. Children are pretty cruel and they would kid me about the eye. I think I started poking fun at myself in self-defense, and that kind of humor became part of my personality and my approach. I learned early on to compensate for that lost eye, and I was an eager beaver. I could do any darn thing that the other kids could do. In my junior and senior years in high school I was editor of the yearbook, quarterback of the football team, led the basketball team in scoring, had my own dance band, and wrote a political column for the weekly newspaper. I had all of this development through living in the small town. When I started to compete with the kids in the bigger cities, I found that I was really better off. I was a generalist. In a little town you could do everything. As a trial lawyer I had to know a little bit about electricity and engineering and medicine and human relationships. I think I was able to be a good generalist because of that exposure to so many things.

There were six children in the family. My father was a superior court judge most of the time I was growing up. Then he became Chief Justice of the Arizona Supreme Court and served about twelve years in that job. My dad always used to say that public service was a rewarding career if you had leadership talents and ability to move people and bring people together. It was a satisfying way to spend your life.

The nicest thing that was ever said about me was at an American Bar Association meeting in Washington when I was on a panel. I was introduced by one of the leaders in the nuclear industry who has to deal with me on a regular basis. He said, "I don't know why it is or just what this guy does, but when he's on your side you win and when he's not, you lose."

The satisfaction of seeing something good happen and the feeling that maybe it wouldn't have happened if I hadn't been a part of it makes it all work for me. In the Alaska Lands Bill, which President Carter signed in 1980, we doubled the national park system in one bill, one stroke of the pen. When Congress finally got through, we had doubled the wilderness system and the game refuges in the country. We disposed of 105 million acres to the people of Alaska. It was the biggest land decision made in the history of the world in terms of resource protection. I was hated and hung in effigy, and it took us six to eight years to put the thing together. But it was all worth it, standing at the White House and being given the pen that the president used to sign that bill. It was very satisfying knowing that I not only had done a good job, but the president and other people said, "We'd never be here if it weren't for this guy's skills. He knows the Congress; he knows how to get things done."

I like to feel that I helped turn things around in Vietnam. We sustained fifty thousand casualties after the 1968 election. It took President Nixon four years to wind down the war. There were others who spoke out before I did, but in my own state I was the first major figure to raise questions about the Vietnam War. I have a feeling that maybe I helped shorten it a little bit.

President Jimmy Carter asked me to help him reform the civil service, which hadn't been touched for a hundred years. I was floor manager of that bill and got it done. President Nixon called me to the White House and asked me to help with his postal reform bill. I took that on for a Republican president. I think it made life a little bit better for a lot of people. I could give you a couple of dozen lesser or greater pieces of legislation that I've handled.

The campaign in 1976 was the best of times and the worst of times; we were up on cloud nine, and we were down in the depths of depression. I think people in our campaign saw me as somebody who was honest in an intellectual sense, who didn't try to fool people or try to fool himself. They probably saw me as somebody who was not perfect but who was a little better than the candidates you sometimes get.

My sense of humor was very attractive to people. This was my great entrée. The night we lost the primary in Michigan I told an old Will Rogers story. Will Rogers is one of my heroes. He said, "Get a few laughs and do the best you can." I said, "We only come here once, and we do the best we can and get a few laughs and live our lives so that even when we lose, we're ahead. I'm ahead in friendships and the support of my family. I'm ahead in having all of you fine people from all over who want to work and give money and help." Our campaign had something to say about the direction the country was going in and what kind of country we were going to have. That's a great satisfaction to me.

I think you take life the way it comes. There's an old piece of philosophy that I first heard attributed to Abraham Lincoln. It's got to be one of those ancient stories. According to the story, an Eastern monarch, one of the most powerful people on earth in ancient times, called together his wise men and told them he wanted them to come up with a slogan or saying, or a piece of advice that was short and simple and would last. It was to be appropriate for all occasions in going through life. They returned months later, having written, "And this, too, shall pass."

When you stop to think about it, it's true. When you're high on the hog and everything's going well and there's laughter, good will, and good feeling, you have to know that's going to pass. There will also be times when you're going to be sad and the breaks go the other way. When you're down you go up, and when you're up you go down. Life itself will pass. Nobody lives forever. That's a pretty good philosophy.

I got Bob Kennedy to use another piece of philosophy I carry around in my head in his campaign of 1968, which touched a lot of lives. He would talk against the defeatist idea that one person can't do anything, the attitude that "this is a big country and what the hell could I do?" He paraphrased an old statement: I am one; I am only one, but I am one. I cannot do everything, but I can do something; and what I can do, I ought to do and what I ought to do, by the grace of God, I will do. Kennedy used that very effectively, and it's a pretty good piece of advice.

I battle Parkinson's disease. No one knows what causes it, and there is no cure, but some medicine helps alleviate the symptoms. There are days when I'm tempted to curse fate and ask, "Why me?" I'm a guy who's been a good, healthy outdoorsman. It's been a challenge to build a life and arrange a regimen, but I can function, I think, quite effectively. It's discouraging some days. You have good days and bad days. There are times in the day or in the week when my medicine doesn't work quite right. Maybe I'm under stress or I've been on one too many airplanes in twenty-four hours. I really feel that the disease is taking hold of me. My muscles ache and my legs are stiff. I can't do a lot of the simple things, such as buttoning a shirt collar and that sort of thing, as well and as quickly as I'd like to.

I remember that this, too, shall pass. I know that some time in the next twenty-four hours I'm going to feel better and the medicine is going to work. When the medicine keeps me in good shape, I remind myself that some time before the day is out, I'm probably going to be miserable for a while. It comes and goes.

I have a physiotherapist who helps my bad back problems. She said, "You're a hero to a lot of people." I thought she was talking politics. I said, "What do you mean?" She said, "You came out front on Parkinson's and made people see that you can live a good life despite it." It's a new mission for me.

Life's basically been good to me and I've been happy. I enjoy what I do. I suspect happiness is in part a conduit in that you don't recognize it at the time. You never sit down and say, "Gee, I'm happy this morning." You feel good, you enjoy the day, you enjoy life. I've had my share.

5 Love/Work/Hope

Three essential elements for happiness are something to do, something to hope for, and someone to love. In our personal lives, it is necessary that we have the opportunity to love another person, or other people. To give to another unconditionally, with no strings attached, is the essence of love. We need to give love and we need to receive love from others. Love is what makes us feel good about ourselves. Love is the key to happiness. We must have others in our lives whom we can love and from whom we can receive love, but we must love ourselves first in order to give love to others. *Do I love myself? Am I secure enough to love others?*

Dr. Joyce Brothers says, "I don't think you can be happy without some love in your life."

Joyce Brothers, Ph.D., is probably America's best-known psychologist. She has frequently appeared on "most admired women" polls conducted by United Press International, Gallup, Roper, and Good Housekeeping *magazine. Joyce broadcasts daily on the NBC radio network's "Newsline"; her daily column appears in more than three hundred and fifty newspapers; and her books, including her latest,* What Every Woman Ought to Know about Love and Marriage, *have been translated into twenty-six languages.*

Joyce Brothers, Ph.D.

You must have some love in your life in order to be happy.
It doesn't have to be love of man for woman. It can be
love of God; it can be love of mankind. Happiness is not
possible without love, although I think you can love and
be very unhappy. You need to be able to give love to be
happy. When you're not getting love, you're unhappy.
Some studies have shown that babies die if they're not
loved.

Relationships with people—friends, partners, those for
whom we'd lay down our lives—can be used to promote
happiness, but not if you seek happiness through them.
The more you pursue happiness, the less likely it is that
you're going to find it.

Self-worth or self-love is really a matter of degree. We
have a continuum of "I hate myself" to "I love myself."
If you love yourself too much, you're incapable of love.
The thing that makes us fall in love is the differential
between what we would like ourselves to be—our idealized image—and the image of ourselves as we think we
are, which is more realistic. Dissatisfaction with the self
makes us fall in love when we find somebody who we
think has cured our problem. If that differential is so
great that we can't bear ourselves, we're not capable of
falling in love.

We've heard over and over, "You can't love somebody
else unless you love yourself." What we're really saying
is that we respect rather than love ourselves. When we feel
comfortable with what we are doing in general, we feel
respect for ourselves. If you demand of your love relationship that happiness pursue you because of it, you're going
to destroy that love relationship. It only happens as a by-
product of your giving and your getting. If you say, "I'm
only going to give because I expect happiness and if I
don't get happiness I'm not going to give," it never happens.

Think of two people with baskets by their side. One
says, "Okay, I'm giving you this to put in your basket, so
now you must give me something to put in my basket and

we have to keep our baskets even.'' In that case happiness is not possible. However, if you sometimes give and sometimes receive, and in the long run the baskets balance out, then happiness is possible. When a relationship gets too far out of kilter, when you are on the giving end all the time, or you're on the receiving end all the time, there's no happiness. There is no happiness for the partner who is given too much, and no happiness for the partner who is giving too much. In any master/slave relationship there's resentment on both sides.

A healthy relationship is like a seesaw. One person isn't always dominant and the other person isn't always submissive. No person is totally independent except a hermit, and a hermit is grossly abnormal. So in any relationship, whether it's friendship, parent/child, or marriage, sometimes one is more dominant than the other, but it evens out in the end.

The link between sexuality and happiness is probably one of the weakest links. You would think that researchers would have conducted enormous numbers of studies of sex in happy marriages, but they never really got around to it until fairly recently. Most of the studies on sexuality and marriage have been done on couples who go to therapists because they have troubled marriages. They find in such populations impotence, frigidity, and premature ejaculation. Now there are studies on sex in a happy marriage, and lo and behold, they've found frigidity, impotence, and premature ejaculation and the same number of problems, the only difference being that the people love each other. It doesn't seem to matter all that much.

A great many priests and nuns who are happy and fulfilled have no sex life at all. Many, many widows and widowers who have loved their husbands and wives dearly have lost their partners. There is no sex in their lives, yet they are content. There are virgin boys and girls who are happy, too. It is possible for gay people to be just as happy as heterosexual people, but I don't think a sex life is necessary for happiness.

Secure people look for something complementary to themselves in their relationships. ''You give me something that I am missing and makes my life more complete, and I will give you something you're missing that makes your life more complete.'' The old Greek myth said, ''Once male and female were one and as a joke the gods divided them into two, and people have been wandering the earth looking for their own lost opposite half.'' There isn't only one half. Lots of people can make that other half, but it is the meshing that increases happiness. Insecure people are looking for security in their relationships, but you can't look for security in a relationship. Nobody can give you security. The insecure person holds on so tightly that the relationship is smothered. You have to be able to bring your half to the relationship, to make it total. The insecure person brings only a quarter to the relationship and asks for three quarters. The purpose of marriage is having someone who cares as much about your success, your happiness, your comfort, and your delight as he or she would care about his or her own.

In terms of what they say about their own happiness, the happiest of all people are married men, then single women, then married women; least happy of all are bachelors. No one really knows for sure why this is so, but many married men enjoy enormous comfort. Who wouldn't want a stereotypical wife? I'd love to come home after a hard day to somebody who makes supper, has my slippers out, and scratches my back. It's really nice to have someone else worry about getting the clothes back from the cleaners. Many married men have the comforts of home. Single women probably expect that life is going to be simply hell for them because they're single in an environment where people are married or paired off. They think their lives are going to be dreadful. They find out they're fulfilled, and very happy, so much better than they thought they would be. I guess that's why they're more satisfied. The women's movement has helped out in this area. A lot of women who should never marry have the option now of not marrying and not being embarrassed by the fact that they're not married.

Marriage, it appears, is good for men but not so hot for women. In marriages husbands really should do more than just help. They should take an equal share and an equal responsibility in making marriage work. Women do much more to keep their marriages together than men do. One area of conflict in relationships arises because we have trained our males not to communicate, to be silent about their emotions. In many cases men and women talk about two different things. So many problems can be resolved by the willingness to talk about them and work them through. Many men are reluctant to talk about things that matter to them. If communication opened up it would be a huge step forward.

Being able to take your partner for granted is a big plus in marriage. When we were young we went away to summer camp and it was fun. When we got home from camp it was different. The feeling was "I'm home, I can relax now." That's what a marriage should be. We go out into the world and do our best, and we have our problems and our triumphs. Marriage should be a situation in which, when we get home, we kick off our shoes, take off our girdles or ties, relax and say with a sigh of relief, "Home." If we have to start charming one another it isn't a relief. That is one of the reasons why the living-together relationship is decreasing in popularity. People are still performing. It's wonderful that the divorce rate is leveling off. People are discovering that you don't get divorced and live happily ever after.

Half of all marriages in America end in divorce. We choose our mates poorly. We confuse love and lust. Perhaps we are looking to someone else to "make us happy." We get involved in relationships that bring us pain. Why we stay in these relationships filled with so much unhappiness is often a mystery. "Till death do us part," the expectations of family and society, and the sacredness of a religious marriage all may play a part. However, we may feel so poorly about ourselves that we accept our misery, believing that this is all we deserve and this is the way relationships are supposed to be. Perhaps as adults we are recreating some of the pain of our childhood. We may have grown up with sadness and pain and unhappiness, so we believe that good relationships include insensitivity, insecurity, rejection, unpredictability, and pain. They don't. *What is the quality of my marriage? Am I trying to control or am I helping to grow? Am I trying to have my own way or am I "adjusting" without effort?*

Edward L. Bernays offers what he feels are the necessary ingredients for a successful and happy marriage. He believes, "If marriage is to be a viable institution, it should be viable twenty-four hours a day."

Edward L. Bernays is respectfully called "the father of public relations." He counseled U.S. presidents from Calvin Coolidge to Dwight Eisenhower and such legendary figures as Enrico Caruso, Thomas Edison, and Henry Ford. A nephew of Sigmund Freud, he was responsible for the early popularization of Freud's writing in America. At ninety-five, he continues an active career as a consultant and lectures throughout America.

Edward L. Bernays

At the universities professors don't teach students anything about outside life. They teach all about the ancient philosophies of Rome and Greece, but at no time do they deal with the realities of present-day living and the interrelationships of people. At no point do the colleges ever talk about job satisfaction or your future life. There are no courses on human relations and no emphasis on parent relationships with children.

Young people ought to be taught to develop personal relationships and to be aware of their social responsibilities as well. Colleges should offer a course called Personal Happiness. It could be created by philosophy departments and be given the same priority as the Greeks and Romans. It would have to be taught by an individual who had mastered physiology, sociology, social psychology, economics, psychoanalytics, and psychiatry. The instructor would have to be a pretty smart person.

If I were asked to create such a course, I would teach the importance of psychological tests at an early age so that people aren't misplaced in jobs. Many are; they change from place to place. I say, "Never permit a dichotomy to rule your life, a dichotomy in which you hate what you do so you can have pleasure in your spare time. Look for a situation in which your work will give you as much happiness as your spare time."

I would also teach the real meaning of a relationship with a mate. You should have with you a companion, a George Gallup; a person who tells you what nobody else tells you, who modifies your attitudes, and who interprets other people to you. You may be the victim or the beneficiary of your behavior without knowing which behavior is important or not. I used to say to my wife, "You're my George Gallup."

I would teach the true place of sexual intercourse in a relationship. Happiness really is based on fundamental values like mutual understanding, empathy, sympathy, adjustment, compromise on little elements without its being called compromise, and having a mutual goal. Something is wrong with the academic process when people think emotional sex is the equivalent of happiness and don't have any idea about the other elements of feeling, emotion, psychological support, mental support, and working together. Young people are ignorant of how happiness is brought about. They see it purely on an emotional plane. The whole boyfriend/girlfriend relationship does not produce happiness. It produces emotional satisfaction and furor without carrying with it the other elements of human understanding.

You and your partner should know that everybody has five ages, not only one age. Understanding the meaning of five ages can contribute to happiness. Chronological age is given all the attention. Everybody also has a physiological age, which is often quite different. My doctor tells me my physiological age is sixty-one and my chronological age is ninety-five. Everybody also have a mental age. You can be a hundred chronologically but have a mental age of six if you are a cretin or a moron. In addition, everybody has a different societal age in terms of being able to adjust to people, events, and situations. I know people who are sixty-five chronologically who, if they were to meet President Reagan, would shiver like a kid of ten. Finally, everybody has an emotional age, which is not necessarily a concomitant of the other ages. It can be much younger or older. The public doesn't recognize these elements in terms of the mating process. That's why there are so many divorces. If two people are looking for happiness they should know whether there's adjustment in all of these ages. Granting that there is, they should have happiness.

In most modern marriages husbands and half the wives leave after breakfast for their jobs. They don't see each other till the evening meal. If they stay home they may have an hour or two together before they go to bed. After whatever fulfillment bedtime gives them they go to sleep, and the same pattern repeats itself the next day. If you really want happiness and you find a person who can give it to you, you get married and go into the same field. Today there are very few fields that you can't go into together. In my own work, my wife was an equal partner. You can work that out at any level. Formerly, it was possible only in mom-and-pop-grocery-store marriages, but today I know a law firm in which there's a husband and wife, I know an accounting firm in which there's a husband and wife, I know a medical practice in which there's a husband and wife, both physicians.

People say, "We need time apart." I'd say, "Then don't get married in the first place." That's undoubtedly why divorces happen, and we know that 43 percent of all marriages end in divorce. Gerontologists say they have no doubt that in the next century life will be sustained up to a hundred and ten years. If marriage is to be a viable institution, it should be viable twenty-four hours a day for as many years as people live.

For most people happiness involves just a small part of a twenty-four hour day. Actually, happiness is a complete adjustment to life. If you work, you adjust yourself to a twelve-hour day of work. If you enjoy exercise, you adjust yourself to that. If you enjoy movies, you adjust to taking two hours off to see a movie. If you're a policeman, you adjust to being shot at. If you want to keep thin, you adjust to not eating sweets. You adjust to marriage; and you adjust to children. The whole basis of life and happiness is to adjust.

In your particular marriage, what are the disagreements between you and your spouse? When do you consider these minor and when do you consider them major? What do you do about major disagreements and what do you do about minor disagreements? That's the way I would get at whether a couple is happy or not. My wife and I didn't resent having to make adjustments because when you're in love you want to live in harmony. There were no such problems as she wanted the window open and I wanted it closed because we'd adjust. If she wanted it closed that was it. We adjusted to each other.

The basis of a good marriage is that if you marry the right person there are no differences anywhere. They don't come up. Differences do come up if you don't marry the right person. If your wife wants the window closed and you want it open, that may become the basis of a divorce. I don't remember a time in the fifty-eight years of our marriage—a twenty-four-hour-a-day relationship—when my wife and I ever had to make a conscious adjustment, which meant doing something we didn't want to do.

Young men and women should gain some knowledge and understanding that sleeping with each other isn't the basic element of happiness or love. In fact, it might really have very little to do with it in terms of the broader aspects of human understanding and human empathy in a relationship. If places like Harvard and other universities would put the emphasis on teaching these things, we wouldn't have the unhappiness that comes not only to the men and women of divorce but especially to their children.

Happiness to me occurs when two people of the opposite sex completely complement each other so they feel comfortably adjusted to life and to each other. That happened to me and to my mate.

Any relationship—but especially marriage—must grow. Rather than being an unhealthy and destructive dependency, a positive relationship must be a liberating experience that allows the partners not only to share their lives, but to realize their individual potential as well. *Is my marriage or relationship a positive growing experience for both of us? Is our relationship getting bitter or getting better?*

Ruby Dee and Ossie Davis worked together in the Broadway production of Jeb *in 1946 and were married two years later. As wife and husband and individually they have built brilliant careers in television, films, and the theater as actors, writers, and producers. They co-starred in* Purlie Victorious, *which Ossie wrote, on Broadway and in the film. Ruby and Ossie are hosts, actors, and producers of the critically acclaimed PBS television series* With Ossie and Ruby *and the PBS special* Martin Luther King: The Dream and the Drum.

Ruby Dee and Ossie Davis look at their marriage and its effect on their happiness.

Ruby Dee

Ossie and I have been married for thirty-seven years. We have three youngsters and four grandchildren. They are the focal point of our lives. They're home. Otherwise I would be out there acting and working with no one to come home to, nobody in particular to whom it mattered. When success comes to you, a family to share with is really gratifying. That to me is a happy, really good feeling.

The wedding is the fact. The marriage is the process. You marry at many levels, many times, sometimes many times a day. If you have more levels at which you can be married and do marry, then marriage has excitement to it. As you grow older you keep finding places to marry, areas to marry anew. There's personal growth, new interests, things upon which you can come together.

We lead separate lives, too. Ossie likes to work alone. I can also work alone. We come together when it's necessary. There is so much we both want to do.

Ossie Davis

If Ruby and I couldn't have become friends, we would have run out of this relationship long ago. You start out as lovers, then you are husband and wife, then you are parents and co-workers, and finally you arrive at being friends. Basically, that is the structure of our relationship. Getting to be friends is the hardest part of all. It is ultimately the most rewarding because all the other elements are subsumed in friendship.

As young folks we are pushed along by biology and culture and genes and inheritance and custom and society and appetites. We find ourselves involved and we find ourselves committed, then we find ourselves married. Nobody ever stops to ask you what you want. You find, either by example or by persuasion, that you are in the middle of something. It is only later that you begin to make hard choices.

Choosing a friend is different from choosing a wife. You have to take a wife because procreation keeps one generation available to replace another. But friendship is all left to you. To find a friend is indeed to find a rare treasure. Of course, you don't know it at the time it happens. Certainly when Ruby and I first met, it wasn't friendship we had in mind. It was acquaintance, attraction, all of those things that young, lusty people see in each other's eyes. But as those fires temper themselves and begin to burn lower and lower, other things come up out of the turmoil that you didn't even know were there. They are central and they are important and our particular friendship is one of them. Our friendship is the crowning glory of my adult life.

A positive, happy relationship is built on trust, respect, and sharing. All relationships, from friendship to mar-

riage, get deeper and better or they become shallow and
fade. Demands, expectations, and the need for approval
are the death knell for any relationship. This type of
relationship is built on getting and not on giving. If the
relationship is built on "what am I getting?" all is lost.
The ideal relationship should be sharing of experiences,
strengths, and hopes—a sharing of our own goodness
with another who appreciates our goodness and shares
his or her goodness with us. The essence of a happy
relationship is the communication of feelings. Self-
revelation carries a relationship to new and deeper levels. By their love, our partners hold up a mirror to us
which affirms our own goodness. *What is the level of
conversation with my partner? Do I feel free enough to
reveal myself and my feelings?*

Margo Howard appreciates the intimacy and sharing in her
own marriage. She says, "My doing something for somebody else is on a very personal level."

Margo Howard has written columns for the Chicago Tribune *and the* Chicago Daily News. *She is the author of*
Eppie: The Story of Ann Landers, *a biography of her
mother. As a magazine journalist she contributes to* The
New Republic, People, The Nation, *and* TV Guide. *Margo
is married to actor Ken Howard.*

Margo Howard

The time I was growing up was a different time for women.
I take the position that it's okay to be at home. If you like
the kiddy action and you like to cook and make beds,
that's fine. The joke was that Margo was going to do it
until she got it right. Not everybody has had three husbands, but I never felt that was a big failure either. "If it
doesn't feel good," I thought, "I am getting out of it."
Each time I said, "I'm never getting married again." I
was a euphoric divorcée. I was always much better on my
own than in a situation that wasn't functional, fun, or re-

warding. I looked. I wanted the perfect partner and I found him.

Ken's a marvelous man. He was raised to like women. He wanted a partner as well and in all this world we found each other. It's an amazing miracle. A computer dating service never would have put us together. I'm older than he is. I'm of another religion, and I had three children trailing after me. We don't really make sense, but people who know us say we do. Ken is my life. We talk all the time. God put two talkers together. We've been married almost nine years, and our conversations are consistently stimulating. We know a lot of the same people now. We've introduced each other into our own worlds. My gift to him was what he calls my intellectual cronies at Cambridge. He's introduced me to a world of theatrical people, more from the stage than from movies. I find the theatrical companies very like family. In his business you re-meet people over the years and it's great fun.

My kids bring me a lot of happiness. Abra, Adam, and Cricket are wonderful people. Adam said to me, "You were a good mom, better than I thought at the time." Then he added, "Probably better than you thought."

We deserve to be happy. The happiness that flows from a loving relationship and the happiness that comes from a rewarding job are exciting to experience. Happy people often have both. They are filled with enthusiasm, optimism, assurance, and confidence in their personal and professional lives. Their positive attitude is contagious. The fact that some people get that prize should set an example for us all. *Am I getting the happiness I deserve personally and professionally?*

Ted Shackelford shares his excitement for his life and his happiness when he says, "I feel better about myself when I am focused on giving to other people, trying to help them grow, and helping them feel better about themselves."

* * *

*Ted Shackelford stars as Gary Ewing on the CBS television
series* Knots Landing. *After discovering theater at the University of Denver and a year-long run in the daytime soap*
Another World, *Ted appeared in a number of television
specials, movies, and series in guest-starring roles before
joining his present series. An active member of the Sierra
Club, he devotes much of his time to publicly supporting
environmental causes.*

Ted Shackelford

I've sort of boiled happiness down to being comfortable,
trying to live in the middle. It's really difficult to do. First
it's trying to be comfortable with me. Everything else emanates from that. This is a new concept for me, living in
the middle and being at peace with myself. Occasionally
I get that feeling, and it brings tears to my eyes. It happened to me recently. I was sitting with a group of people
and I just felt so at one with everybody, with God, and
with the world. It felt wonderful! It wasn't a great high, it
was peace.

I really love acting. I just love it. It's a kick, it's fun,
it's exciting, it's dull, it's anger-provoking, it's everything,
it's wonderful, *I just love it!* I've had work before but I
didn't have love. I've had what I thought was love but I
didn't have the work. Without both it's just miserable for
me. I've got both now. I've got a terrific relationship with
my wife, Jan. She is my lover and my friend, my best
friend. I'm very dependent on her. I don't go out and try
to be with other people as much as I should because I'm
really able to isolate more with her. I can't think of anybody I'd rather spend time with. It's nice, it's warm, it's
comfortable, peaceful, funny, and crazy. I can be me.
Whoever I am at any given moment of time, I can be that
person with her and it's okay. It's fabulous. I can even be
totally bananas and it's okay. I know she loves me. I know
that for certain. I don't know anything else for a fact, but
that I do know.

As an actor, I have never doubted my talent. That's
never been my problem. I'm capable of doing much

more than I have done so far. The problem for me is all
the externals. It's the externals of "getting the job,"
which is not acting, which is difficult for me. I'm certainly not the first actor to say "I can't do auditions and
I can't do interviews. Just give me the words, man, I
can act anything." Well, that's not the way the system
works. You've got to go through all of that in order to
get to the golden fleece.

The first time I acted was in high school and it was a
lark. My first dramatic role was at the end of my freshman year in college. I played Ben Gant in *Look Home-
ward, Angel,* the older brother who smokes too much,
drinks too much coffee, and drinks too much liquor. I
was eighteen when I did it and it was as if all of a
sudden my head opened up and all the stuff poured in.
I got instant approval. I could be angry; and rather than
people telling me anger was an inappropriate reaction,
rather than somebody saying, "Go to your room,"
rather than somebody saying, "We're going to put you
in jail," they applauded. It was like wow! Talk about
an instant narcotic. I was hooked. On a psychological
level it was fabulous. I could be anybody I wanted to
be. I could be all the things I ever wanted to be without
having to leave my body. The audience didn't know that.
Those people watching would not know it was really
me. Ben Gant was me, Gary Ewing is me. All the roles
I've ever played are me.

As an actor, you've got to keep everything right on
the edge so you can have those emotions there immediately. I guess maybe that's part of what I like about
acting. I can have all those emotions and it's all right.
If I were a policeman or a fireman or a doctor or a
lawyer, and I went around with my emotions on the
edge like that, I wouldn't last long. They'd take me away
real fast. But because I'm an "artist" it's all right, because that's what I do. I sell my emotions. I'm a kid
about it. I fooled them all. I never had to grow up. They
didn't think I could do it, but I did.

I count myself as one of the luckiest people in the world.
I have the best job in the world because I'm doing what I

love doing. How many people can say that? How many people go to work every day with a smile on their face saying, "Oh boy, can't wait to get there"? I'm acting and that's what I love doing. It's what gives me the greatest happiness, my work and Jan. At this point in my life, I've got it made.

Because of our own insecurities we are often afraid of losing another's exclusive devotion to us or we are hostile toward others who seem to be better off than we are. We measure our own lives against what we imagine the lives of others to be. Their youth, popularity, status, looks, success, and security are the yardsticks by which we judge ourselves. Jealousy and envy are the causes of tremendous unhappiness. Our happiness is really tied to our sense of self, the quality of our personal relationships, and the firm belief that we are making a contribution to the lives of others because we are who we are and through our work. *Do I compare? Am I envious of other people's apparent success and happiness? What am I doing to promote my own happiness?*

Helen Thomas asks the important questions about happiness and then reviews—from her vantage point—the happiness of our recent presidents. Of her own work, she states, "I truly do like the news. It isn't a question of seeing my by-line. I'm trying to keep people informed."

Helen Thomas is the United Press International bureau chief at the White House, which she has been covering for twenty-five years. She was the first woman to close a presidential news conference with the traditional "Thank you, Mr. President." Since then she has opened and closed many news conferences in ensuing presidencies. She paved the way for women in journalism as president of the Women's National Press Club and as the first woman officer of the White House Correspondents Association. She has traveled around the world several times with Presidents Richard Nixon, Gerald Ford, and Ronald Reagan.

Helen Thomas

If I were to do an interview to find out if someone was happy my first question would be "Do you like your job?"

I'll go with President John F. Kennedy's definition of happiness. He quoted from the Greeks, saying, "Happiness is the fullest use of one's powers along the lines of excellence." When you consider the amount of time and the amount of dedication that a good job requires, if you're happy in that, I think it is very rewarding and very satisfying. Then I would ask, "How's your love life?" Most people would ask these questions in exactly the reverse order: "How's your love life and how's your job?" But I've spent so much time on my job and I really have felt great reward. There's lots of frustration, of course; nothing's going to be all gravy in any sense. When you get up in the morning you should really want to go to work. If it's exciting and you have some sense that you're going to learn something and be a part of something, I think that's one of the most fulfilling rewards in life. My job does make me happy.

Of course, there's nothing in the world like love and good companionship and the combination of the two. Love can make you happy if everything goes right. But you have less control over love than over what you make of yourself. In work maybe you have better leverage on happiness in the sense of fulfilling what you are. Good luck and a lot of other things make true love possible. You have to go through a lot of bad moments in love to really know what true love is. Great love has to have a tremendous sense of confidence, faith, and your esteem for the other person.

Unhappiness may come through frustration if one side of your life is not being fulfilled.

I think President Kennedy was a happy man. He was also a very sad man. There is no question in my mind that he knew he was going to die; he had a sense of his own mortality. He had been given the last rites three times. You can't go through life like that without knowing you're on borrowed time. He definitely had a sense of his destiny in that regard. He also had a sense of vision of where he wanted the country to go. He was idealistic in the sense of what could happen to the country. He was a man of peace. He realized how important peace was because he had known war. He believed that public service could be a badge of honor. He really did believe that he had reached the height of fulfillment in terms of being president.

President Lyndon Johnson was probably the most insecure president I've ever known. He was happy when things went right for him and when he had his successes, but there was never enough. Nothing could truly convince him that he was a great man, which he was, at least in the domestic field. He wrote the most significant domestic legislation that has ever helped this country—the war on poverty, Medicare, civil rights, voting rights, minimum wage, the environmental laws, aid to education. His contribution is monumental.

He never felt that people truly appreciated him and he thought at times that he was being ridiculed rather than admired. I think his own insecurity drove him to the presidency in the first place. He always thought he had to be bigger than life to be a real person. As a consequence, I think, he never knew true happiness, great happiness. When he died he was not a happy man. He really almost drove himself to it because power to him was happiness, or so he thought. He thought power would give him the elixir that makes one truly happy. When power was taken away from him, he was not a happy man anymore. I'm sure he had moments of happiness, but I don't think it was a sustained thing because he didn't have true confidence in himself.

President Richard Nixon was also a very insecure man. He was probably happiest when he was walking on the beach with Bebe Reboso, who was his friend and whom he could trust. His own sense of fulfillment, of course, was to arrive at the presidency after defeat and an eight-year hiatus from 1960 to 1968. You never did really feel that he was a truly happy man in office. He certainly loved to be involved in foreign affairs and walk with the top statesmen. I think that he had a happy moment when our astronauts landed on the moon and he got credit for it even though it had been Kennedy's commitment and Johnson had been a part of the space program.

Of course, the way he had to leave was a total tragedy, but he's proved that he's like the phoenix; rising out of the ashes, he'll always fight to come back and never give up. He could never be happy if he was not involved and in the limelight, but I think that's true of most presidents. They can hardly stand being past presidents. President Dwight Eisenhower enjoyed golf and his farm became a mecca. Everyone came and bowed at the shrine; other past presidents have not achieved that.

President Gerald Ford was a happy man in the sense that destiny or fate delivered a wonderful gift that he certainly never expected in his wildest dreams when he became president of the United States. He fit in the shoes and sat in the chair very well. He was disappointed, of course, and deeply hurt when he was defeated, because he felt he had done a good job. Fulfillment, however, must be constantly renewed with him; he doesn't stop traveling. He's on the road several times a week. All the grandeur of a million-dollar estate in Palm Springs is not fulfilling for him. He is a people person. It's not enough for him to just retire and say, "Well, I did a good job." He must constantly be in the spotlight in the sense that he wanted to be doing something.

President Jimmy Carter certainly was thrilled to become president of the United States, but I think he had other fish to fry, really. He has kind of a special religious aspect to him. I think he truly would also have been happy as a Sunday school teacher. Teaching is kind of his role. Of all the past presidents, he is the one who truly accepted retirement and has found it satisfying. He can write, he can work in wood and build furniture. He can travel. It's a part of the ego that former presidents still want to walk into palaces and be recognized.

Out of sight, out of mind is the way Washington treats you. One minute after you're no longer president or senator, that's it. It's pretty devastating. You get a certain amount of fan mail for a little while, but basically you have to keep yourself in the limelight or you're forgotten.

The Carters have a very close relationship. They are in tandem in the things they do and in their ambitions. Their ambitions aren't over, far from it. Carter is more of a man who understands himself and knows what meets his own needs, but he's not a great people person.

President Ronald Reagan is definitely a happy man. I think that he loves being president. He considers it a piece of cake. In his macromanagement style everything is delegated, so he's not bored or worried about the nitty-gritty of running a colossal government. Win, lose, or draw, he feels that he has accomplished a lot. He has turned the country to the right. The Reagan revolution has really restored what he thinks is individualism in the country. It's morning in America. There'd be very little to get this man down. He is what he reflects. His sense of optimism is good, but I think the lack of compassion that accompanies it is not. The attitude seems to be, ''If you can't make it, tough.'' That's what is on the debit side.

In Washington it's not difficult to have a sense of self, but I think that you also have a sense that all is fleeting. You have to keep your eyes and ears open, because if you are here only by virtue of being elected, you know you are accountable and subservient to your constituency. In journalism, you know you're only as good as your last story. A sense of being comes from security, and I don't think people in this town always have a tremendous sense of security.

A trouble shared is a trouble cut in half. A life shared is twice blessed. We need someone in our life who is a close confidant, someone who knows everything about us and

loves us. The essence of a good relationship is not a reporting of the facts, but a sharing of who we are. It has
to do with sharing feelings. It is our feelings that make us
unique. To love and be loved is happiness, a state of well-
being and contentment. We can experience that comfort
with a special friend. *Would my friends say I am a happy
person? Do I have a close relationship in which I can be
me?*

May Sarton looks at the passion of love and her passion
for work.

*May Sarton, novelist and nonfiction writer, is the author
of forty-seven books. Among her best-known works are*
Journal of Solitude *and* At Seventy: A Journal. *May was
born in Belgium; her parents came to the United States as
refugees during World War I. She has received twelve honorary doctorates from various universities and colleges. A
collection of her poetry appears in* Selected Poems of May
Sarton.

May Sarton

There is a great difference between joy and happiness. I'm
happier than I've ever been, but I don't have the intensity
of joy that I used to have. "Joy and woe are woven fine
in the human soul divine," Blake says. The poet is the
person of joy and woe. There's an enormous amount of
anguish involved in being a poet. You're so vulnerable;
you have to keep yourself very open. I'm less vulnerable
than I used to be and happier, but I don't have the same
intensity. That has to do with being in love.
    Love is often a marvelous experience, but I would not
call it happiness except with a woman with whom I lived
for fifteen years, Judy Mattlak, who died of Alzheimer's
disease. When I think about Judy as happiness—and she
really gave it to me—I think about her coming home at
four o'clock and our having tea together. The cats would
be there and then we would go for a little walk around
Cambridge. We'd look up at the lighted houses where stu-

dents were on the third floor working away. We would go get the food for supper. It was sort of an ambling walk, not hurrying, and then we'd come home. I miss that terribly in living alone. There is not that moment of communion and quiet enjoyment with somebody that I used to have—a sharing of the day.

When you're first in love everything is so marvelous; the whole world has changed. In a more stable relationship that lasts, you get times of very peaceful communion, and I loved that. That I would call happiness. If love is very intense, it's very painful. There's an enormous amount of pain involved in love. If it's true love, you have to give up a part of yourself, and that's always very difficult. You have to adjust to somebody else's rhythm. I've been in therapy three times. Each time it revolved around an unhappy love affair and depression. The intense passionate relationships don't last, usually. You have to be willing to let go. It's very hard to let go if you're that involved.

Pain is the great teacher. There's no doubt about it. You learn more through pain. It makes you examine life, it makes you think awfully hard. It makes you face yourself. In happiness, you're freed from this; that's what happiness is in a way. You don't have to face yourself, you're just being.

I welcome anything that I've not experienced before, because I'll learn something from it. That's what we're on earth for, to learn—to make our souls. I always felt that what I felt deeply was right. I never had any doubt about that. What I felt for the women I loved was very deep—whether it lasted or not. I always thought that being able to write a poem was a sort of blessing from God, because it was a gift.

I never had moral doubts. I'm European, and in Europe these things are accepted in a way that they're not here. Americans are very mixed up about their sexuality. I think it's the fear of feeling. You're going to get hurt if you feel, if you allow yourself to be vulnerable. Many Americans will not allow themselves a deep relationship. They will allow themselves a love affair which is purely sexual, or almost entirely sexual, because that's safe. Feeling is dangerous because then you're going to learn, you're going to grow, and you're going to make your soul. The poet Keats talks about it. "Life is a vale of soul making" is his phrase. It's a different, more mystical way of saying something about creating oneself as an identity. Each human being is a creation and soul making is really creating yourself.

Life is like a game of solitaire, and in my case it has been coming out in the last years of my life. It's rather nice. I'm seventy-four now.

Happiness is not something you can find like a stone in the road that has a beautiful color. It is the by-product of your being completely yourself and being very much aware, and it can happen at any moment.

I don't think happiness is a lasting thing. I think it's moments. Happiness has to do with not being under pressure as far as time goes. In other words, having time to be. For example, looking at the light on the flowers is something I do when I'm alone. When you're alone you're fully yourself; you're not trying to respond to somebody else. You're not putting out feelers. If you're very responsive and sensitive to other people, as I believe I am, it's more tiring. The more sensitive you are to other people, the more they take out of you. It's because you're thinking about the other person. When you're alone you can simply be.

My definition of happiness is writing a poem. I'm absolutely alone then and I'm in a state of great intensity of feeling and intellect. I'm perfectly balanced and nothing else exists. Time doesn't exist. Happiness has a lot to do with timelessness—those times when you are not pressured by the feeling "I've got to get somewhere." Maybe you're just sitting out in the sun and just being. What I was most meant to do was write poetry. If you're a poet, that comes first. Nothing else matters. If I were in solitary confinement, I would write poems. Poems are given to some extent. You can't do them at will. You really are an instrument of something far greater than yourself, and it doesn't have to be named God. You are an instrument for forces. You have to be open to receive. Then you still have to work on the poem. It isn't given in the sense that you write it all down. You work very hard, but while you're working you're so excited. For me it's like playing three sets of tennis, which I can't do now. But I can still write poems.

You can't force poetry. You can't say, "I'm going to write a poem next Wednesday." It's terribly hard work. Sometimes a poem goes through sixty drafts. But because you're in such a state of awareness and excitement, it doesn't feel like work, it feels like a game. You have to think as well as feel to write a good poem. It starts with a collision between you and something that hits you very hard where you live.

Ninety percent of people do work that doesn't fulfill anything in them. They do work that simply brings in a paycheck. To me this is hell. To me the most important thing is to discover early enough what you really mean about your life. Money's a by-product, just like happiness. I'm now making money. I never thought I ever would. I never had money as the goal in my mind at all. I was determined to write certain things and I've had better things to say, deeper things to say, as I got older. I was lucky because I knew, very young, what I wanted to do. I sold my first poem when I was seventeen. It was so exciting to get paid for a poem. It isn't that money is not important—it's terribly important—but if you say, "I'm going to make money," you probably never will.

If you are an artist or a writer, each new thing stretches you. It's got to be better than anything you've done. This is good; it keeps you alive. It's wonderful. Robert Frost called a poem "a momentary stay against confusion." That's a lovely definition. A poem lasts. It's so moving to me that a poem I wrote forty years ago can cause somebody to write to me and say, "How did you know this is just how I feel?" It's absolutely fresh to that person who finds it.

I wrote "The Work of Happiness" a long time ago, but I still feel it's right. It's still what I mean.

I thought of happiness, how it is woven
Out of the silence in the empty house each day
And how it is not sudden and it is not given
But is creation itself like the growth of a tree.
No one has seen it happen, but inside the bark
Another circle is growing in the expanding ring.
No one has heard the root go deeper in the dark,
But the tree is lifted by this inward work
And its plumes shine, and its leaves are glittering.

So happiness is woven out of the peace of hours
And strikes its roots deep in the house alone:
The old chest in the corner, cool waxed floors,
White curtains softly and continually blown
As the free air moves quietly about the room;
A shelf of books, a table, and the white-washed
  wall—
These are the dear familiar gods of home,
And here the work of faith can best be done,
The growing tree is green and musical.

For what is happiness but growth in peace,
The timeless sense of time when furniture
Has stood a life's span in a single place,
And as the air moves, so the old dreams stir
The shining leaves of present happiness?
No one has heard thought or listened to a mind,
But where people have lived in inwardness
The air is charged with blessing and does bless;
Windows look out on mountains and the walls are
  kind.

Work is important to our happiness as a creative outlet for
our special gifts. It is vital to work at something we love.
Work must provide not only economic reward, but also
personal satisfaction for our efforts. If we are doing our
jobs only for money, we are cutting off one of the principal
avenues for happiness. Our jobs should enhance our self-

esteem and make us feel good about ourselves. *Do I look forward to going to work each day? Am I bored?*

Ken Kragen can't wait to get to work in the morning, and he reaps the rewards of his efforts. Ken declares, "I work hard because I enjoy it and it's fun."

Ken Kragen was the organizer of Hands Across America to benefit starving Americans on the Sunday of Memorial Day Weekend 1986. He also put together the most famous recording session in the history of music, USA for Africa, which gathered forty-five major recording artists to benefit the starving people of Africa. That event raised over $150 million. Ken manages the careers of singers Kenny Rogers and Lionel Ritchie.

Ken Kragen

The only area of displeasure in my whole life is lack of enough time. That's true of almost any successful executive in any business, not just the entertainment business. I'm a Harvard Business School graduate. On the very first day of classes, the dean of students said, "Your business career starts today, not two years from now. As of today, you will always have more work than it's humanly possible to do. Those of you who are successful will have figured out what to do and what not to do." In truth, probably 50 percent of what comes to me can't get done, even with a staff of thirty people.

Sometimes I have a longing for the earlier, simpler times. I remember in my earlier days managing the Limelighters. I did everything for them, but I was focused on one project. Now I'm constantly shifting gears, constantly changing. I have to make very fast decisions. I can't give things quite the same personal attention that I want. On the other hand, I'm involved in much more and there's more excitement, more diversity, more enjoyment. You learn to go home and not feel guilty about the fact that you haven't been able to accomplish everything. I catch myself at times making lists, then feeling pure pleasure at being able to cross off items regardless of how insignificant they are.

I have a tremendous compulsion to fulfill my obligations, to live up to what I promise people I will do, to make the careers of the people I work for successful, to make the projects successful, to fill the line on Hands Across America, to be sure that the money the people sent to USA for Africa goes to really help people. I am a person who works with a tremendous amount of enthusiasm. I am excited to try to make something successful. I have to avoid seeing too much because if I get enthusiastic about something, it's hard for me not to participate in it. The time just isn't there. New ideas and new talent always turn me on.

I produced the musical play *Hair* in California. I remember after the opening, when it was clearly on its way to being a smash, going home and feeling a certain letdown. I go on a tremendous high up to an accomplishment and then there's always a little bit of down afterward. Interestingly it didn't happen with "We Are the World," mainly because there wasn't time. I went home after "We Are the World" at eight in the morning. I was the last person to leave. I got home and crawled into bed. My wife had left the session at about three in the morning and I said to her, "You should have stayed all night. It was great." I went to sleep for two hours, got up, and was in the office at eleven that morning, working on things. It was that way from then on, virtually through the year. We were putting an album together. We had to bring all the tracks in. It had to be edited. All the clearances with all the artists had to be done. The video had to be put together. The record company had to be negotiated with and all the record companies were represented. I had to deal with all the artists, all the managers, all the lawyers. We also got out a book, shirts, and other materials. We did a year's worth of work in a month. It was literally eighteen hours a day.

I've always been a very up and enthusiastic person, totally optimistic. I came from wonderful, loving parents who rarely ever said, "Don't do this" or "Don't do that."

They allowed me to make my own mistakes, but they were always there, helpful and participatory. I was very close to them and I continue to be close to them. Yet I was very independent. I was working at age thirteen. I worked all through school. My dad is a professor of law at Berkeley. He loves his work. He did a very, very significant thing early in my life that had tremendous influence on me later. He was a successful attorney, a senior partner in a large law firm in Los Angeles. It was during the forties and he was making what was then a huge sum of money—$36,000 a year. He was offered $12,000 a year to teach at the University of California at Berkeley. He took it. He left the law practice to go back to what he loved, which was the university and teaching. He had been a professor of history at the university prior to going to law school and he had loved it. At seventy-eight he's still there, and he's still teaching. From him I learned that you don't just do things in your life for the money; you do them to enjoy your life. If you do that, the rest usually comes. He went for the right reasons and I've pretty much had the same pattern all my life. I don't work for the money. I work for the fun and excitement of it. Everything else seems to flow.

I learned another important lesson from an ex-partner of mine, Tom Carroll, who has since passed away. He said that the only thing that matters is your reputation. If you have the best reputation in town, business will beat a path to your door. If you focus on being the most professional, the most honest, and provide things that build a credible reputation for delivering, you don't have to worry about the money side of it. It will come in the door. He said, "Let's go to Los Angeles and we'll build a business based on being the most honest guys in town. From what we've seen, we'll stand out." I was always a totally honest person, but it was as though I had suddenly discovered that honesty is one of the great gimmicks of the world. It absolutely works. It works for you in every situation in an amazing way. For example, if I really screw up and fail to do something important for one of my clients, I can try to cover it up, à la Richard Nixon, or I can pick up the telephone and call up a client and say, "You know, I really screwed this up. I forgot it." I just confess it right there and then. It goes away in thirty seconds. In fact the clients admire me for doing that. Even in the tremendous conflicts that I had to deal with, I've just gone head-on in there with my good-old-boy honesty and it's worked. It almost disarms people. I do it in negotiations all the time. It's a nice way to live your life. It makes things a lot simpler.

I remember as a little kid stealing a water gun. I had bought a water gun at the five-and-ten around the corner and it broke the first or second day. So I went back and stole another one. I got caught as I was coming out of the store; the owner grabbed me, reprimanded me terribly, and took it back. I was crying and I went home. I wouldn't tell my folks. Then later that night I just couldn't help it. It was really bothering me, so I started crying. I was six or seven years old. I confessed to them that I had done this awful thing, I had stolen this gun. Where I learned that stealing was awful, I don't remember. I also wish I could remember what they said, but I do recall that it was okay and everything was all right. I was traumatized by that incident—the idea of being caught stealing something.

I'm very driven by honesty and something else that was very significant. When I was fifteen years old, I was attending the Wilshire Boulevard Temple in Los Angeles, and Rabbi Edgar F. Magnin, who was very famous, took aside five of us fifteen-year-olds before our confirmation ceremony. We were sitting in a room with him and we started asking him questions. One of us asked, "Is there afterlife?" He said, "I don't know that there's anything beyond this life. You really don't have much or any awareness of anything before you are born and I don't think you're going to have any awareness of anything after you die." At the age of fifteen, having that imparted by a man of God, in a setting like that, had an unbelievable impact on me in a variety of ways. It's been a motivator for all my life. If you believe this is it, this life is it, which I absolutely do, you'd better make the best out of it. You can take a very self-centered, materialistic, everything-for-me kind of attitude. Why I didn't do that I don't know. But I did take a very strong attitude that I didn't want to waste any of my life. I always wanted to be doing things I enjoyed doing or that I felt were productive, and I wanted to do something in this life that was meaningful, that had greater meaning than just earning a living. That's why I think this past year has been the most satisfying of my life, because of my feeling that organizing USA for Africa and Hands Across America might make a real difference, one that could last beyond my own existence. That meeting with Rabbi Magnin was probably the most significant moment in my life.

Happiness for me has a direct relationship to the freedom in life to make choices, to do the things I want to do. If I have freedom in my life, and I do have that, it's a happy life. I have financial freedom and I have personal freedom. I have certain obligations obviously, but I'm really free to make my life what I want to make of it. I'm running my life. I'm in charge of my life. I'm in control of my life.

Although I am not a heavy person, I always would like to be thinner. My weight goes up and it goes down. It is never that bad, but it always feels bad to me. But in almost every other area, other than that and the fact I'm not very good at remembering names, I think that I am totally secure and feel totally comfortable with myself and with what's happening.

I've had the fortunate opportunity to have experienced events that bring home how lucky I am. You can't go to Africa and not come back with a sense of the almost incredible quality of our life here compared to the quality of life on so much of the planet. That, in itself, changed my whole appreciation. Arriving in Ethiopia, getting off the plane, knowing that we'd brought 270,000 pounds of food and that we had realized the first step of a dream of feeding people and solving problems, was an extremely emotional moment. The U.S.A. for Africa recording session itself was a wonderful high point.

Another great moment for me was standing in front of

ninety thousand people at the Live Aid concert in Philadelphia, with millions watching on television, and singing
"We Are the World" while holding on to Peter, Paul, and
Mary. I felt that those of us who had tried to change the
establishment from the outside in the sixties were now
suddenly the establishment, and we were making a real
difference.

On one occasion I was honored at a dinner for the Boys
Club. It was probably one of the single best moments of
the last few years for me. After the dinner I got into the
car with my mom and dad, and she was crying. I asked,
"What's wrong?" Through her tears she said, "It was one
of the best nights of my entire life." Of her life? I was
the one who was honored.

Most of us, I think, do things to make our parents
proud of us or to make our parents happy. My dad said,
"I'm so proud of you. I'm so happy we lived long enough
to see this." Kenny Rogers presented me the award that
night—and this was another one of my best moments. He
took the microphone and said, "You know, Ken Kragen
has managed my career for nineteen years, and not all of
them have been good years." I leaned over his shoulder
and spontaneously said, "Yes, but it wasn't my fault."
The place came apart. People fell on the floor. It was the
biggest roar of laughter I've ever created and almost ever
heard in my life. I was standing there and it was all coming at me. People laughed and laughed and laughed, and
I felt just great. I felt that I understood why a comedian
goes out and stands on a stage and likes the laughter.

It was a big moment to receive the UN Peace Medal.
Only once before had it been given to a private citizen. I
was really emotionally moved by it. Another significant
moment, as I think back, was at Lincoln Center, having
Geoff Nightingale of Burson-Marsteller, the public relations firm, say to me, "What if we strung millions of
people holding hands from one end of the country to the
other, from the Atlantic Ocean to the Pacific Ocean?"
And I said, "Why not?"

I want to have a profound effect on the world, there's
no question about that. But I can't feel that as an obli-

gation. I have to give myself room to say "Maybe it's going to happen, maybe it's not." Winston Churchill said, "The price of greatness is responsibility." And Robert Frost said, "The reward of daring should be still to dare." A wonderful, wonderful thought that I like very much. I think that I sit in one of the best positions to bring about change. People come to me and say, "You sound like you're running for office" or "You ought to run for office." I don't think that's the only way to make social change. From the outside, in a nonpartisan approach, I can have tremendous impact on getting something done. I played a big part in getting the government to give free cheese to poor people a few years ago. I did it as one individual by mobilizing my industry and particularly by mobilizing the president's supporters to say that this is something we ought to do.

My situation is something I love which is fun. It leaves me in a position to really make some difference.

What's been happening in my life recently proves to me absolutely conclusively that you get back more than you give. If you want to get something back, give altruistically of yourself in a way that will really help someone or something. Give of yourself unselfishly. I've gotten back much more than I put in on every level: certainly on the levels of recognition, emotional satisfaction, enjoyment, and my feelings of self-worth—just priceless things. It's come back by the truckload.

Work should be an opportunity for us to challenge ourselves and help us to grow. If we played the piano and practiced often, we would not only expect to get better, but our ability to play more difficult pieces successfully would bring us greater happiness. *Does my work stretch me? Am I getting better? Does my work make me happy?*

Julia Child enthusiastically states, "I'm certainly getting better at my work all the time."

* * *

Julia Child is the popular television personality and author known by the name of her original program on PBS, The French Chef. *Her cooking shows have aired without interruption for more than twenty years. After graduating from Smith College, Julia joined the OSS "to become a spy." On her first overseas assignment in Ceylon she met her future husband, Paul. An Emmy Award winner, Julia is a co-author of* Mastering the Art of French Cooking, *served as food editor of* Parade *magazine, and is a regular guest on* Good Morning America.

Julia Child

I'm a ham. I grew up in a very lively, jocular family, so that probably came with it.

I know I'm happy. I was very fortunate in my family background because I had a very loving, supportive family. We had no conflict. My sister was five years younger and we had a brother halfway between us, so we never had any sibling rivalry. My parents were happy; we were not rich, but comfortably well-off.

My mother thought everything we did was absolutely marvelous. I think your background makes an awful lot of difference. I don't know what you do if you've been abused, or haven't been praised enough so that you don't feel that you're okay. I was very fortunate in having such a happy background.

I was never brilliant in school, but I never had any problems either, so I didn't feel inferior. I did have the problem of being twice as tall as anyone else, but that didn't seem to make any difference because my mother always said we were so wonderful, no matter what.

To be happy, it's terribly important to find the kind of work you really love to do, so that it's a real hobby. When children are growing up, if their famililes are clever, they would encourage hobbies so that people have a real passionate interest in something—rock collecting, butterflies, chemistry, anything. Find something you love to do. If you're going to go into a profession, you've got to love it and work very hard. You can't go into it halfway or you'll never get anywhere.

When my husband, Paul, and I got over to France and I took one bite of that food, I realized it was for me. Fortunately, the Cordon Bleu was going and I was able to apply. I found that the regular course was just for housewives, but they were having a group of GIs, so I joined them. They didn't object at all. I never had any feeling of inferiority about being a woman, because I was not competing with them.

I had a wonderful time learning my trade and I'm continually learning and progressing. It's tremendously creative. You can use everything you've got in the way of intellectual equipment because cooking is a science and it also has a history. You can never be smart enough to do all that you can with it. Cooking is definitely a science, just as wine making is a science. It's rather like architecture and painting in that you have manual dexterity as well as intellectual dexterity. And then there's all the experimenting that you have to do.

You can never be creative enough in cooking. The more background you have, the more you're able to solve problems that arise or create new things. I never talk to a really good chef who doesn't say, "Just about every day I learn something new." Cooking is alive as well as everything else. It is life itself that you're using. Live things, like grain and meat and vegetables. You're turning them into another form and it's life giving itself.

Eating is part of a beautiful experience, like attending an opera or listening to a beautiful symphony or looking at a beautiful painting. That's the way civilized people should consider food. People who are really interested in gastronomy take immense pleasure in eating a lovely meal with people who converse beautifully. Food, like a symphony, should really be orchestrated to make a meal.

There is a direct link between work and happiness. We do what we do for many reasons. Some of us think it is what we should be doing; some of us are in careers or professions to please other people; some of us think our jobs are the ticket to money and success. More people work today than ever before, and we spend most of our waking hours during the work week on the job. Yet most people are doing work they hate in jobs in which they feel trapped. We invest time and effort in a career that gives no personal satisfaction, uses little of our talents and abilities, and guarantees us nothing but unhappiness. *What are my real feelings about my job? Does my job bring me happiness? Am I trapped?*

Tom Peters recalls, "There's a wonderful story of a musician—it may have been Pablo Casals—who died at almost one hundred years of age. The morning he died he was downstairs practicing his notes at 6:00 A.M. That's just lovely."

Tom Peters is a co-author of the only two number one bestselling books on management, In Search of Excellence *and* A Passion for Excellence. *He is the founder of the Tom Peters Group, a management consultant, research, and seminar organization. Tom writes a regular column for* U.S. News & World Report *and a syndicated weekly newspaper column distributed by Tribune Media Services.*

Tom Peters

Happiness, at all levels of the workplace, has to do with being engaged. Whether it's making a Chrysler, going to see your route if you're a bus driver, or battling in the internal politics of the company where you work, you want to get up in the morning and do it. It's almost action for action's sake. Probably the closest operating definition to loneliness or unhappiness I can invent is not being engaged in whatever it is that you're doing. Years ago I was a lieutenant in the Navy. I did my thing in Vietnam, and then, as a very young man, came back to the Pentagon. I was with a much maligned class of Grade 9 or Grade 11 civil servants. It was an intriguing thing for me to watch. Those people all found something to engage themselves.

Most often, because of the stupid organization at work, it wasn't what they were being paid to do. Whether it was shopping for tires or being engaged in a small entrepreneurial venture they had going in their garage, there was just a quest to have something that would turn their light on.

Being engaged literally means being excited in any sense of the word about any task. If I were putting on my corporate observation hat, I would say it's nice to be associated with good products instead of crappy products. I might even talk about pride. That's part of it too. But there's something else. It's that excitement about what you're doing that makes you want to trot to work, looking forward to whatever it is you're doing.

A man would never admit that he wants to be a middle manager at General Motors for the next forty years. Indeed, as a youngster he was probably an excited potential entrepreneur with his own lemonade stand. If I were Secretary of the Treasury I'd rather have him doing his own entrepreneurial thing than punching buttons at General Motors. But I'm still guessing that whatever the guy is doing at GM, he's engaged. I'm guessing that people find something compelling even in jobs that we'd call very routine and work like hell to put meaning into their jobs even though a person from Mars or Kansas City would say it's a waste of good talent. I know there are a lot of people who are on the production line who think, "Life isn't engaging." That's true. There are a lot of people whom we never ask to contribute intellectually. But there are a whole bunch of managers, staff people, and blue-collar employees who some would say are non-productive, but who can put meaning into a job and into a situation.

Too much of it may have to do with our definition of what happiness is supposed to be. Look at me. I live in the Bay area—the greatest place in the world. In theory, by the definitions I was taught as a kid and things that I've read as a grown-up, the happiest thing in the world would be to have a ten-acre vineyard in Sonoma County with great Chardonnay grapes that win triple gold medals from Paris to Moscow to Napa Valley. My guess is that if I were running a ten-acre vineyard in Napa Valley, given where I've been for the last twenty years, I would go completely crazy in about three weeks. So what's the model for happiness? If you looked at my life, you could say, "It's sheer madness." I do lots of things to make sure it's not sheer madness, but nonetheless the person from Mars is completely accurate in classifying it as sheer madness. But I like it in lots of respects. If I didn't, I suspect I would do something about it to change it. Kenny Blanchard, the *One Minute Manager* guy, and I had a nauseating conversation. He said, "You travel because you like to travel." I said, "I hate to travel." He said, "You're wrong. If you hated to travel so much, you wouldn't travel." There's a lot of truth in what he's saying.

I don't think happiness has much to do with the fairy-tale kind of stuff that says run in the vineyard. After I got out of the Navy the first guy I worked for at Peat, Marwick, Mitchell and Company in Washington was a tough old son of a gun, a classic consultant. Three years later I heard that he had retired and was building furniture in Maine. That sounds like heaven to me, because that's what you're supposed to define as heaven. That's happiness. I've not talked to him so he may be thrilled or he may be bored stiff. He may have done it for only six months. It strikes me that we've got some little nodules that get implanted at a very young age; they say, "This is happiness." That may not have a lot to do with what it really is. Retirement or not being engaged is unhappiness to the point of close to instant death in a lot of cases.

Money certainly buy options. Options are better than no options. That's my personal feeling. However, if your world has been defined differently, you can probably do just fine. There's a man in Palo Alto, who has the UPS route, and UPS is a pretty good company. Being a UPS driver is not what average striving parents want for their kids. However, I'm not willing to say that he is less happy than I am, because he gets a hell of a kick out of that route. I talk to high school students a lot and I say, "Do something you like. Don't do something your parents want you to do. I'd much rather see you be a happy UPS driver

at $19,300 a year than an unhappy accountant at $42,500.''
I love the idea of happiness as having more options rather
than fewer options, but I think people can create infinite
options out of things that I call nothing.

Again, if I were playing the role of Secretary of the
Treasury I would rather have people be happy with their
jobs. If you're in a really horrible job where you've got to
work your forty hours and you feel you don't have any
option (which I happen to think is crap) it's most exciting
to find that a person in this situation is also the world's
number one East Coast duck carver on the side. At least
he's engaged in life that way.

The sort of advice I've given people relative to a job
they hate is "Don't be afraid to quit." Obviously quitting
anything is frightening, but the worst thing is to be in
something that's totally dead-ended. There's so much experience to support this. For example, after a recession or
depression or the white-collar layoffs that we've had in the
last few years, a lot of people have found out the greatest
thing that ever happened to them was to have been laid
off. Incidentally, if they were on the list for laying off,
either they were being sleepy or the company was sleepy,
but somehow it was a situation that wasn't very happy. To
make the change is key.

If you're in a rotten job and must stay or decide to
stay, the other advice I've given is "For God's sake, find
something in the damn job that you can try to improve
on." If you happen to hate the post office or Ford or
Hewlett-Packard, the main person who's getting screwed
if you're unhappy is you. The reality is that we spend the
largest number of our waking hours in that thing called
the job; and given the still not totally developed state of
biotechnology, we don't get to go around twice. Look
for something within the context of those hours that you
can learn to do better, that you can try to do better. Don't
do it for reasons of the great American economy or the
great Ford Motor Corporation; do it out of sheer selfishness. It may end up that accidentally you'll also be good
to your employer, but don't do it for that reason. Do it
for you.

Sometimes you see people sitting in the middle of a miserable, slimy, rotten plant with the highest accident rate in the state of California. Yet you look at these people when they come to life after work on the bowling team, or making birdhouses, and you see that you're obviously dealing with incredibly vital people. I say to them, "You're probably still making a big mistake in the sense that you're still writing off the largest number of waking hours, but at least you're better off if you're engaged in the external world." There may be some happiness which is totally legitimate if you feel you're ripping off your employer and using the money to have some joy in the rest of your life. There's a lot to say for that because at least there's the notion of a whole person.

Hope is the commitment of time and energy to the future. We need our hopes and dreams, our short-term and long-term goals. To achieve goals requires effort, and to reach those goals brings satisfaction and happiness. To have no dreams is to have no hope, and to have no hope is to have no reason to live. We must have something to live for or we die. *What are my dreams? Am I willing to put in the effort to get there?*

Ossie Davis surveys his own life, his dreams, and eloquently expresses his frustrations and a sense of helplessness for those without hope.

Ossie Davis has appeared in such noted Broadway plays as A Raisin in the Sun *and* Green Pastures *and on television in* All God's Children, Roots, The Next Generation, *and* King, *for which he won an Emmy nomination. His film work includes* Harry & Son *and* The Cardinal *as an actor and* Cotton Comes to Harlem, *among others, as director. Besides* Purlie Victorious, *his other published work includes* Langston *and* Escape to Freedom.

* * *

Ossie Davis

It was a happy childhood. As a matter of fact I get blamed for it sometimes now because I'm a rather docile, placid, cowlike person. I think it's because most of my experiences as a child were happy ones. I don't think anybody sat me down and said. "This is the way to be happy." We learned from our parents and we learned by observation. Although I grew up in the Depression and I knew the hard times, it never seemed to be a time in which, even though we were hungry, we suffered. There was always humor. There was always something substantially funny about our plight. My dad and momma were religious people in the context that all the world made sense to them, both this world and the world hereafter. They knew that there was a place in heaven that had to be earned, but it could be earned. There was a deep satisfaction in that.

In my childhood there were no areas of fear and anguish which were not put to rest by what the family did or how the family did it or by the jokes or by whatever. I grew up in a community that was essentially black. The father figures were black. The power figures were black. The people in the church were black. The people in the schools were black. My companions were black. We lived a pretty full life. Living in Waycross, Georgia, we knew the Ku Klux Klan was always nearby and that the threat of death was a real and live one. There were many things that disturbed us deeply, but the community in which I lived provided a ritual by which all of these devils were exorcised. They never seemed anything that pinned me individually into a corner so that even if there were horrible things or somebody was lynched or there was a storm in Florida and my aunt got blown away, it always came to me cushioned by the culture and my father and my mother explaining things. My pastor explained things or my teacher explained things in such a way that they didn't wind up being threatening. We knew there were mean white folks. But we also knew there were good white folks.

As a child I didn't go around thinking about happiness

or even thinking about what was important. I took my cues from my elders. But as a person who has worked with humor, who has struggled with it, who has talked about it to others, I have come to appreciate, even more deeply, humor as a saving grace. That was available to people no matter what the problems were or the depths of the misery in which they found themselves. The culture always provided them with a humor that enabled them to put things into some kind of perspective and make them palatable.

Upon reflection on my life and on the life of those around me, I am now aware that awful things went on. Both culturally and individually we gave up some important parts of our personality and character, let alone our rights, in order to survive. At the time it didn't seem onerous to me. It didn't seem degrading. My own life was never lacking in dignity in terms of models and the behavior of people who were around me. There was suffering. There was deprivation. But there was laughter and there was warmth and there was camaraderie and there were picnics and there was love. There was also hate and death. All of those things danced around me, but none of them tested me closely. People in my family didn't do much dying. One or two friends died and some neighbors died, but death wasn't always trying to get me. I was a happy child because the things that were awful in my life tended to let me alone.

The bitterness I experienced as a child was the bitterness the group experienced. Certainly when things happened, when there was a lynching, I would listen to my parents around the dinner table. I would hear about it and note their prayers. Sometimes the pastor would say something different from what he usually said. So I took my cue from my environment and my companions. We looked and we saw denial around us based on who and what we were, but I personally was never a bitter person. I knew people who were bitter, but there was never really bitterness in my family, in my father, in my mother and my group. I don't think a person who is truly bitter can have a working sense of humor. The two wouldn't really go together. Though there was anger, though there was hostility, though there was a group hatred of those who would destroy us and there was bitterness in being rejected, still it seldom kept us from getting to the dinner table and at the dinner table there was a good meal and a nice joke. The hated enemy, if such were the case, was forgotten before bedtime. I was not scarred by bitterness.

There were two low points in my life. The first was when I went to college at Howard University. I was away from home and family and community and I was exposed to a very noncaring, cold environment, which did not recognize me as a person. I almost took the nonrecognition as rejection. The closest I ever came to thinking about suicide was at that time. It really was a horrible thing and it was the discovery of two or three people on campus who made the difference. They made a difference in a personal sense.

The second was when I left college and came to New York. It was at the onset of World War II and the racial prejudice that went along with it. To look across at what was happening in Europe, and knowing what was happening to the Jews was frightening. If they got the Jews, I thought, next down the line they would be coming for me. That shock changed my whole concept of religion. What my parents had given me was a coherent world, supervised and reigned over by a God who, though he was inscrutable, never let a sparrow fall without taking note. To find all those millions of people being killed and knowing about the bombing of Ethiopians by Mussolini meant the personal God was suddenly absent. It was a great loss and a great shock to me. I went into the Army. I suppose a part of my motivation for joining the Army was a personal depression. I never expected to come back alive, although I wasn't going to invite death. Before I left I made sure that the Creator knew that if this is the way he was going to run the world, and these were his values, I certainly wanted no part of it. God could go his way and I would go mine. If we never met, it really didn't matter to me. So the hopelessness that I faced was hopelessness that was shared not only by black people, but by a lot of people.

Coming out of the Depression we went into a war with Hitler rampant and seemingly victorious. That really gave us all a sting.

In April 1945 Franklin Roosevelt died, and that seemed to be the bottom of a long period of depression. Then, on August 7, the bomb fell on Hiroshima, and that really opened up the bottomless pits to me. I was still in the Army at the time. I became rebellious and drunk. As a matter of fact, I think it was only because the war was over that very serious charges against me and a group of soldiers were dropped. I don't remember what we did. It had something to do with taking a truck and doing some kind of nonsense out of drunkenness and frustration.

After I left the Army I went home again and ultimately came back to New York and got into theater. Hope came alive to me because there were people in the theater who took an active part in the fight against fascism, the fight against racism, the fight against hunger. People like Paul Robeson and Canada Lee, whom I got to know, and others whose lives were orderly and directed influenced me. They knew of struggle. I also met W. E. B. Du Bois. Hope became possible as a result of meeting these people at that stage in my career. I got to know them personally and I had the chance to talk to them, to question them, to mentally wrestle with them. They showed me that desolation and despair was a luxury that a black man could not afford. "If you don't need your life personally, your people need it," they said. The message was "Damn it, get up off your ass. Keep crying if you want to, but while you are crying, get out there and fight and strike a blow for something."

I don't think anybody lit a bonfire under me. It was a slow fuse. It was almost like spontaneous combustion in a pile of wet hay. It took a long time. I went along but at a distance. I observed. I even participated. It took a long time for me to jump into the middle of the circle and say, "Hallelujah, I'm free." It took a long time.

I've been thinking a lot about the number of young people who commit suicide in our country every day. I almost take it as a personal affront. I have been asking myself, "Ossie, what did you do, or did you not do, that you let these golden young people slip out of your hands, waste their lives, and dash themselves against death? Why didn't you stop it?" Life is infinitely precious, and the struggle to preserve it only makes it more precious. The gold shines best when it's burnished and buffed and roughed and rubbed against something. We need conflict. We need struggle. We even need disaster to tell us who we are. But once having gone through that, once having risen above all of that, what we see beyond justifies all of it a thousand times. "Hang on, hang in, and fight like hell until the bitter end." That's what I would say to myself and that's what I say to my young friends who love death more than they love life. I feel. I'm upset by what is happening, but I don't know what I can do. I must do something. These youthful suicides to me are more tragic than those faces of the children who starve in Ethiopia. They have no choice. But our golden young people have everything in front of them. Choose to reach up and turn out the light? No. No. No. Life is infinitely worth it and struggle glorifies the life that you struggle to redeem.

The life I lived was full of struggle—meaningful struggle—but I also developed as a person in the theater. I met and married Ruby. That, too, was a part of the richness and the wonder of my growing up. I became a parent. All those things tied together did give me satisfaction, did give me contentment, and if you can't find a better word, I'd say it did give me happiness too.

There is only one additional step that I need to take. All of these things, past and present, should be woven into something that can be expressed by me as a writer. I have had the benefit of the longest childhood God ever granted anybody. I think the time has come for me to put away childish things and to take up the pen and become a writer. If I am granted that privilege, then no man who ever lived will be able to say that he was a happier or a more fulfilled man. I sit here and I look at a shelf that contains things I wrote when I came out of the war, things from three to three hundred pages long. Plays that have been done five

times and stories that remain yet unwritten. It's not one
thing that I want to do. I really want to do all those things
that I attempted and somehow left unfinished because
something deep within me told me, "You are not ready.
You can't do that. You aren't big enough to tackle that
subject." What I need now is time, and there is plenty of
that. Health, I've got enough of that. Some plain paper
and a lot of pencils is all I need. I think my ultimate joy—
my ultimate epitaph—will be "I really was a writer."

. . . will never know complete fulfillment or be . . . they will never know what it is to be giv . . . an unalterable thing that over 27 percent of

6   Health

Most happy people put health near the top of their happiness list. However, the majority of us do not take care of our bodies. We take health for granted. We abuse our bodies with poor diets, alcohol, drugs, and cigarettes. We get little or no exercise, too little sleep, live with incredible amounts of stress, and exist in a polluted environment.

The leading causes of sickness and death in America are heart disease, cancer, and alcoholism, followed by accidents, pulmonary disease and influenza, diabetes, and suicide. We push ourselves to the limit and realize too late that much of the illness we experience we have visited on ourselves. *Do I take care of my body? Do I exercise regularly?*

Dr. Joe Arends lays out his priorities: "My personal value system is: number one, God; number two, my physical well-being; number three, my family; number four, my career."

Joseph Arends, M.D., is in the practice of preventive medicine and assistant professor in the Department of Family Medicine at the Wayne State University School of Medicine in Detroit, Michigan. He has completed ten marathons, including Pike's Peak and the Boston Marathon twice. Joe serves as a senior medical examiner for the Federal Aviation Administration and is a lieutenant commander in the U.S. Navy Medical Corps.

126

Joseph Arends, M.D.

Most people will never know complete fulfillment or be happy because they will never know what it is to be physically fit. It is an unfortunate thing that over 97 percent of our females and over 50 percent of our males have never been fit once in their entire lives. Only about 10 to 15 percent of our population is fit.

There are a number of major forces operating on people which make them the way they are. The strongest and most pervasive influence is parents. If your parents smoked, you have about a 65 to 75 percent chance of being a smoker also. If alcohol was very important in their lives, you have a greater chance of becoming an alcoholic. If they were sedentary and fat, you will tend to be sedentary and fat. In 65 to 75 percent of cases children will track as their parents track.

The first four or five years of elementary school are also very important, and the educational system lets us down. Those are very critical years in anybody's development. What most children get exposed to as far as physical well-being is concerned is sports. The majority of kids are not athletes in the strict sense of the definition. Most kids are not well coordinated enough to go on to play football, baseball, or basketball in the pros. They're just not that good. Only 3 percent of children are playing any kind of sports by the age of thirteen. Ninety-seven percent of our kids have been programmed to believe that they are inadequate in regard to sports activity. The way kids, and you and I, interpret that is, "Well, sports are not for me. I'm not physically able; I am somehow physically inadequate." We come to believe that we are physically inferior, we are lesser beings. Just because we're not super athletes doesn't make us inferior, but we don't provide any alternatives for kids to feel good about themselves physically, to feel good about their physical self-esteem. You can be in super condition and be a lousy athlete. We don't provide other avenues for our kids to do that. Consequently, most adults are sort of turned off the idea of taking good care of themselves and experiencing the full quality of physical well-being. Adults don't separate athletics from fitness. Those are two separate entities.

In my opinion the majority of people haven't enough moxie to face the truth. I was a fat guy. I weighed 160 pounds at age twelve. I was obese. I was always looking for a magic answer. I tried some diet pills. I lost twenty pounds for a while, but I didn't solve the problem. I went right back. By the time I was in the Navy I weighed 240 pounds and asked, "Where's it going to stop?" Finally I had to sit down and talk to myself and say, "The problem is mine. It's nobody else's problem and I've got to confront the fact that I am overweight." When I admitted that to myself I was able to start a program to control it.

People love to talk about weight control; they love to talk about getting off Valium and Librium, getting off alcohol, quitting cigarettes—even getting some exercise. They love to talk about it but few ever accomplish that because they're not willing to take action. It is a matter of priorities and values in your mind. Until you go out and take that first step, until you go out and walk half a mile, you're not going to make it long term.

All people have a responsibility for their own lives. You choose to be as happy as you wish to be. You can make a choice and stay in that rut or you can make a choice and say, "I will be different. I will not follow the path of my parents or my friends or the average American. I don't want to be an average American. I want to be different." Everybody has a right to make that choice.

People can make themselves happier by concentrating on physical fitness. You start with the action step. You cycle or play a little tennis, but the easiest thing for anybody to do is walk.

At age eighteen, when you finish high school, you should be able to run two miles in sixteen minutes. Any adult ought to be able to run two miles in seventeen minutes till age sixty. That's basic physical fitness. We can equate that to walking three miles in forty-two minutes. You can achieve physical fitness, the kind of physical well-being I'm talking about, either in high-intensity exercise of short duration—two miles in seventeen minutes—or lower-intensity exercise of longer duration, like walking or backpacking. It makes no difference.

For the adult population I prefer to stress the lower-intensity exercise of longer duration. It's easier on joints, and you're going to arrive at the same end point with less chance of injury. It's very difficult to give absolute criteria for those over age sixty. I would suggest that you talk to a physician who is prevention-oriented, who can give you a stress test, and who can write a personal exercise prescription for you. Even if you are handicapped you should exercise, but you should get professional advice on what constitutes an appropriate exercise program.

The common American pattern is to go out and exercise seven days a week for thirty days, say, "Well, I can't do this the rest of my life," and then quit. What you have to do is set realistic goals for yourself when you begin. You have to say to yourself, "What do I see myself doing now and what do I see myself doing ten years from now?" Set up realistic habit patterns. We know from scientific studies that you have to exercise at least three days a week. You give me those three days and all I'm going to ask you for is roughly twenty to thirty minutes per day. Let's pick twenty-five minutes as a median number. You give me twenty-five minutes, three times a week, and at the end of one year you'll say, "Doctor, I have exercised 156 times in the last year—three times per week for fifty-two weeks." That's outstanding.

If you just do that in one year, you're changing your whole philosophy of life. You're saying to yourself and you're demonstrating to yourself and to me: "My physical activity time is one of my highest priorities. I am creating time in my week to take care of my physical well-being, which is important to me." A woman once asked me, "Doctor, how come you're so consistent with your physical activity and I am not?" We got talking about her life and I found out that on Tuesdays at six o'clock she gets her hair done. She's gone through snowstorms, power blackouts, hail, and ice storms. One time, she said, she had a fever of 104 degrees, yet she sat in that chair. If Christmas and New Year's fell on a Tuesday, she got her hair done on Monday. She never missed a hair appointment in twenty-five years. I said, "That's the answer: your hair is the most important thing in your week. I'm not saying that's wrong; I'm saying that's your value system."

The most important times in my whole week are Tuesday, Thursday, Saturday, and Sunday at five o'clock, when I run or play racquetball. Everything else falls around that. Dinnertime falls around that, career falls around that, patients fall around that. Nothing transgresses that exercise time. I set that priority back in 1968 when I started to lose my excess weight. I said that nothing would interfere and nothing ever has. There's no reason you can't do it. It's a basic value system, a philosophy of life. Physical time for myself will not be compromised. Everything else can go by the wayside, but nothing will compromise my exercise time.

There's a lot of misinformation around. One belief is that exercise lowers blood cholesterol. Jim Fixx, the running expert, ran forty to fifty miles a week, but he died of a coronary because he had high blood cholesterol. Anything over 180 is too high. Blood cholesterol is fat in the blood which is deposited in the coronary arteries. It starts to build at the age of ten. If I could exorcise five foods from the American diet they would be bacon, pork sausage, hot dogs, butter, and cheese. They affect blood cholesterol, which causes heart attack and stroke. As for sleeping, a small percentage of people can get by with five or six hours, but they are very rare; most folks need at least seven, and the majority need eight hours' sleep every night. If they're not getting the seven or eight they generally wind up getting chronically fatigued over a period of time and they're commonly irritable. When you're irritable you're not happy.

By and large, the primary value of exercise for most people is stress release. If you don't exercise you will deteriorate, I can guarantee that. In this country we accept deterioration because of what we see around us. Everybody else is going downhill, everybody's gaining twenty pounds. We accept the fact that this is normal. That's not what normal is. That's a very sick population. We are the most obese nation in the world and we're number five in heart attacks. We're a very abusive society and we perceive that to be normal. It isn't. If you can't walk up a flight of stairs without getting exhausted, that's not what I call happiness. You need the physical energy, and energy is tied into exercise.

As a doctor who is interested in your happiness and physical well-being, I might ask you the following questions.

1. Are you fit?
2. Do you exercise?
3. Are you obese?
4. Do you smoke?
5. Do you use drugs?
6. Is your blood pressure normal (120/70)?
7. Is your blood cholesterol under 180?
8. Do you have some kind of balance between yourself, your personal relations, and your career?

Being physically fit is going to have a profound impact on your happiness.

Some of us are so devoted to success and accomplishment that they become the measure by which we value ourselves. A life of stress is not a happy life, and success and stress seem to go together. Exercise, proper diet, sleep, relaxation, play, fun, and lack of stress are all essential to happiness. Continued stress over a long period of time can take a horrible toll on our health. *Is my life in balance or am I living a life of stress? Why am I so hell-bent on success?*

Agnes de Mille believes, "If you don't want to be a clod at seventy-five, start working to avoid it when you're six years old. If you're a clod at ten, you're a decayed clod at seventy-five. You've got to be curious. You've got to be interested in other people and alert to other things. There's no rule that at any age you stop, until the mind goes. Then you just hope for a quick rubbing out.''

Agnes de Mille has distinguished herself in ballet and theater as a dancer, director, author, lecturer, and one of America's finest choreographers. Audiences know her work from the Broadway musicals Oklahoma, One Touch of Venus, Carousel, Brigadoon, Gentlemen Prefer Blondes, Paint Your Wagon, *and* 110 in the Shade. *Among the many ballets she created are* Fall River Legend, Three Virgins and a Devil, *and* Rodeo, *which premiered at the Metropolitan Opera House. In that ballet, Agnes danced the lead, received twenty-two curtain calls, and was paid $15 for her performance. She is the author of eleven books, including* Reprieve, *which details her cerebral hemorrhage of May 15, 1975, her rehabilitation, and insights into her need to succeed.*

Agnes de Mille

In May of 1975 I was going to give a big lecture demonstration called ''Conversations about the Dance,'' which was a rather fancy piece of work. I had a company of twenty-four dancers, an orchestra, and various other embellishments. It was about the history of dancing in this country and how it reflected the history and the sociology of America. The production was very complicated and there were lots of problems. It was mayhem in my theater, just an hour before we were to take the stage. It got so hairy and horrible that I went upstairs, put my head in my hands, and thought, ''You've got to be quiet. Keep your cool. Let them fall down and break their necks, but you be all right.''

I came back into the auditorium and was told that the boy who was going to do the Irish clog, one of the champions in the world, had sent word that he couldn't come. He had sent a substitute. This made me pretty mad. I said, ''Come here, Victor, and sign the contract and I'll sign with you.'' I picked up a pen to sign the contract, but I couldn't write my name. That was the first I knew anything had happened. I said, "I can't write. I simply cannot write. I can't control the pen." The pen dropped on the floor and the pianist said, "Sit down and take it easy. You've had a rotten afternoon." Then I said to my assistant, "I can't feel. I can't feel in my right hand. I can't feel at all in my right leg." My assistant called for a nurse, who immediately called an ambulance. It came and the ambulance men lifted me up, put me in a chair, and carried me out. By the time I got to the exit, my head was rolling, and by the time I got down the steps to the ambulance I was beginning to drool.

In the ambulance my right arm dropped and fell off the stretcher; I've never moved it again with any feeling. That was eleven years ago. At the hospital they didn't know at first whether it was a hemorrhage or a clot. Actually, it was both, but the problem was that what was marvelous for the hemorrhage was deadly for the clot. It was terrifying. I spent three and a half months in the hospital. I nearly died two or three times.

I was a very well-known choreographer, but I didn't think I was as good as I wanted to be. I hadn't done the ballets I wanted to do. I hadn't even done the shows I wanted to do. I was writing, and I always looked on myself as an amateur as a writer. I was so dissatisfied with myself. I was very restless all the time. I was always straining to do a better, more perfect work.

Today the right side of my body has no feeling and there's no coordination. I can grip with my hand, but that's all I can do. I've learned to use my left hand, as my master hand, and my right hand simply feeds it like a machine. I can't use my right hand to write with or to play the piano or to button my dress. When I have to make up my face, it's mud-pie time. My left hand puts on the mouth, and I just hope it lands on the mouth and not over by the ear.

I practiced my exercises most faithfully every day and I had therapy twice a week, but I never could feel. After eight and a half years the pain just grew from the arthritis and I thought, "What the hell am I doing all this for? It's boring, it's tiring, it's defeating." I just stopped. I don't think it's praiseworthy, but that's a fact. Whenever I go

out I use a wheelchair. In the house I have my paths all
the way through, so I can get about by myself.

Self-love and pride are linked to the body. When I was
a little girl I knew I had beautiful golden hair and that I
was very pert, quick, and pretty. When I became an adolescent, my nose developed, which I thought was hid-
eous, and I was told in Hollywood it was a disaster. You
do think of yourself as inhabiting this machine and it's
identified with you. I always prided myself on my agility
and I was proud of my strength. Until way into my sixties,
I could kick over my head with a straight supporting knee.
I was never vain about my face—obviously I couldn't be—
but I was vain about my hair. As I've gotten older, my
hair's turned perfectly white and it's getting very thin. Everybody's does, but I wasn't prepared for mine to. My feet
were my joy and my legs were strong as iron, but that's
gone now. Under these circumstances you realize that's
not why people have loved you, or that's not why people
care about preserving you, and that's not why you're having a good time in life.

When I came home from the hospital I experienced the
marvelous sense of rebirth. "My God, I can do all these
things." A day will break every day. I wake up. I have
breakfast. People are kind. My family is wonderful. I felt
another life starting, one with different values and different
goals. It was going to be fun. The biggest insight was that
I didn't have to meet standards that I had quite falsely set
for myself. The secret of life is that you set good standards
for yourself, but not impossible standards which my
mother and father had done for me.

My mother always wanted a genius for a daughter. In
fact, in the little memory book of my childhood, my
mother wrote, "I, who have always been known as the
daughter of my father and the wife of my husband, hope
that I may someday be known as the mother of my daughter." I was about ten. My father wrote, "My firstborn
child, you are. But that's nothing. I'd rather love you for
what you do than because you are mine." Well now, come
on. I couldn't sit down. I was just pushing, pushing, pushing, and they expected it, too. I graduated from college

cum laude. "Well, why didn't you get summa cum laude?" I'd come home with five B's and four A's. "Why aren't they all A's? Why not A+'s?"

I did everything. In high school I was the editor of the school paper. I was the captain of the tennis team. I was the best student in dramatics. I bossed everybody. I simply bossed the pants off them. I didn't care. I had my own friends and they were the oddnicks. I was unpopular with boys. When I got to the university, believe me, it was something quite different. I remember my first day there. The freshman class assembled in the auditorium and was addressed by the chancellor. My class took up every seat and filled every aisle and crowded the sides of the aisles. I realized there were thousands of people there and I was only one. I was nothing. The relief that came over me was simply prodigious. I wasn't responsible for the whole thing. I could join.

I had that same feeling when I realized I was pregnant. I felt I was going to drop into the mainstream of biological development and be a normal person. Making a baby was the easiest thing I ever did in my life. I didn't have to count music. I didn't have to figure out one problem. I didn't have to move anybody. I didn't have to tell anybody anything. Fingernails were being made, eyelashes were being made, intestines were being made, all without my trouble. I didn't have to do it. Somebody else was taking care of it, Mother Nature.

It's extraordinary that the human mechanism can continue to change, to adopt, to acclimatize itself. I think that is remarkable. Maybe these doors could have opened earlier, but I was too frenetic and caught up with what I was doing. I think you do change. Life's a marvelous plant. It can get along in this new soil now whereas it couldn't have done that earlier. In the past I couldn't forgive myself because I didn't think I'd done what I meant to do. I thought I'd failed. Now I have come to the conclusion that I've done the best I could and I can't do better.

In recovery, the care and love of my family, chiefly my husband, were extraordinary. I was enduring and it was persistent. All during my convalescence my husband's fun, his humor, and his relentless pushing of me never stopped. His kidding of me and keeping me going was just merciless and marvelous. I learned that my husband loved me, which I hadn't really believed before. If you don't love with trust, I think there's no happiness. I had to learn to trust him.

I am relatively happy today. I seem to be much more contented. It seems insane, but I don't expect as much. I don't demand as much. Partly, I guess, it's growing older. I don't want to do things all the time. I'm perfectly content to just stay home. I look forward to the six o'clock news and *60 Minutes*, reading a little bit and going to sleep. That's my idea of a fine evening.

Contributors' Comments

Two contributors offer their own prescriptions for a healthy life.

Dick Gregory on Health Habits

A real secret of being happy is good health. It's diet, proper rest, proper maintenance of the body, proper exercise, and proper amount of water. If you drink eight glasses of water—clean water, not tap water—every day, in one week you'll see things start changing. Most folks are the way they are because they don't drink enough water. We're 97 percent liquid against 3 percent solid. One day somebody is going to be wise enough to say "I've got to put that ratio in my body." Once you start doing this there's a joy.

One of the worst things you can do is jog. Why was jogging so beautiful? It beat doing nothing. The best thing one can do is walk. Jogging messes up the body. Look at joggers when they run; they're not happy. I always said that if jogging was so good you'd wake your family up and take them with you. Walking, walking, and walking gets the body in shape. The body's throwing off certain diseases and certain stresses. Rest, rest, rest. When you get that proper rest everything is there. Children get the exercise, they get the proper rest, and they leap out of the bed ready to take on the day. If you look for children's shoes at night, you can't find them because they do not go to bed prearranging getting up. Adults do. We almost can't go to bed. Children jump into the bed and that's the end of it. When they wake up the next day, "Wow." That's happiness, man.

Shelley Duvall on Exercise

When I was an actress I was doing very physical things in movies. I was on my feet all the time, running around outdoors and indoors, so I felt that my health was being taken care of. Since I've become a producer I spend much more time sitting at a desk. It builds anxiety and stress to sit all day. Physical activity lessens that.

Lately I have been exercising; it's a choice I've made. I've rediscovered how good it feels. I work out on the Nautilus equipment at the YMCA, and I try to go three days a week. I try to play tennis now as much as possible, too. This is a very new thing in my life. I used to resist tennis because I thought it was such a ritzy sport. It costs money to go play on a court, but since I can afford it and it gives me pleasure and good health, I think it's worth it. When I play tennis, I spend a lot of time picking up balls, but I enjoy the running around and working up a sweat.

People spend a large amount of money on houses and cars and other material things, but they forget about investing money in their own body to feel good.

Exercise really makes me feel good. Now with the Nautilus, tennis, and taking walks, I feel better and I think I'm looking a little better.

7　Spirituality

There is a spiritual dimension to the lives of most happy people. Minimally, there is a feeling of participating in the oneness of humanity. At the other end of the spectrum are those who believe with conviction that there is a God, that God created the universe, and that humans can join God in an afterlife. Most often, the greater the faith, the greater the happiness. It is wonderful to watch people of great faith in action. They seem so secure. They begin with the premise that God loves them exactly as they are, and they experience life as if it is exactly the way God intended it to be. Faith isn't something they have; faith is something they do. The true believers demonstrate their faith through actions and then they sit back, relax, and let God do the rest. Regardless of the type and level of faith, spirituality brings a sense of order and purpose to the lives of many. *Is there a God? Does God love me? What am I doing to love God?*

Willard Scott's faith is the primary reason for his happiness.

Willard Scott is the weather reporter for NBC-TV's Today *show. His "act" was developed at WRC-TV in Washington, D.C. As a long-time radio and television personality in that market, Willard distinguished himself through his public service efforts. A graduate of American University, he holds degrees in both philosophy and religion. Named one of the ten most huggable persons by the International Hug Center, Willard made broadcasting history on August*

22, 1983, when he appeared on Today *dressed as Carmen Miranda, performed an original musical number, and delivered the weather report in costume in an effort to raise money for the USO.*

Willard Scott

One key to happiness, of course, is that you're healthy. To me, that's one of the foremost things. Another key is to be appreciative of the things you have. You have to be grateful and have a sense of appreciation and not be one of those who say, "What's next?" or "Is there anything else?" and "What are you going to do for me tomorrow?" Appreciate and enjoy what you have today. The third thing is to be honest. Be honest in every single respect: honest with yourself; honest in your relationships with other people; don't delude yourself; don't lie to people; don't try to pull a fast one over on friends, business, or family. Be a straight shooter. If you are honest you eliminate a whole parcelful of worries and anxieties. You don't have to stay on your toes all the time to cover a lie. If you tell a lie, deep down underneath you're always going to be concerned about how you're going to cover that lie. Always let your conscience be your guide. I remember as a kid I saw *Pinocchio,* and it had a tremendous influence on me. Jiminy Cricket was my first philosophical hero.

Some people have an incredible ability to block out their conscience, but I think that if you listen for it, it's always there. There's only one right and wrong. We've analyzed, scrutinized, and tried to dissect morals and truth and values. I believe in a set of absolutes, and I think that if you listen they're there.

I believe that we are all children of God, and I'm a big believer in faith. I don't want to come off as a Goody Two-shoes because I'm not one of those by a long shot. But the real honest-to-God faith has been a tremendous influence in my life.

The essence of happiness, of course, is love. Jesus Christ taught one thing. Again, his teachings have been

convoluted, twisted, used for political purposes, and used
to make moral judgments. There's only one message that
Christ taught, and that was love, simple and pure. Love
is a form of respect, consideration, and kindness. That's
the secret. It comes down to that.

That's why I believed in the beginning that I had something more to offer than just to do the weather or to be
funny or silly or make a stupid remark or put on a dress—
the dumb things that I've done for an act. It's amazing the
people who have gotten it. I don't get up there and preach.
I don't sit up there with a choir behind me, but I've been
able to get the message across by the way that I conduct
myself, the things that I talk about, the things that I show
respect for. I think you can get much more done that way
than you can sometimes when you hit people over the head
with a message. People love to watch other people have a
good time, and people sense that I enjoy what I do.

In some cases, some people don't understand quite what
I'm all about. At a cocktail party or on the street somebody will stop me and say, "I watch you every day and I
think you're terrific. You just seem to be so happy. Why
are you so happy?" They keep asking me, "Why do you
enjoy yourself?" Then I tell them, "I love my job. I love
my family. I've got a good wife. I've been healthy. Why
shouldn't I be happy?" Then I'll throw in the fact that I
believe in the teachings of Jesus Christ and the faith I
believe in has served me well. That's when they start to
back off and say, "Hey, hey, hey, one of those. Look
out!" It's the old bit again. They don't consider that so-
phisticated and they're afraid. They resist it because people tend to resist the simple truth when that really is 90
percent of the answer for everything. Things are not that
complicated. Many people resist it because they think that
anytime you talk about God you're trying to convert them.
There's a natural cynicism or reluctance to accept religion
as a means to happiness. People feel that they're going to
be considered Bible thumpers. There's ego there, too. They
don't ever want to admit that there's something stronger
than they are.

In the last hundred years we have come to think of ourselves as the God. We control our own air-conditioning systems, our own television systems, we drive, and we fly. It's almost like Who needs deity to direct us? We can direct ourselves. Why can't we direct our personal lives and our emotions? The problem is just that—we can't. That's what I think they resist.

All of the things that people need to make their lives happy, I think you can find in the basic precepts of Christian faith. Now I'm not sure some little Arab child who is a Moslem couldn't find the same thing in his set of beliefs to make his life fulfilled. I just happen to have been born into the Christian faith and accepted it as an older person and had it work for me. Happiness is the answer that everybody's after and a lot of it's found in faith.

There's no question that I'm happy right now, I really am. I think happiness includes enough common sense to know what makes you happy and what doesn't and then to follow up on it. Everybody between forty-five and fifty-five starts to look and take inventory. Time is the most precious commodity that we have, and simplification is definitely the big key.

I should start thinking now about slowly unwinding and getting out of this business because I've had a wonderful run. I think there are other things in store for me. Now that I've received some national recognition, I can go around and do a little preaching and teaching. I can see myself down the road in a couple of years doing a nice little cable show that's not competitive, that's not in a ratings war, a do-or-die situation. I'll just sit down and talk with somebody and the show will be fun.

I see myself going to Omaha, where I make a speech at the Kiwanis Club and then stay in town for a couple of days. Maybe I'll do a guest shot at the Baptist Church on a Sunday and make a little testimonial and share with people the very thing that I'm talking about right here.

I know this faith business has worked for me and I want to share that with others. I'm sure there are plenty of people who would find that faith can work for them, too.

* * *

The me-oriented goals of money, sex, power, status, and success do not bring happiness. To pursue them for their own sake or for the purpose of our own ego gratification can only result in unhappiness. Many have tried and been humbled. If we gain any of those goals as a by-product of unselfish actions, they can be experienced in a positive way in a balanced life. What does bring happiness to many is not a life devoted to worldly possessions, but a life dedicated to spiritual principles set down by the great religious leaders throughout history. Life becomes the sincere attempt to do God's work. "Thy will, not mine, be done." *Is God or some higher power at the center of my universe? What is his will for me?*

Chuck Colson remembers, "When I got out of prison, I had some very good offers, but I really believe that God was calling me to do what I am doing."

Charles W. Colson is the founder and chairman of the board of the Prison Fellowship Ministries, a unique group that serves inmates and former convicts and their families. It is also an advocacy organization dedicated to criminal justice reform. An attorney, Chuck was special counsel to President Richard M. Nixon and served seven months on a one-to-three-year federal prison sentence after pleading guilty to a Watergate-related charge in 1974.

Charles W. Colson

When you finally come to terms with who you are and understand your relationship first to God and second to your fellow men, then you can begin to live in the world. You can't really live while you are chasing something that you will never find. I believe it was Pascal, the mathematician and philosopher and Christian writer of three centuries ago, who said that there is a hole in every human being. His argument was that it was a God-shaped hole. You can try to fill it with drugs and alcohol and sex and power and money and achievement, but you can't fill it up because it won't fit. It's putting something into the hole that isn't shaped right.

You are really at peace with God when you have come to the understanding that you didn't arise out of a chance collision of atoms and that you didn't just come out of mud. If I see that there is a moral purpose to man, and that what I am doing is what God has called me to do in life, I'm at peace. It doesn't matter whether I'm working with dying people in the streets of Calcutta, as Mother Theresa is, or walking out of the White House. My security comes not from what I do. My security comes from the knowledge that I am created and I am doing what my Creator has called me to do. I don't know how else you can be at peace. I've tried just about everything else.

The search of self can only be consummated in the death of self. The apostle Paul, in Scripture, writes, "I die daily." His problem, we can reasonably conclude from his writings, was pride. What he was talking about was the need to kill his pride every day in order to survive that day. There's a great deal of truth that unless you die daily, you are going to be carried away by the siren song that you hear in the culture from every angle, principally, of course, from the electronic media.

Television tells us that material goals provide all the satisfaction and meaning of life. Look at the ads for everything from beer to automobiles to kitchen appliances. The theme is that if you just have a particular product, you'll find happiness in life. Don't you think you deserve a Buick? Live life with gusto. As if the meaning of life is related to material things. If that's all there is to life, life is bankrupt because those things don't fill the hole that Pascal talked about. The most significant questions that exist inside every human being are Who am I? Why am I? Where did I come from? and Where am I going?

I grew up a poor kid in the Depression, the grandson of an immigrant. Nobody in my family had gone to college, and I thought my identity would be found in success and going to the right school. I won a scholarship to an Ivy League college; I was a captain in the Marines; I earned a doctorate and became a lawyer. I thought all of these things would give me some distinction, all of these things would give me some identity, all of these things would give me a sense of fulfillment. I felt I would meet the demands of my inner questioning by living on the fast track; the cocktail party circuit with the six-figure income, the yachts, the limousines, politics, "Hail to the Chief," and Air Force One. I went the distance. You can't do a great deal more than I did in thirty-nine or forty years. But then I discovered a terrible emptiness inside.

I found myself waking up in the morning not feeling happy about myself, not feeling that my life was worth a whole lot, not feeling that I'd accomplished much, not feeling satisfied. I was not getting any thrill out of getting into the back seat of a black Lincoln Continental, sitting behind a driver who picked me up every morning. I had a feeling that all of these things were a drag. I wasn't finding what my life was all about. I wasn't feeling content.

I felt unclean about things and I didn't feel that I had been the kind of person to other people that I really wanted them to be to me. I didn't feel that my life was all it was cracked up to be. I had people looking up to me and saluting me and thinking I was a big shot. I didn't feel that way inside. I felt kind of phony.

This was really pre-Watergate. It was at a time when I was not the target of the investigators; in fact, I'd been told I wasn't. Yet I hated to go to my office. A client would come in and sign up with a hundred-thousand-dollar retainer and you'd think I'd feel jubilant. Instead, I'd go out and take a walk around the block and try to get a deep breath of air because it just didn't mean anything. I knew the client wanted me for my influence and that made it even worse. At that time I had the classic midlife crisis. I began to realize that my life, which was the perfect success story, was not going to make me happy. I was not going to be able to live the rest of my life that way.

I had been feeling that way for several months when I met a friend who told me what had happened in his life in an almost parallel situation. He had surrendered his life to Christ one night and had found fulfillment. Watergate was the crisis that forced me to face things, but for a year before Watergate, I had been wrestling inside. I had been feeling the hole. I had been unhappy with my life. Something was not right and I knew it was not right. Watergate brought me to the point of having to face it. I might have postponed it for a long time.

The conviction of sin that comes across us creates emotional distress which causes us to recognize our need for a relationship with the God who created us. This is the basis of conversion. A conversion is a change. A conversion is not an instant. Most people think that conversions are blinding flashes. Conversion is a process that people go through in their lives. It is an experience in which you first come to terms with yourself and discover that you aren't your own creator; you do not really control your own destiny and you need something larger than yourself.

Conversion for most people is a process whereby they first begin to look at themselves and at the nature of life and the universe. They begin to see, in a Christian conversion at least, that much of life is determined by invisible forces. There is a spiritual as well as a temporal realm in which we live, and Christ is bringing a message that has meaning and gives meaning and dignity to life. If they begin to go a little bit further, they'll discover that historical evidence validates the historicity of Christ's life. For a while some of the modern scholars said Christ never lived. But if you look at the Roman secular pagan authors, there's more written about the life of Jesus than any other character in that period. There's no question there was a historic Jesus who lived. There's no question on the evidence of the Resurrection—the eyewitness accounts of the twelve apostles who were with Jesus and who saw him. For forty years they never denied him and they went through all sorts of persecution. The apostles were subjected to all kinds of torture and beatings and prison. All but one died a martyr's death, and the evidence, both biblical and extrabiblical in terms of the secular accounts of the day, are that these men never denied that they had seen Christ rise from the dead.

If you look at the fact of the Resurrection, unique in

human history, I believe it to be the fulfillment of the ancient Hebrew Scriptures. Therefore, the prophecies were validated, and thus, what we find in biblical writings is true. And if it is true, that's a fact of history that changes life.

For me, it was surrendering my life to the teachings of Jesus Christ. I decided that God really is in charge of this world and he wanted me to live according to his teaching. When I started doing that, things really began to happen. My whole relationship with my family was one of the most dramatic changes. I figured my job in life was to make money and be successful and give my kids money and get them through the best schools. That's not my job at all. I've discovered what it really means to love each other as a family and love other people. I realize now that I used to use people and maybe I still do, but I've discovered a real feeling for people I never had before. I know I've been blessed. I've not had material wants in my life, but I think I could live in any circumstance with the same peace.

I spent seven months in prison. It was not pleasant but I lived with the same peace inside. I was restless every day and I wanted to get out, but I still had that assurance inside. I still had that comfort, that peace, and the feeling about relationships with other people. Conversion is beginning to experience that. I believe my own conversion process is continuing today. Theologians use the term *regeneration* to denote the moment that God convicts you of your sin and gives you a new life. Regeneration is the moment of belief. It is the moment when you come to a point of faith, and that's a moment that exists in every life. Some people don't recognize it. They come to faith gradually. It's like being on a train between Pennsylvania and New York. Unless you've seen a WELCOME TO NEW YORK sign, you don't know that you've left Pennsylvania and gone into New York. You don't necessarily know it, but there was an instant when you passed over the state line. God regenerates in that sense at that moment, but the conversion is a process.

Historic Christianity teaches that you come to Christ

surrendering yourself. You are turning yourself over to God for his use. Life is not going to be easy or better. You won't go through life with a plastic, frozen smile because God's going to put you on a magic carpet and let you float through life without experiencing the things other people experience. The Bible says that it rains on the just and the unjust alike. You're going to experience all the things in life everybody else experiences. The difference is that you're going to have the assurance of knowing who you are, where you've come from, what you're doing, who you belong to, and where you're going to end up.

I have met a few people in their forties and fifties who tell me that they have no relationship with God, they're self-sufficient and they got where they are by themselves. However, I believe there has to be crisis in everybody's life.

I gave a speech in Hobe Sound, Florida, the watering spot of the international jet set. A lovely Christian woman hosted a meeting for me. Because I'm a curiosity, everybody in Hobe Sound came. She had a tent set up on her lawn and I spent thirty minutes explaining the story of my life and what had happened. Then there was a half-hour question-and-answer period. The scene was a sloping lawn leading down to the beautiful inland waterway that runs just behind Hobe Sound, which was bumper to bumper with huge yachts. White-coated waiters served punch, which disappointed most of the guests because it was five-thirty in the afternoon of a beautiful March day and the sun was setting. People were getting restless because it was martini time.

A man in a white jacket was standing in the back, getting ready to go to a party. He said, "Mr. Colson, I can fully understand what happened to you. You went from the White House to prison and you obviously needed God, but look around here." He pointed to the yachts and the lawn. "What do you have to say to people like us who have never had a crisis in our lives and who have everything that everybody could ever want?" I said, "Well, the first answer is that if you've never had a crisis in your life, get ready because there has to be one. It is absolutely inevitable because it's part of the cycle of life and death. It may not come until you're lying on your deathbed and you realize that all these things that you're pointing to right now can do you absolutely no good. It's then that you may have to hear the words of Jesus, 'He who believes in me has eternal life.' Second, I disagree with your assumption. I don't believe there's anybody here who has not experienced a crisis or is not facing one right now.'' I sat down.

It was like a bellows letting air out; everybody said, ''Ohhhhhhhhhh.'' For the next hour and a half I couldn't get out of that tent. People—all in their sixties and seventies—kept coming up and saying, ''My husband is running off with another woman. I don't know what to do.'' ''I have two sons who are on drugs.'' ''My wife is an alcoholic.'' These people were realizing that all the values upon which they were hanging their lives were empty, they were meaningless. They had beautiful homes and beautiful boats and beautiful cars, but you can't get up in the morning and walk around and say, ''Wow, my life is fulfilled in this home.'' It isn't. Boats are great to go cruising on, except that even if you have a lot of money, you still have trouble getting help to run them. Life's got a lot of problems and those things just don't give you that fulfillment. People who are involved in a relationship with God are happier people. Happy in the sense of the joy of salvation, the assurance of their relationship with God and the understanding of themselves. Not happy in the sense of giddy, but with a sense of peace and security.

One hundred million Americans say—I'm quoting a Gallup poll here—that they never pick up a Bible. I think that's dumb because this book has endured in its present form for hundreds of years. The sacred writings it contains have endured for three thousand years. Anybody with any intelligence has to conclude that the Bible is a pretty remarkable book. It's remained the best seller for years and years, outselling all books. There's got to be something there.

Most people take the Bible home and stick it on a table and press flowers in it. They keep family records in it and have it around to show in case anybody comes in. They never open it. If you are honest with yourself, you ought to take a look at it and begin to ask, Could this be true? If it could be true, it changes your whole life. It changes the entire frame of reference of life. If Jesus was, in fact, resurrected from the dead, that has to be the single most important event of all human history. That has to be the pivotal point of history. That has to change all the ground rules. The story of Christ's life and resurrection is contained in the New Testament. You have to read the New Testament in conjunction with the Old Testament in order to understand who Christ was.

My only appeal to people is that if you have a modicum of intelligence and a desire to understand life, at least expose yourself to the Bible and see whether it could possibly be true. I always run into people who say, "Well, I think it's a collection of fables and old wives' tales and legends." I say, "Great. That's exactly the way I started." Start reading some of the literature about the historical evidence in support of the Bible and it's absolutely amazing what you begin to discover. It's extraordinary.

A group of Orthodox Jews on an archeological expedition to Syria found the remains of the kingdom of Ebla. The only historical evidence for the existence of that kingdom was in the Bible. It's in no other literature. Fifty years ago, most scholars in America would have said the Bible is in error when it talks about the Hittites because there is no evidence anywhere of the Hittite empire. Then we discover the ruins of a whole empire. A University of Chicago professor published a vocabulary of the Hittite language. No scholar today would ever say the Hittite empire didn't exist. It's an accepted fact at all universities. The Bible is a remarkable book and you at least ought to look at its claims if you're looking for the meaning for life. Freud said that anyone who searches for the meaning of life is mentally unbalanced because there is no meaning to life. If you want to accept that, okay. Ernest Hemingway did and blew his brains out as the only logical conclusion. He was, in effect, asserting meaning over life because he was saying, "I can assert meaning by taking my life.'' If you really believe Freud is right, that anybody who seeks the meaning of life is mentally unbalanced, then just drift right on through. Get what you can. Look for the pleasures of the moment. I don't believe anybody really feels that way. I believe in everybody's heart of hearts is a desire to know: "Could there be a God?" The place to begin to look is in the Bible.

If you're looking for happiness, I believe that you cannot find it through yourself or through material things around you because true happiness is peace in your heart, peace in your soul, the "peace of God which passeth all understanding." True happiness is the fulfillment of life—not the filling up of life—the fulfillment in meaning and purpose and identity which I believe comes outside of yourself and through Jesus Christ.

Contributor's Comment

Ruby Dee on Miracles

We are moving toward some kind of marvelous realization that has to do with love and light and the recognition that we're all one. Some people don't acknowledge it, but they've got God. It's a universal force. People in the Soviet Union and Africa have the same genes as we have in the United States. We've got a whole lot in common. So whether we acknowledge our connectedness as a species with definite tangible or intangible things in common, it doesn't matter. We are creatures. We are miracles. Each of us is an absolute astonishment. So whether you believe in miracles or not, we still are. We still partake of "miracledom.''

8 Humanness

Most of us look at life as a journey upward. We move through our childhoods, schooling, careers, and families. We get older. Others around us who are part of our lives die. We realize we will die. We see happiness as the prize and continually strive to achieve it. We should understand that life is a journey, but the journey is inward, not upward. We are human. We wrestle with our humanness. Some of us struggle with ego; some struggle with insecurity or inferiority; some deal with emotional, mental or sexual problems. Poverty, illness, and physical disability test us. Many feel the pain of sexual, racial, or ethnic prejudice. It's as if each of us is given a special task or challenge to work on as part of life. It is the joy of discovering ourselves as human beings, our personal growth, sharing of our love with others, and the contribution we make to others' lives that make the process of life so exciting. The journey inward is life. Each of us must find his or her own way. *Do I understand the life process? Do I see that happiness is just a part of my journey?*

Dr. Daryl Race examines the life process. "If you don't keep growing, you deteriorate emotionally, mentally, and intellectually."

Daryl Race, M.D., is a psychiatrist in private practice, the medical director of Charter Lane Psychiatric Hospital in Austin, Texas, and a member of the American Psychiatric Association.

* * *

Daryl Race, M.D.

Everybody believes that when you're a teenager you go through an identity crisis and that's it. That isn't it. These crises go on about every decade. An identity crisis is the concept of a person as an entity recognizing and defining himself in the larger world around him and also defining his inner world, the concept of the self. In adolescence the challenge for a person is the movement from being a child to being an adult—"Who am I as a big person?" "Who am I as a sexual person?" "Who am I going to be as a working person?" In adolescence you see the trying on of adult roles while trying to avoid them.

The twenties is a time when we are expected to leave home, make our own way, and, it is hoped, develop some of the beginning levels of intimacy. Leaving home is moving out from the parents' dominion and separating from them and their direct influence. That is when young people get their own apartments or are off at school living in a dorm. Autonomy is developing. Who am I as an adult away from my family at large? It's a scary period. People tend to find others going through the same thing. They can mutually feel: "We're different from our families but we support each other." A lot of people get married, start careers and families and the personal development of "Who am I?" is continuing. Contentment in this period is usually seen to be something in the future. Adolescents construct a career ladder by wondering, "What am I going to be when I grow up?" In the twenties, when people start a career, they begin thinking, "Okay, here I am and I'm willing to do what needs to be done. I can see those guys up there at thirty and forty and fifty and I want to get there faster." Women have a bi-mobile work curve. They start a career ladder and then they may have another compelling desire to have a family. Frequently after they get married they drop off the work ladder and do their family agenda. Later, when the children are ten, twelve, fourteen, and women are in their late thirties or forties they return to the work ladder.

At about thirty, these adults hit another crisis. For couples it used to be called the seven-year itch. One or the other is dissatisfied in the relationship. One blames it on the spouse because it's easier to blame than to look within. The developmental tasks that need to be accomplished at about thirty have to do with climbing your ladder, building your family, making your fortune, and looking at your future. The inner sense of self should be "I'm happy with who I am and where I am at this time in my life"—or "I'm not."

Also at thirty a realization hits, and you say, "I've done everything the way I was supposed to do, done everything I thought I'd do when I was a teenager and young adult, and I'm still not happy. I don't know what's going on. What is it?" The internal unrest is not "What's going on with me or my life or where am I going," but it's focused on the external, the spouse. "The thrill, the magic, the excitement, the romance are gone. There's somebody else out there who thinks I'm pretty neat. The things that made me feel good when I was younger no longer do, so I'll find somebody else or I'll just ignore it." At this time there's a lot of divorce, separation, running around, and entry into alcoholism and therapy.

The successful resolution of this is "I've done everything I was supposed to do, but I still don't feel okay." So the person comes up with the realization, "I've done it their way. Now I'm going to do it for myself. I'm going to be a little more openminded, be flexible, try different things that seem to fit me, that I like, not what my parents wanted." People who successfully conclude that stage end up feeling much more content with themselves. Many may make a career shift, a marriage shift, a hobby or free-time shift. They may focus more on the priorities in their lives. Where before it might have been the work, now it might be focused more on the family or friends or the church or other activities they may have neglected, such as physical exercise.

The forties is the big banana, the big bazooka. Why is that so tough? It has to do with the ultimate issue everybody has to deal with, which is "I'm going to die. My body's going. I'm getting gray hair. I'm bald. I'm fat. My friends are dying. I've got high blood pressure. I've got arthritis. I've got diabetes.'' Women typically get face jobs and breast and bottom lifts and men are out exercising. A very high incidence of entry into alcoholism and drug abuse, as well as therapy, occurs at this time. ''Who am I? Where am I going? What does my life mean to me? I've got the trappings of material success, professional recognition, and the family seem to be doing well, but I'm still not happy.'' The kids are leaving home and mothers frequently re-enter the work force. This is a time when people can be very helpful to the younger folks coming up, being a mentor, an all-loving, knowing big brother or sister who provides the way for someone younger. You can feel productive. You feel better about yourself, giving to the younger folks coming up in the firm or to the younger mothers on the block. The younger people really appreciate that leading guidance. In the forties the priorities can get shaken up.

The crisis of the fifties is realization that you don't have a whole lot of other options, particularly in the vocational world. You are looking forward to another ten or fifteen years of productivity. You may not be able to change jobs very easily at that age. There should be a sense of ''I'm pretty well on the main track in my life in work or in love.'' If you don't like it or never liked it or did it for the wrong reasons, it's a pretty tough spot to be in, particularly if you're vulnerable to getting fired or getting replaced or if health problems come along. That's a real crisis. You have to deal with the external reality and the inner feelings of ''I can't really change my life as much as I might have in my fantasy or I could in my earlier years.'' Ideally, you've achieved a sense of accomplishment in that period of time.

In the sixties the new crisis is the prospect of letting go—letting go of all that made you ''you'' in the work world or in your own life. ''I was the leader of the pack or I was in this position in my company or my field and I was here with my family. People are beginning to say 'Yes, sir' and to treat me as if I'm older, as if I'm not worth as much in the mercantile world.'' In the inner world if you thought of yourself as being potent physically or dynamic with other people or sexual with women, it's a terrible strain. For people who have tied up too much of their life happiness in the concept of being on the occupational ladder, especially if they left the rest of their life still to be developed—the family life, the hobbies, the religious pursuits, the physical things, the political activities, all the things that make us human—what does that leave? If you've left those to atrophy and just focused on work, when you think about letting go, that can be a devastating, despairing nothingness.

It's a time of tremendous onset of alcoholism and less entry into therapy. A lot of depression comes on and there's a fairly high instance of people having heart attacks and dying from stress. The so-called golden years of retirement frequently are not very golden. Our society has a huge vice called ageism. Because you're older, you can't do as much, can't see as well, can't hear as well. You're going to be sick, your memory is going, and sexually you're not going to have the same life. This is a real crisis to deal with—the external society's expectations, that you can't do as much as you used to, and your own expectations, your inner awareness that tells you you're physically unable to keep up.

If you can successfully come to grips with that period of the sixties, letting go and re-establishing what's important to you and what seems to be satisfying to you in your free time with your family or spouse or friends, then you move on to the seventies, eighties, nineties, and beyond. Those years haven't been well studied.

In the seventies and eighties you hope to look back on your life and be able to say "I made a lot of mistakes and there were problems, but by and large, at the time I did those things, I didn't have other information and I would probably have done it again. Basically, I did the best I could and I made the best of it and I can be at peace with myself. I can forgive myself for the bad things I've done; I can accept myself for the good things I've done. I can recommit myself to doing more positive things for myself and for my world now."

These developmental stages are there. Each one is built

upon the successful resolution of the previous one. We talk about a crisis as an opportunity. It's not a negative thing, it's an opportunity to go forward or to go backward. At the time of each crisis our mechanisms are shaken up like crazy. It's like the old snowflake Christmas ball—when you shake it up the snowflakes go up. Your defenses are up in the air in a crisis and it blows you away, but you have an opportunity as they settle back down into a stronger, more crystallized foundation, or into more chaos like ashes in a pile. Crisis defines who we are and helps us be able to shake out and drop some of the old unwanted baggage, neurotic patterns, and poor self-esteem. It should leave us with a feeling that life will come out right and we can help the process and learn to grow.

Happiness is the journey, not the destination. It's doing what you want to do, not being there one day. You should be happy doing what you're doing—and doing what you want to do. The percentage of people who are doing what they want to do with their lives emotionally, vocationally, having fun, keeping friends, is not the majority. It's a minority of folks. People may experience happiness during brief periods, but how many are content for long periods in their lives, and generally happy, saying, "My life's okay"? Probably only 15 to 20 percent.

Our lives are complex journeys made up of periods of searching and growth. As we mature we evaluate our needs and often shift our focus. During periods of transition we discover new qualities in ourselves and achieve a greater appreciation of the life process. As we grow older we tend to be more self-accepting and less concerned with our accomplishments. If success has ruled our lives and the human element is missing, there is often major change toward bringing more people into our lives, which in turn brings greater happiness. *What are my own needs? Am I being good to myself?*

Dr. Pierre Mornell surveys his own life and states, "For me to go out into the world and put food on the table and come home to nobody I loved would seem very empty.''

Pierre Mornell, M.D., is a recognized expert on interpersonal relationships and the problem of success. A faculty member of the University of California and a diplomate of the American Board of Psychiatry, Pierre divides his time among lecturing, consulting, the private practice of psychiatry in Mill Valley, California, and writing. His latest book is Thank God It's Monday or How to Prevent Success from Ruining Your Marriage.

Pierre Mornell, M.D.

One definition of happiness could be the enjoyment of pleasure without pain. I don't think there can be pleasure without pain. There can't be a point without a counterpoint, an ebb without a flow. I wouldn't understand happiness without some unhappiness. For example, the appreciation of health is only in contrast to being ill.

The best story about happiness that I remember was told by Isaac Bashevis Singer, long before he won the Nobel Prize. In the Yiddish folk tale a farmer complains that he's unhappy because he lives in a small room with his wife and two children and a dog. He goes to the rabbi and says, ''Rabbi, I'm unhappy. What can I do?'' The rabbi says to him, ''You have a goat outside?'' The man says yes. ''Bring it into the house,'' says the rabbi. The next week, the man goes back and says, ''Rabbi, it's terrible. The goat's there and it's even more crowded. What should I do?'' The rabbi says, ''Bring in the cow.'' The third Friday it's bring in the chickens; the fourth it's bring in the rabbits; and the fifth it's bring in the horses. Finally the man says, ''I can't stand it anymore. What should I do?'' So on the sixth week the rabbi says, ''Get rid of the horses.'' The seventh week, the rabbits, then the chickens, and it goes right back down the line. Finally the man is back to where he started out and he says, ''Rabbi, I'm so happy.'' Happiness is perceived only through contrast.

Happiness is, of course, different for every person. Tolstoy's opening line for *Anna Karenina* is "Happy families are all alike; every unhappy family is unhappy in its own way." It's a very catchy line, but I don't think it's true. We're all different and we're happy in our own fashion.

Happiness usually comes as a surprise to me. It comes out of the blue and it comes in short bursts. Often I am functioning on automatic pilot, seeing patients, dealing with my kids, paying the bills, and when I have a burst of happiness it's a fleeting and wonderful moment. It's not a chronic state. A poet in Berkeley wrote that happiness is like a Chinese meal where sorrow provides constant nourishment.

I was close to my mother. When she died my view of the world changed in a positive way. In the weeks that followed I would be driving along and see the sunrise. We live near a large wildlife lagoon and I'd actually stop and look. I had been driving the route for fifteen years and had rarely pulled over to watch the sunrise or look at the color of the lagoon or watch the seals getting ready to warm themselves as the sun was coming up. But when I did I was appreciating that I was alive. It was a beautiful thing.

Happiness is also good health and spirituality and a family and work I love. It's some sort of psychological well-being. People who look for one key to unlock one door behind which lie all the answers are looking at the wrong metaphor. For me happiness is a puzzle with a lot of different pieces. I keep moving those pieces around and sometimes they fit. In my early life, it was one picture, but that blurred and changed. The two most significant aspects of my happiness today are my children and my wife—their love and my relationships with them. It's family, it's sexuality, it's affection, and it's meaningfulness in contrast to any kind of loneliness I've experienced in my life. I would also say that the most unhappy and painful times have been in my marriage and with my children. The happy times are a contrast to that.

You can't buy happiness or seek it. It's a by-product of other activity. When I go running in the morning, it's not to be happy, because it's hard to get up. It's a pain and it's boring, but when I get through there's a sense of happiness. Happiness obviously changes at different stages and phases in life. Along the way in my life it's been playing basketball in high school, traveling to India, making Phi Beta Kappa in college, and getting discharged from the Army. Later on it was getting in and graduating from medical school, meeting my wife, my children's births, seeing patients, having my first book published, and making speeches.

At this point in my life I am turning my need for applause, approval, accomplishment, and acceptance from the outer world to do what's important to me. I'm trying to focus on my own values and my own acceptance and develop my feeling side and my inner resources. Yet as I think about the intangibles of my life there are certain things I find difficult to capture in words. Whether it's with my patients or with my kids, I know I'm doing some sort of service that I enjoy, and it gives me a great deal of pleasure. Also when I speak or consult with a corporation, I feel I'm doing something worthwhile and I feel very happy that I have done it. What I've left out of this are words like *compassion* and *honor* and *sacrifice* and words like *pride, pity, courage, honor,* and *hope.* I think they're in the mix somewhere.

I think there really is something quite wonderful about people. It's important to tune into the contrast. Out of crisis, good things come; out of illness, we can appreciate health; out of crazy and chaotic lives we can appreciate solitude; out of obscurity we can appreciate fame; and out of fame we can appreciate obscurity and simplicity. To see this ebb and flow, this point and counterpoint, this contrast in life, can give us an inordinate amount of pleasure. In my own life it goes way beyond my mother's death as an event that allowed me to open my eyes for the first time and see the lagoon and the light, the fish and the birds. It takes a rare moment or a rare person to shake people out of the furrow they're plowing and appreciate life. It's been my experience that it takes a major life event to have people appreciate life.

* * *

Pain is a part of life, part of the human equation. We will all experience some pain—physical, mental, emotional, or spiritual. To expect life to be pain-free is to deny our humanness. Most of us never learn from pain. We experience it and are so relieved when it is over, we never look at it. We learn our greatest lessons about ourselves and life from not only facing painful situations but examining the pain. Through pain, we define who we are. A painful situation is an opportunity to grow. *What was the last really painful situation I faced? What did I learn about myself?*

Pat Carroll feels: "Living here is all lessons. Lots of things are hard and some are even dreadful. No matter how much we buck them and fight them at the moment, they're all to our good eventually. It's all learning."

Pat Carroll is a well-known actress and comedienne whose talents have been utilized on television situation comedies, variety and panel shows, and in cabaret acts and stage productions. Pat, who once called herself "the dowager queen of the game shows," has received critical praise and delighted theatergoers in New York and around the country with her one-woman show, Gertrude Stein, Gertrude Stein, Gertrude Stein. *She has played opposite many of the great comedy talents of America, including Red Buttons, Eddie Albert, Ben Blue, Sid Caesar, Jimmy Durante, Mickey Rooney, Danny Thomas, and Mary Tyler Moore. She appears on television's* Ted Knight Show.

Pat Carroll

People who expect to be happy all the time are out of their minds. To learn to deal with the pain of the loss of happiness and know it can come around again is the most important thing. Be optimistic enough to know that it's normal and human not to be happy every second of your life. The lesson of now is going to lead us to the next happiness. The happiness will be different as we build the layers of our lives. Why at fifty-eight would I expect the same happinesses that I thought were my happinesses at fifteen? I see my mother at eighty finding different but new happiness. I find other older friends of mine who have had to adjust their lives to the limitations of aging and death ahead. Death is ahead the minute we are born. We don't want to accept that pain either. Aren't the lessons all there to teach us how to die?

I have stopped taking Valium since I stopped trying to run away from pain, and I have accepted the pain of rejection in this business. I've been in show business almost forty years. If I couldn't accept rejection, I would have been out of it in five minutes. It's not pleasant. It hurts. That's what pain is about. It teaches you something. I am a devout coward about physical, emotional, or mental pain. But after taking away the body suit of Valium, booze, and cigarettes—all of my no-no's that protected me from pain— I found out that pain exists and it's real and I deal with it. I get depressed about it. But I say, "Hey, what's the lesson here? You are going to keep being rejected because you are in a profession of rejection, but look behind you at the years you have built up. Does it mean you're not going to work again? I don't think so. Maybe things aren't going fantastically right this minute. But you can't throw away the years that you have put into something. You can't throw away what you know, what you have to give, and what you want to give." It's the handling of pain that's the most important thing—to accept it.

I do see value in pain because when we have pain in our body it tells us that something is wrong. "What am I doing? Why was I rejected? Why did they turn me down for that job?" You begin to examine. Pain kicks you into activity, if you don't pull the cover over your head. Pain kicks you if you aren't protected, if you don't have the pills or the booze or whatever protects you. It kicks you into examination, the examination of conscience. "What didn't I do right? Did I make a schmuck of myself? Was my approach wrong? Didn't I read the material well? Why didn't I read the material well?" If you are objective about that and not twisting the knife in yourself you call people and ask, "Could you tell me, because I'm driving myself nuts over here, why I didn't get the job? I'm not going to bomb the place. It's driving me nuts.'' I think people understand that and they respond. The burden is off me.

Pain stinks. Almost two years ago I was walking with a cane. I weighed 250 pounds. My blood pressure was so high I was to be hospitalized. I was a veritable mess. One day I sat down and said, ''Why am I killing myself? Why am I doing this to myself? I love using my body. I love playing tennis. I love horseback riding. I love swimming. Why am I doing this to myself? I can't play tennis. I can't do the things I used to do.'' Why is it that our pain is so many times self-inflicted?

Thank God I went to a place where I corrected it and dropped sixty-five pounds. I worked damn hard to take it off. With each pound that came off I could move, I could walk. I started with just a couple of steps. That's all I could do without a cane. The next day it was five steps. The next day it was six steps. In two weeks it was a mile. In ten weeks, it was three miles. It's brick on brick on brick.

We all want it this instant. Let the castle rise. The castle isn't going to rise in twenty-four hours. You have to take one brick, another brick, two bricks together. It's slow and tedious, but if you are stubborn and you're determined you keep plodding ahead, one foot in front of the other. By God, it's the only way. There is pain along the road but you accept it and deal with it.

At my mother's eightieth birthday celebration I made a little speech. I said what was in my heart. ''We're all in this place at this time because of a little woman who has affected all of our lives. Since I was a kid there were two things that Mother said and they made such sense. One dictum was 'Never envy anybody.' It sounds simple, sounds real cliché. But think about it. Never envy anybody. I remember asking my mother one time, 'What does that mean? Suzie has a pretty dress and I don't have a pretty dress.' She said, 'It goes beyond that because you don't see everything about a person's life. You never know all there is to know. You are only seeing externals. Since we don't know everything about other people, don't envy them for anything, whether it is what they have materially, what they have in their spirit or their character, or what they own, or what they are talented with. Never envy anybody.'

"The other idea was far simpler than that. She not only said it, but lived it in her life: 'Always do one thing every day for another person.' She made no distinction for whom—your family, your husband, your children, or your neighbors. Just do one thing for someone else. Do you know how hard that is to do? I have seen it in my mother's life. It could be a get-well card to a person she doesn't know very well, a phone call to someone who is very depressed or very sad, or running an errand for someone who is just too pressurized. My mother had lit little candles."

Every one of the 115 people in that room had been a recipient of her philosophy. I said, "We all know, all of us—I as her daughter in a greater way—that her funny little philosophy works. Think about yourself. Every person here is here because he or she is a friend of my mother's. That goes for her brothers, her sister-in-law, her grandchildren, and me. We are her friends because she has been our friend. She has done one thing at some point or another for every one of us in this room." One of my aunts was in absolute tears. We all cried because we recognized how wonderful and how simple it is.

It's like multiplication. You don't have to go out and do big things. The big things we leave to the president at the summit or Lee Iacocca at Chrysler. We are not presidents. We are not heads of companies. We are simple human beings who live our lives day to day, wanting to be happy.

Most people don't know what feeling happy is about, or don't know how to effect it in other people's lives. Many times I think those tiny little nuggets are better than the big bricks. Those tiny little pieces mean so much more to those of us who aren't going to get the big nuggets. We're going to have the tiny things but, boy, when they're rubbed together, do they make a sound. That becomes a whirlwind, and it comes back.

One of the few theological principles that I have ever

really felt in my gut is the communion of saints. It's a tremendous feeling between those who have gone to the beyond and those who are here. What goes around, comes around. Do you remember that thing, about good goes around in a circle? It's not to return the good that somebody else has done to you, but to keep the good going, to pass it on. Remember the old saying, "Pass it on, pass it on." To pass on good I think is more important than to return it to the person who gave it to you. In my life, when somebody has done something spectacularly marvelous for me, the best of those people have always said, "Pass it on. Don't try to repay me. Do it for somebody else, because that's the way I got it."

We Christians talk a great philosophy, but we don't live it. Jews live it. They're the first people to give to charities, not only with money, but with time, enthusiasm, and passion. They have an absolute passion to do this because their heaven is here on earth. I sometimes think that the Jews are right. The good that you do here is your heaven. It isn't because Christianity has been tried and found wanting; it is that it hasn't been tried. People say, "I want to be happy, I want to be happy." They haven't tried it.

Our responsibility is to be happy. It's not your parents' responsibility. It's not your teachers' responsibility. It's not your neighbors' responsibility. It's your responsibility to be happy.

We grow older. Our bodies change. We are human and we are aging. We gain the wisdom and maturity of our years, but we lose the spontaneity and vitality of youth. In our culture we do not deal with age very well. Jokingly we say, "Youth is wasted on the young." However, a positive attitude can do a great deal to offset the negative messages of society and an acceptance of our humanness can make the aging process a more positive experience. *How do I really feel about getting older? Do I accept my humanness?*

* * *

Burt Bacharach has a positive attitude and says, "One of the ways you can slow down the process of getting older a little bit is by making it all count all the time."

Burt Bacharach has become a legend in the music business as a composer and performer over the past three decades. With Dionne Warwick alone, Burt, with lyricist Hal David, scored an incredible thirty-nine chart records in ten years. The same collaboration was responsible for the smash Broadway musical Promises, Promises. *Burt has scored many films and received two Academy Awards for* Butch Cassidy and the Sundance Kid *and one for "Arthur's Theme," which he wrote with his wife, Carole Bayer Sager, Peter Allen, and Christopher Cross.*

Burt Bacharach

My mother and father gave me the nickname Happy. I thought I'd better try to be happy because that was what was expected of me to deserve that name. The name followed me to school, but I don't remember feeling particularly happy in school. I didn't feel very connected to the kids. I was alone most of the time. I was an only child and I was very small. I was the smallest kid in the school. There were three thousand kids and I couldn't find a girl who was shorter than I. It's almost like having a defect. You're called Shorty or Shrimp. I tended to split off and be by myself. You can be happy by yourself.

I had a lot of good times by myself, but in retrospect I'd surely rather have been with my peers. Being an only child, you're prone to more isolation, but my parents were very good to me. I think it's interesting that I had a name like Happy. I don't know how happy I was. I don't think I was very happy. My dad was a top college football player and I worshiped the ground that he walked on. I gave up football in my mind when I saw how rough the game was. My family doctor told me one time I was getting beat up too much just playing after school.

I was training to become a serious composer, writing classical music, but I never really got close to it. You starve when you do that. When I was working with the Ames brothers I used to see the songs that came in and they looked so deceptively simple. I said, "Let me get off the road and go back to New York. I could write three or four of these a day and have a couple of hits." One year later I hadn't had a hit.

Winning the Academy Award gives you a happy moment, the highest kind of feeling, totally on top of the world. Euphoric. You wanted it, you've missed it before, you were nominated, you finally get it. You finally win two Academy Awards—not one, but two. You walk out of the Chandler Pavilion, you're the happiest person in the world. You stay happy through the night. The next day you put those two Oscars up there on the mantelpiece above the fireplace. Three days after you win the Academy Awards, you go through the whole day without thinking about them or even noticing them in the living room. The externals don't work, they just are temporary things.

You've got to get inner peace to be happy. It's really important to not be looking backward or forward. That's looking for something that's going to happen in a couple of days that's going to make you happy. It gets there and it's not so good. Then you've got to look for the next thing. You've got to stay right in the present. I tell my daughter not to dwell on the rock concert she's going to see in two weeks. I tell her she's just losing a lot of present time. Then I find that I don't take my own advice.

I used to go to the theater when I was in New York. I'd be watching a show that I really wanted to see after writing all day, maybe an orchestration or a song. I'd sit in the theater watching the show, but only partially watching it. The other part of me would be thinking about trying to resolve the song. I'd walk out of the theater not having resolved a thing. I didn't get it done and it took time away from seeing the show. I thought it was a natural process but now in retrospect I realize that that's not the smart way to go. If you're going to a show, let it go. When you work, work, and when you play, play.

The music is hard, but I like going back to the room and writing. I'm happy because I push myself into a discipline. I get into a groove where I'm playing the piano and melodies start to flow and I'm happy. Then I become not so happy because I beat myself up trying to make it perfect.

I'm very lucky in having met Carole and sharing my life with her. She's very, very sensitive, very, very smart, and very supportive of me. I'm really supportive of her as well, and I just feel lucky.

I'm happy in our house. I've never thought where you lived mattered too much. I was always happy to rent an apartment or a house. I was never much into owning houses. When I met Carole I was living in a rented apartment, but this is great. I love it. It feels wonderful here. I wake up in the morning and say to myself, "Look at this. Look where you're living, this is very beautiful. Look at the city. You can see the ocean." There are days I stop seeing it and I've got to say "Don't be a fool, don't take it for granted."

One of the things that can stop that appreciation is me. It's an attitude of what today's going to be like for *me,* not what it's going to be like for Carole. There is something special about it when I can really give. It's a very happy process.

Music is a wonderful tool with which to reach out and make people happy. One of the things that I feel really terrific about is when people come up to me and say, "Your music has meant a lot to me." Or "It got me through some very difficult times." It's a very good feeling to make people feel things, and I feel happy that I contributed to somebody's life, even for a minute.

I probably had more "good times"—what I thought were happy times—when I really was floating around, having drinks with the guys. I was involved with musicians and singers, playing in celebrity tennis tournaments every weekend. When you wake up and start looking at things, there's a lot of things that are really tough to see that you've been able to avoid by going to those tennis tournaments every weekend.

It's all within. The majority of people don't want to look inside. They think, "Let me take some drugs so I don't have to look inside. Let's keep it moving fast. Let's keep the television on so there's some sound. Let's keep the radio on so I don't have to think. Let's keep the Musak playing in the elevator so nobody really has to be bored for one second.''

You've got to keep working with yourself. My daughter said to me, ''You're so together.'' I thought, ''I'm never together; I've got to keep growing.'' In music if you stop writing, if you stop exploring, you're fat, you're dead, it's over. In life you have to continue expanding and stretching and being aware and being conscious and reading and thinking and not sitting back and getting fat. If you do, I don't think you'll be happy.

Fear is a powerful emotion. It is caused by the anticipation or awareness of danger. Fear performs a very important and useful function in our lives. However, the sense of ''bad things to come'' can inhibit us so much that we exist in a very small comfort zone. Excessive worry can immobilize us. We feel threatened. In our interpersonal relationships we fear rejection. On the job we fear disapproval. On the dance floor or ski slopes, we fear looking like a fool. Our fears are often self-centered. We are overly concerned with the real or imagined judgments of others. Because we are human we are all insecure. To understand this vulnerability and imperfection is to accept ourselves. *Is it okay for me to be insecure? Is fear keeping me from doing the things I want to do?*

Ivan Bloch has found the answer. ''It has made me very happy to find out that everybody is insecure, because I don't feel all alone.''

Ivan Bloch is a Tony Award–winning Broadway theater producer, real estate entrepreneur, political fund raiser, and philanthropist. He co-produced the musical TinTypes *and* The Real Thing *and produced* Master Harold . . . and the Boys, Hurly Burly, Ma Rainey's Black Bottom, *and* Joe Egg. *Ivan, the chairman of Uniprop, a real estate equity investment firm, is a recipient of the State of Israel Peace Medal and is the brother-in-law of Julia Chang Bloch, who appears earlier in this book.*

Ivan Bloch

I left home when I was seventeen. My folks were divorced. My older brother, who is my hero, was gone. My younger brother was living with my dad. My sister was married. It was time for me to go. I wanted to be in show business. My whole childhood was difficult. I was very unsure of myself and very shy. I was terrible in school. I didn't like myself at all. I thought I was not cool. Nobody mistreated me or anything, I just wasn't a happy kid. I had this gorgeous older sister whom everybody fawned over. I had a good-looking, popular brother. My younger brother was a genius. My mother was beautiful. My father was good looking. We were always called the beautiful family. I was overweight. My childhood was confusing because of all that. I thought surfaces were more important than what's inside. Good looks— blond hair and blue eyes, tall and thin—I didn't fill any of those requirements. My folks had actually divorced and remarried three times. It was hectic. My mother was an alcoholic, but I didn't know it. I was very close to her because I was very sick as a child. She's adorable, my mother. She doesn't drink at all now. She's wonderful.

I always knew I would turn out to be something. I haven't yet, but someday I will. Someday I may do something that will contribute something. I was going to be a famous singer. Everybody was going to fall at my feet. I was great on stage. At home I was so bashful my dad used to make me pick up the phone and call people for him. I never asked a girl out because I was very shy, but I was real good on stage. I was very sure of myself about singing. I was hot. I won't deny that with false modesty. I was good. I held an audience. I knew what I was doing.

I made a record on Decca, "Your Photograph," which was good. It sold some copies. I was signed the same day as Ricky Nelson and Brenda Lee. Of course, you've never heard of them again, and I became famous.

I married a wonderful girl. She had gone to college when she was fourteen—really brilliant, very quiet, and very calm. She gave me a lot of stability. We were on the road together, which was totally new to her. We were in Orlando, Florida, where I was working and I was not real happy. I had gotten a little lazy. I wasn't going anywhere. I was getting a little tired of it. We went to a furniture store one day and I thought, "Gee, it would be nice to have a place and furnish it and be a regular person." So I said to her, "I'm quitting." And she said, "When?" I said, "Now. I don't have anything after Saturday night. I'm not going to call my agent. I'm done. I'm finished." I told my group and I quit. We got an apartment in Orlando and we furnished it. It was fun and nice. We were madly in love.

I went to work for my brother in real estate, but I wasn't crazy about Florida. I wanted to come back home. I also made that decision totally rationally. I said "We're going home." She said, "When?" I said, "Tomorrow. Pack up." So that's what we did. I have always made decisions quickly. I have always felt I wasn't smart enough to do a lot of logical thinking about what to do. I've always gone with my feelings. I've never been afraid of making a move. It just never occurred to me to be afraid. My father taught me that. "Let's buy a house on the lake," he'd say, and he'd go and buy a house on the lake. I think that's what you should do.

Do what you think you should do. You're not hurting anybody as long as you provide for your family if you have one. Just go. It's more interesting anyhow. Lots of adults I know say, "When I was a kid my father and mother used to move here and there." They're happy kids. Nothing says you have to live in the same place and do the same thing. I have always said that every seven or eight years you should change what you are doing. I get bored real easy. That's something that causes problems in my life. But I do get bored, so I go do something else.

My success in real estate brought me some recognition, which brought me happiness. It also brought me some proof that I was capable of doing something and that brought me happiness. But the success directly? No. What difference does it make? It just provided me with the financial opportunity to go into the theater.

The thing that makes me happiest is that I can do what I want in the theater. I don't have to make a living at it. So I can really take chances on shows like *Master Harold*, *Ma Rainey, Joe Egg*. The interesting thing is that those seem to be the plays I get most rewarded for, not with money but with awards. *Hurly Burly* didn't win any awards but was an enormous financial success. *The Real Thing* was financially successful and got a lot of awards. *The Real Thing* and *Hurly Burly* gave me the courage and the reputation and the ability to do a *Ma Rainey*, which deserved to be produced. It was an incredible opportunity to be able to do it. That's what I like the best. August Wilson, a young playwright, has two other plays that are eventually going to Broadway. To think that I was the one who gave him his first opportunity to be on Broadway is great. Danny Glover, the guy who played Whoopi Goldberg's husband in *The Color Purple* and is a big star now, is another case in point. I gave him his first job with *Master Harold . . . and the Boys*. I even gave him the money to bring his mother to New York, to come to the opening. She said to me, ''Master Harold washed the floor almost the whole play. I washed floors all my life to send my son to New York and now he's in New York washing floors.'' To be a part of their lives really makes me happy. That gives me a lot of joy.

I like to make an audience think. That's what it's all about. Theater is something you should work at. You can't lean forward and turn up the dial. You have to listen. It's a live experience and theater's an interplay between the actors and the audience. If you don't work at it with the actors then you are not getting the experience. It's sad because a lot of people don't and they miss something. Success makes me happy, sure, because it's an achievement.

I found out something interesting, though, that being successful in the theater gives you a certain kind of public profile. I work for a lot of charitable causes and I found that I can do a lot more because I'm known. Now when I speak at a dinner, I can raise more money. People listen to me. Funny, I know the same things I knew before, but it's nice to be able to use celebrity in the right way. I'm always hollering at people who are celebrities, "You really should do more. You have no idea of the power of what you can do." To put back into this community or this world is something important. You should use it. Actually it's a debt.

To cope with failure, I mourn for seventy-two hours with no guilt. I get mad and aggravated and I scream at the critics and I tell everybody they were wrong and I was right. *Boys of Winter* is a good example. A play about Vietnam, it was brutally criticized. Unfairly, I thought, because the critics didn't review the actors. I dwelled on it for three days and then I was over with it. I separated myself from it. My life gets me out of it. I'm too busy. I can't waste my time.

I'm a doer more than a thinker. Thinking becomes an excuse for people. People don't make moves because they want to think about it. They wind up thinking about it for too long. People say, "You know, I've been thinking about moving to California for twenty years and now it's too late." Thinking becomes a crutch or excuse not to take the action. Some people are afraid of making the wrong decision. I think they're afraid of what people will think of their decision, which is probably one of the most powerful things to stop people from doing something. All kinds of things such as money and family might be involved in it, so they don't make a decision. In not making the decision they've made one. Not doing something is the same as doing it.

The doers are the happy people. But a lot of people who sit around in think tanks may also lead very wonderful, calm lives. They sit in their libraries reading their books and they live long lives. They decided that that's what they wanted to do. I couldn't do that. That's not for me. Maybe they're satisfied, which is happiness.

My kids bring me happiness because they are great kids and I like them. I have a son who is in college who is as wacky as any teenager. He's a trip. I have a lot of faith in him. He's going to be okay. My daughter is a very special person. She fascinates me. I can't wait to see how her life turns out. My wife and I have been married twenty-three years. We have had enormous fights and a great love affair. We're two totally different kinds of people. She is a true intellectual who reads and studies. She went to law school, got her law degree, and graduated at the top of her class. She was awarded a dean's scholarship.

We have had lots of strains and lots of problems in our marriage. We have been separated. Back together. Separated again. Back together again. But we love each other, and we like each other, too. I could do a whole book on her. It works well even when it doesn't work. We're both Russian, Polish, and German, so we have incredible tempers. But that's fun. You don't love somebody if you don't argue. She's my best friend, no doubt about it. Absolutely. I really like her.

I guess I'm involved in Jewish causes because that's where I can do the most good in the community. The Jewish community knows me. I'm thankful that I have the opportunity to really be involved in it and put something back. I would feel very empty without it. Everybody·has an obligation. The more you get, the bigger your obligation is. We don't do enough. None of us does. You have to try.

I had a conversation with Averell Harriman at Senator Teddy Kennedy's house. He could walk into an restaurant and nobody would know him. He's probably one of the most important Americans living today. He's my idol. He said to me at dinner, ''I don't know how you do it all.'' And I said, ''Governor Harriman, I have never in my life been so awed and so complimented at the same time. I can't believe that you said that to me.'' Just previous to that remark we had been talking about his visit, as a young man, with Tolstoy, and later with Stalin. I learned something that night because I thought about it a lot. He's not taken with himself. He listens and that gives him the ability to do what he does. He focuses on other people and

what's going on around him. I wish I could do that. It's
got to be the greatest gift.

Sometimes when I think about life I think it's the silliest
thing I could possible imagine, all those human beings
running around building buildings, going to the bathroom,
screaming and hollering, driving cars. Is this what it's for?
I don't know. I'd love to try to figure life out. My religion
says the biggest sin you can commit is not doing something with your life. That's waste. God made us in his
image. I don't think he made us in his physical image, but
I think he made us in his moral and spiritual image. You
say, "Why are so many people starving?" That's not God's
fault. There is enough food in the world to feed everybody. It's our fault because we don't care enough to get it
to them. You have a responsibility to give back. Those two
go together. If everybody in the world felt that way, good
things would happen.

Being happy is relative. I'm pretty happy. I have the
ability to do what I want and that's kind of nice. But I'm
also pretty sad about what goes on that's wasteful. There
are so many people starving. You walk around the streets
in New York and you see people who are desperate. A
Russian lady who is famous around the theater and Broadway tells fortunes before you open a show. She was in my
office and I said, "I don't believe in that garbage." A
woman in the office said, "Let her come in and talk to
you." So I said, "All right." She started telling me about
the influence of an older woman in my life—my great-
grandmother—which is true. Then she said to me, "The
problem you have with being happy"—and I will never
forget this—"is that when you walk down the street, you
don't notice the buildings like most people do, but you are
looking at all the people and it bothers you." That was a
little freaky and she started to tell me about how I feel
about things. She said, "You can be happy as anything,
but then all of a sudden something will enter your mind
that makes you feel bad." She's right. In my happiest moments I get almost depressed. The only one who understands it is my wife. Both times I've won a Tony, I was
miserable. I felt like "Big deal, so I mounted a play; any-

body could have done that. They give me an award, so what good did it do anybody?'' So I was on television and some advertiser and producer made millions of dollars and damn it, what did it do for anybody? Everybody says, ''Isn't that great?'' But really, what are we doing? It's not that it wasn't nice to get them.

There was a wonderful article about me in *Michigan* magazine. The previous week there had been an article about a man who feeds many starving children. I got a lot of favorable comments about the article on me, and I wondered if the man who really was doing something received as many. That bothered me. Why do people want to read about me? It doesn't mean a lot. I'm not putting it down. Theater is an art. On the other hand, the other man is feeding hundreds or thousands of children. To follow him was trite.

It would be like following Mahatma Gandhi on a speaker's platform. He'd get up and speak about the world, and I would get up and talk about producing a Broadway show. I mean, it's ridiculous. Dr. Doolittle or Albert Einstein? When I was invited to Senator Kennedy's house I sat between Averell Harriman and Carl Sagan. I thought, ''I'm not going to have a thing to say.'' I couldn't believe I was with these two men and they were fascinated with the theater business.

I'm very insecure. I believe that most people are. I learned that because a lot of people I talk to tell me they are. I ask them. I recognize it. I admit it. I know a lot of other people are and I go on. Actually, it has made me very happy to find out that everybody is insecure, because now I don't feel all alone.

Contributors' Comments

We think that we are the only ones who struggle. We feel that we are the only ones who wrestle with our humanness. We believe that everybody else is moving along through life effortlessly and we are the only ones with difficulties. Some of the contributors whom you have already met share themselves and their humanness.

John Naisbitt on Unhappy Memories

I grew up in real poverty. We didn't have any money. My father, bless his heart, refused to join the WPA (Work Projects Administration). I have images of all the WPA guys building the curbs and the streets in Salt Lake. My father had too much pride for that. He would go around and knock on doors to see if he could shovel snow or do odd jobs. I remember as a kid we lived for quite a number of days on just flour and water, to have something stick to our stomachs. I remember being teased by my schoolmates for the shabbiness of my clothes. I decided somewhere along the line I had to get through. I vowed at the time that I would never be that poor.

Ted Shackelford on Anger and Fear

When I'm ill-tempered, ill-mannered, and snippy, it means that I'm afraid of something. My anger is a cover for a lot of things. It's a cover for fear, it's a cover for pain, or it's a cover for being hurt. When I'm angry I have to know, "Why am I angry? What's making me angry? Am I angry because I'm afraid? Why am I afraid? What do I have to be afraid of? Is it the situation that's making me afraid? Do I have enough information? Am I angry because I'm hurt? Did a person hurt my feelings? Why didn't I confront that person?" I can still confront that person and say, "Listen, I've got to tell you something. You made me angry and the reason you made me angry is because you hurt me and you hurt me because of this . . . That's how I reacted to it, those are my feelings, and I would appreciate it if you wouldn't do it again."

My biggest fear is other people. I am more afraid of other people than anything in the world. I think it's because I don't know who I am. It's an ongoing thing. I'm becoming less and less afraid of people and less and less afraid of new situations. I haven't quite gotten to the point where I welcome change with open arms, but I don't shun it either. I'm trying to look at change as an adventure.

Dr. Joyce Brothers on Arguments

My husband and I have fought over air conditioning for thirty-six years. I am the only woman who spends her summers and winters with a chapped face. That's never going to get resolved. I will probably die and be buried with a little heater over my grave.

Gloria Steinem on Little Things

I'm really good in emergencies but I'm not too good in everyday life. I can't handle things like fixing up my apartment, getting my clothes from the cleaners, or organizing routine things. I get inundated by the detail of undone tasks and I get depressed by that. I know other people in my situation who do manage and orchestrate all those details, people who are just as busy as I am. People do have neat desks and files and pick up their clothes and plan ahead and do all those things that I don't do.

Willard Scott on Ego

We had done a TV pilot and it was not a success. I couldn't figure out why. Everything was right. My commercial acceptance is high, my personal ratings are high, I'm booked up for a year in advance for speeches. I just couldn't understand it and it was driving me crazy. I had a problem that I just couldn't seem to solve. I sat there and for just a minute I closed my eyes. I didn't fall to my knees and I didn't offer up any great word. I just sat there. I may have thought to myself, "What is wrong and what am I doing wrong?" It was like a wave that came over me that just said, "The only thing that you're doing wrong is you're letting your ego stand in the way of continuing to produce some kind of a program. You're questioning too many things. Just quit trying to figure out why this failed and go on and do something else." It was amazing how the whole thing was lifted. From that minute on, the frustration I'd had for a month absolutely, totally disappeared.

Ego was the center of that problem. Letting go with faith was the solution.

Julia Child on Growing Older

I have to get my knee fixed and Paul had a heart bypass but he's doing pretty well. I'm sorry that we're getting older. That's my only regret. But you have to accept that. You're not going to stop getting old.

Some things you absolutely cannot change. If you're a man, you're a man; if you're tall, you're tall; if you're getting older, you're getting older. You'd better learn to accept it and do something with it. Accept what you have. That's a key to life.

Congressman Morris K. Udall on Expressing Feelings

Hubert Humphrey had cancer and went home to Minneapolis. He was given a big reception, and all his old friends were there. People who had fought the fights with him and been with him when he lost in 1968 were on hand. They said a lot of kind things, and just before he was introduced Hubert choked up. He was known for shedding tears publicly, and that is viewed as a sign of a wimp or weak guy by some people. Hubert got up, wiped the tears from his eyes, and he said, "A man who has no tears has no heart." I've used that many times. I don't think it's bad for grown men to show emotion. I was an introvert in some ways and not anxious to push myself forward or be in emotional situations. I think I've improved on that a great deal.

Helen Thomas on Death

My husband died in 1982. I certainly had a period of adjustment and lots of emotion, but gradually you live with the reality. Time is a great healer, but you don't ever forget. We had such a good relationship that I always feel he's there. I had a happy marriage and I can feed on that. I have happy memories.

Leo F. Buscaglia on Letting Go

One of my greatest moments of despair was when my mother, with whom I had an enormous relationship, was dying in the hospital. We were all taking shifts because we didn't want her to die alone. My classes were very late in the afternoon, so I could stay with her early in the morning when all my brothers and sisters couldn't. I was sitting there and thinking of losing her—this personification of joy—and how sad that made me. I was crying and she opened her eyes. She took my hand and asked, "Felice, what are you holding on to?" At that moment I had an incredible, wondrous insight. I realized that life is a process and we are constantly interfering with that process. Here was this eighty-two-year-old woman who had lived a joyous, wonderful life, who was ready to die and was at peace with death.

Indeed, what was I holding on to? That moment of release caused me to lift out of this possessive, ego-centered concept of love in which one holds on to things. I opened my arms. It made all the difference. Since then, because of that rapturous moment, it's been impossible for me to hold on to anything. I had talked a great deal before that moment about letting go, but I know a lot of it was talk and I was not letting go. I wasn't letting go of life, I wasn't letting go of pain, I wasn't letting go of anything. I was holding on. That wonderful experience changed my life.

Dick Gregory on Values

I took my oldest son to Mexico to a place where there is no electricity. We lived in a hut. I was in the hut one night when my son ran in and said, "Dad, Dad come here. Come here, I'm scared. I want to show you something." I went out and my son showed me the stars. It dawned on me that, having been born and raised in Chicago, he'd never seen a sky full of stars. I lay on my back with a straw in my mouth, and we looked at the Big Dipper and the Milky Way. We saw shooting stars too. I cried that night—not for him, he'd never seen that many stars—but for me. I grew up looking at the stars and got so hooked into the vicious cycle, I never remembered the day they left. I got so hooked into this chase that I never missed the stars.

9   Acceptance and Gratitude

Happy people have a deep appreciation for the gift of life, an attitude of gratitude, and a true understanding of the concept of acceptance. Rather than focus on what they don't have, happy people savor what they do have. They do have desires, but their needs are few. If I ask happy people what they need, they will probably respond, "Nothing" or "Not much." Happy people count their blessings over and over again. Their enthusiasm for what is in their lives is exciting. They seem to go with the flow, take with appreciation what life offers them, and find some positive meaning and significance for even those things that most of us would see as negative, horrible, or sad. Happy people plan actions, they don't plan results. It's as if they enter every situation knowing that all they can do is give it their best shot and accept the outcome, whatever it is. *Do I have an attitude of gratitude? Do I accept what I cannot change?*

According to Max Cleland, "One of the ways I have found happiness is to have seen the purpose of my own suffering. I try to share that to encourage others to survive and affirm that there's life on the other side of the valley."

Max Cleland, the Secretary of State of Georgia, was the administrator of the United States Veterans Administration under President Jimmy Carter. Max is a triple amputee, the result of a war injury he suffered while serving in Vietnam. His life story, including his eighteen months of rehabilitation after a grenade explosion cost him both legs and an arm, is set down in his book, Strong at the Broken Places. *In addition to receiving military honors, Max was chosen as one of the ten outstanding Vietnam Veterans in 1985 by the National Vietnam Veterans Network.*

Max Cleland

Adlai Stevenson sent a prayer as his Christmas card after he was defeated by Eisenhower. One of the people who received the Christmas card was the famed Dr. Howard Rusk, the founder of the Rusk Institute of Rehabilitation Medicine in New York City. Rusk had the prayer, which was then known as "The Prayer of an Unknown Confederate Soldier," placed in bronze and entitled it "A Creed for the Disabled." That creed has been in the lobby of the Rusk Institute for thirty years.

When I became head of the VA, *60 Minutes* did a story on me. One of the segments it covered was a speech that I made to the Spanish-American War veterans. The average age of those veterans was ninety-eight; one man was a hundred and one. I had never spoken to a group of Spanish-American War veterans. I had talked to Vietnam veterans, Korean veterans, World War II veterans, and World War I veterans, but the Spanish-American War really challenged me.

I had been a history major in college, and I realized that these veterans had been young men in the wake of the Civil War and grew up hearing stories of that war. I thought something from the Civil War might be of interest to them. I was really speaking to them, but I was speaking generically to all veterans. I read this prayer, which probably identifies me most in the public mind throughout the country.

I asked God for strength that I might achieve.
I was made weak that I might learn humbly to obey.
I asked for health that I might do greater things.
I was given infirmity that I might do better things.
I asked for riches that I might be happy.
I was given poverty that I might be wise.

I asked for power that I might have the praise of men.
I was given weakness that I might feel the need of God.
I asked for all things that I might enjoy life.
I was given life that I might enjoy all things.
I got nothing that I asked for, but everything I had hoped
    for.
Almost despite myself, my unspoken prayers were an-
    swered.
I am, among all men, most richly blessed.

That is my prayer. That's what I would answer if you ask,
"What about this happiness and you, Cleland?" That's
what I would say. I am now able to more fully relate to
the final line, which is happiness as defined in the prayer—
"I am, among all men, most richly blessed."

The very effort to make sense out of pain or hurt or
tragedy or defeat or setback is an incredible act of faith,
belief, and assertion. Victor Frankel, the marvelous psychiatrist who was in a concentration camp, was stripped
of everything, even his gold wedding ring. The Nazis took
away all his possessions, but Frankel said he came to the
awesome conclusion that they could strip him of everything but they couldn't deny him the freedom to choose
how he reacted to that situation. That's the basis for possibility thinking, for positive thinking. Aldous Huxley, a
British author, put it another way: "The experience is not
what happens to a man, it's what a man does with what
happens to him." That is a cornerstone of my belief.

Victor Frankel says in his book *Man's Search for Meaning,* "To live is to suffer, to survive is to find meaning in
suffering." The amazing thing about life is if you look for
it, you can find people who have discovered some sense
of meaning and purpose in suffering. They've turned their
minuses into pluses. They've turned their stumbling blocks
into steppingstones. In a perverse or contradictory or incredible way, problems become the basis for solutions.
The pain shakes you out of your complacency to challenge
you to a higher level of living, and the man who has ten
problems is twice as alive as the man who has only five.

I identify with every line in the poem. "I asked God

for strength that I might achieve." I'm an achiever. I'm an only child, what a psychologist calls an unrescued firstborn. General George Patton was a firstborn of a firstborn of a firstborn. General Douglas MacArthur was a firstborn. I'm not only a firstborn, I'm a unrescued firstborn. I'm a male firstborn only child. My aunt said when I was growing up that I was either going to become the largest mass murderer in the history of the United States or president, she didn't know which. I was an achiever. I received a trophy as the outstanding student in my high school; I was runner-up in the state tennis championship and I played basketball. I did everything. For me, that's life. For me, that's happiness, going all out. Objectively, it's crazy; if I couldn't do that, I'd be less of a person. I would change some of the things that happened to me, but I wouldn't change the response to what has happened to me. Nobody volunteers for pain, but one volunteers for a certain risk in life. One hopes to be able to overcome some fears so that one can get out beyond the eddies in the harbors into the open sea and find out what it's all about. I did that. I've done that all my life. That's been my style.

Nobody wins all the time. That's unrealistic. We are human, we can be broken, we are vulnerable. Ernest Hemingway acknowledged this in a book he wrote ten years after his war, World War I. *A Farewell to Arms*, published in 1929, is probably the finest war novel by an American. He said, "Life breaks us all but afterwards many are strong at the broken places."

"I was made weak that I might learn humbly to obey." I don't obey anybody. I'm bullheaded. My grandmother called me hardheaded. She said, "You're going to run out in the street and a car's going to run over you and there ain't going to be nothing left of you but a little greasy spot." It's been hard for me to obey; but "I was made weak that I might learn humbly to obey." There are some rules out there, and you learn them one way or the other. I learned them the other. I've now learned to obey a little bit better and follow some other instincts.

"I asked for health that I might do greater things." I always wanted to do great things in my life and that's not bad. To want to be great, to do great, is not bad; but "I was given infirmity that I might do better things." Doors closed on me. I didn't ask for them to close. I didn't volunteer for them to close. I volunteered for Vietnam, but I didn't volunteer to get wounded. Nobody volunteers for that. People volunteer because they think they should or they think they ought to share the suffering or take the risks. I don't think anybody really wants to get in harm's way just for the hell of it.

There's no doubt in my mind that had I not been wounded in Vietnam, I would have come back with a master's degree in history, ended up as a volunteer in several political campaigns, and gotten a job teaching history in a small junior college. Beyond that, I don't know what my life would have turned out to be. But being wounded and spending a year and a half in military and VA hospitals took me on a course that I would never have volunteered for and that I didn't want to go on. I found myself on that course and I had two choices—survive or not. I had to find meaning out of suffering and to decide if I was going to be a survivor. Was I going to find some meaning out of suffering, was I going to move through the valley and make some sense of it, or was I not? That suffering made me tougher and stronger. I decided I wanted to live.

I knew a lot of other men who wanted to live but weren't able to. They made it back to Walter Reed Hospital but weren't able to survive. It's one thing to see body bags on the field in Vietnam, to see casualties on the field; it's another to see them back in the hospital after surviving and then still not make it. Winston Churchill once said that he had a great appreciation of life because he had known "the deprivation of the trenches." I decided I wanted to live, and little things made life pleasant, more bearable. I picked up a sense of humor through it all. I had to because it was either laugh or cry. The wounded tried to laugh as much as possible. That broke the tension; jokes gave us a sense of perspective. There was lots of gallows humor. We'd be lying on the ward, saying, "What are they going to do with us if we're bad boys here, send us to Vietnam?"

I came back and followed an interest I had picked up in my early twenties, which was politics. When I came back to Georgia after the hospitalization, I ran for the state Senate and was elected; I was the youngest member at the age of twenty-eight. I was still working through a lot of that Vietnam stuff. I still had a lot of hostility, frustration, and bitterness, so I wasn't a good politician. I was a loose cannon on deck. I was a maverick.

I ran and lost a race for lieutenant governor in 1974 and thought politics was all over for me. Believe it or not, out of defeat comes victory. I've seen it happen in my life over and over again. Rod McKuen says, ''There's a brighter day ahead.'' I thought the doors were closed; I thought it was all over. The only job offer I had was in Washington with the staff of the Senate Committee on Veterans' Affairs. I went up to Washington in 1975. I had been there for two years when all of a sudden Jimmy Carter became president of the United States. That was a bona fide, certified, twenty-four karat miracle. I was making $19,500 a year on Capitol Hill with no desk, one phone, and two pencils, and Jimmy Carter offered me the job of running the Veterans Administration with 230,000 employees and a budget of $19 billion and a salary of $57,500 a year, when I was thirty-four. I thought for a minute and then I said yes.

''I was given infirmity that I might do better things.'' I was able then as head of the VA to transfer and translate all of that pain and hurt and suffering and struggle into making the VA a more appropriate vehicle for dealing with my generation of Vietnam veterans and certainly for all those veterans who had been hurt or felt they'd been hurt by their government at war or by history. That became a mission, and I threw myself into it. Someone once asked me, ''What is your best contribution in Washington?'' I said, ''Survival, and beyond that it was creating the Vet Center Program, the readjustment counseling program.'' By the late seventies the physical injuries had pretty much healed up for me and for thousands of others, but the emotional, spiritual, and personal wounds were still very much open and very raw, but there was no acknowledgment that they were there. We now have some two hundred Vet Centers in the nation, and some half a million Vietnam veterans and their families have received counseling in that program. That's my single best contribution. I wouldn't have been able to do that had I come back and been a junior college history teacher.

"I asked for riches that I might be happy." Well, I've never had riches, but I've never been poor either. I did spend a lot of time thinking of building up job security and trying to get a little money in the bank. That's not a bad goal; but "I was given poverty that I might be wise." The poverty for me was getting beaten. It was like getting wounded. You never think you're going to get wounded and you really don't think you're really human and can bleed. You really don't think you can make mistakes either, at least I didn't, and then you do. I had a poverty of spirit. I was down. I was given poverty and that gave me a perspective on riches, on winning, on success, on happiness, that I might know what would really make me happy and what wouldn't.

"I asked for power that I might have the praise of men." When I was running for the state Senate, that was just part of the climbing up the ladder. I'm blessed now because I was separated from that. I had to find an identity separate from that climbing in the political world. It's always, "What's the next race?" It's a treadmill. Politics can be a rat race, a maze. Some humorist said, "The thing about the rat race is even if you win the race, you're still a rat." I was out there running and winning, but I was still a rat. "I asked for power that I might have the praise of men." I was beaten. I was right down at the bottom. "I was given weakness that I might feel the need of God." It was really the first time I appropriated the Christian faith to my life.

There's a story in the New Testament about two men. One's in the fold and he says, "I'm wonderful." The other's outside the fold and he's beating his breast, saying, "God forgive me, I'm a sinner." That's where I was. That, for me, is where it began. It was the first time I really felt the need of God. I had burned out. I was at the end of the rope and I found out that "I asked for all things that I might enjoy life,'' but I realized later, and certainly now, that ''I was given life that I might enjoy all things.'' You know you go through all this and you're amazed that you have survived. I now have an appreciation for life, for the grace of God, and for the help of friends. I realized what's really important. ''I was given life that I might enjoy all things.'' My appetite for life is now more keen than it has ever been. I appreciate all things more. ''I got nothing that I asked for, but everything I had hoped for.'' I achieved happiness, kicking and screaming and coming in the back door.

''Almost despite myself, my unspoken prayers were answered.'' Now I can say, ''I am, among all men, most richly blessed.'' It's an incredible perspective to have on life. Who is to say that the valleys were not supposed to be there? Who's to say that the hurt and the pain didn't later contribute to a deeper sense of happiness and awareness and love and respect? Who's to say that the contradictions don't ultimately make sense? I'm just glad to be alive now and glad to do what I can. Sometimes happiness just comes your way despite yourself.

Contributors' Comments

Happy people find their greatest pleasure not in spectacular events or incredible moments, but in life's very simple things. Their happiness is found in play, recreation, hobbies, interests, and people. Quiet, solitude, and nature often contribute to a sense of peace and contentment for many happy people. Some of the contributors share their happiness and gratitude.

Margo Howard on Little Things
One of the sources of my happiness is small things. I get great joy from absolute nonsense. I'm very weather reactive. A sunny day can just start things wonderfully. I also love encounters with strangers that bespeak a kind of human warmth. It makes me happy.

I'm a great reader. I get pleasure from reading something that I think is just wonderfully done. I care how the words get together. I can feel on top of the world sitting around with a good newspaper and a cup of coffee and killing three hours. It's a great luxury not to have anything else I must do.

Congressman Morris K. Udall on Nature

I have a near religious feeling about the land. Like the American Indians, I have a feeling of reverence for it. We're stewards of it; we turn it over to the next generation. I really do get peace and satisfaction from visits to the wilderness and the forest. One of the most important influences on my life has been this closeness to nature. That's why it's been so terribly satisfying to have something to do with the important environmental laws that we've passed.

Shelley Duvall on Music

I bought a piano years ago, and it makes me very happy. I've never taken lessons. I really don't know how to play the piano. I don't know the keys. I have to find them, hunting and pecking just as I do on the typewriter. I play when I'm alone. The music that comes out of me on that piano sounds so pretty, so soothing. It gives me a great feeling of peace. I find very little more relaxing than that. I don't often do it, but when I do, I sincerely and thoroughly enjoy it. All the songs I play sound Scottish and sad and beautiful simply because I can't play fast. Playing the piano gives me great peace, great peace. That makes me feel very good, almost better than anything.

Helen Thomas on Family and Friends

I constantly told myself, from my teens on, that I should always try to know when I am happy. I thought there would be times when I wouldn't be happy so I should never feel denied. Always take a special enjoyment and realization when you really are happy. Know it and say, ''I'm happy and I do know it.'' You also have to be thankful, because life won't always be happy. You want to have some sense of gratitude and some sense that you have not been short-changed. To know when you are happy is really to give it that extra snap.

I love good conversation. I love to be with my friends. When you talk shop in Washington, you talk about the world; you talk about the news. Not that you don't gossip also. Everything you talk about involves what is happening. I love to go out to dinner. I love good wine. I love music.

I love my family very much. As you get older you really appreciate members of your family more and realize the ties. I have been so lucky. That's part of fulfillment as a person to know they are there with mutual love and respect.

Og Mandino on Being Alive

I'm at peace. It's so nice. I'm so damn laid back. My family asked me what I wanted for Christmas. I had to make up things to want, to keep them happy. I don't want anything from them. I've got all I want. I just hope I'm around awhile to enjoy a few more years with them. I'm so lucky. I go out to the golf course, get out on the first tee, and think, "God, thank you. Isn't this great? I've got another one."

Dr. Benjamin Spock on Contentment

Sailing is a challenge and a comfort to me. It's the challenge of getting to the next harbor by using the winds right, and it's a comfort in that I forget all my other troubles when I sail.

John Naisbitt on Solitude

A lot of people go to the ocean. I've gone back to the Rocky Mountains, where I was born. The majesty and beauty of them are really uplifting.

May Sarton on Hobbies

Reading the mail is one of the best things in my life. Answering it is one of the worst things. You can't have one without the other.

Gardening is happiness. One of the happiest things is

ordering seeds, because then you're not doing any work. You're just dreaming this wonderful garden, which is never going to exist. You go out in a rage against the world and after you've pulled up weeds for an hour, everything is smoothed out. I mean, what does it matter if the *New York Times* gave me a bad review?

Gardening is for middle-aged people. It's not for the young because you've got to be patient. You sow and six weeks later you may get a result and you probably won't. You have to be very philosophical to be a gardner, and wildly extravagant also. You buy plants that never do well. Every year I spend a fortune.

Agnes de Mille on Family
My son gives me enormous pleasure. He's a professor of history at Emory University. He's a scholar and he's a good one. His book *The Coming of Industrial Order* was published by Cambridge University Press. In scholastic circles it's a sellout. So that's nice. He's married to a perfectly lovely young woman who is a professor of French and they have a young child who's quite wonderful. Family brings me great pleasure. Any day that my husband's well enough to enjoy himself is a good day.

Dr. Joyce Brothers on Happiness
When you look at your life, the greatest happinesses are family happinesses.

10   Taking Inventory

Peace of mind and contentment should be the real goals
in our quest for happiness. To believe that life is an endless
parade of fun and games is to fail to comprehend what life
is all about and to miss the opportunity for growth. We
may work too hard at obtaining happiness or even try to
be too happy. We have been led to think that we can
be happy twenty-four hours a day if we do the "right"
things, know the "right" people, and acquire the "right"
possessions. Happiness is only part of the puzzle. Self-
knowledge, self-worth, the freedom to be ourselves,
self-acceptance, and the inner security to be able to
give to others without looking for a reward seem to be
what life is asking from us. *What is my definition of happiness? Am I trying too hard to be happy?*

Dr. Robert Jarvik offers a fascinating theory about happiness.

*Robert K. Jarvik, M.D., is one of the developers of the
Jarvik-7, the artificial heart that bears his name. He is
assistant research professor of surgery at the University of
Utah and president of Symbion, Inc., a company that man-
ufactures the prosthetic heart and other artificial organs.*

Robert K. Jarvik, M.D.

The presumption is that there is some sort of cultural illusion about happiness that people are chasing. That's a
tough one from the point of view of semantics. Probably

happiness is an inept word to describe it. People might be chasing something totally illusory and frustrating because they are trying to achieve something that's impossible. Maybe some other word or term, such as "personal fulfillment," should replace the term "happiness." I was trying to think about this, asking myself whether there is a state of mind that we identity as happiness. I wondered further if that state of mind is triggered, it feels good and makes people feel happy—a physical, mental, and emotional sensation. It is possible regardless of the input from a person's life or experience or interaction or luck; if one has triggered a certain activity in the brain perceived as happiness, it doesn't matter what makes it happen.

We know that when you stimulate a certain electrical area of the brain, a person feels something. We know from our work with artificial hearing devices that when you stimulate nerve fibers in the ear, a signal goes to the brain and the subjects hear the sound. They don't know whether there actually was a sound out there; all they know is that they hear a sound. The nerves in their brains have been activated by an electrical impulse. It is disconnected from reality. There is a state of activation in those nerves that, to those people, is sound.

I think there may be a pattern of nervous system activity that is happiness. There are a lot of different states of good feeling. But just as there is something that people understand and accept as depression, maybe there is a state that's happiness. Just as there are people who get depressed, maybe there are people who just get happy. Maybe happiness is not so much a physiological function as a brain function, an inborn pattern of nervous-system activity. Then maybe happiness is reachable in many ways.

I remember that my former wife became very happy when she was pregnant. She felt really good about herself and about everything. A lot of people get sick when they're pregnant, but there was a definite hormonal change in her and she knew it and she felt very happy. She felt very good. She said she never felt better in her life. What was it? It wasn't anything that she was really doing for gratification or achievement. It was some sort of physiological thing that triggered it, probably a chemical change in her brain, that led to happiness. Some people, of course, take drugs to make them "happy."

What I'm trying to get at is the idea that there is a state of happiness or a state of generalized good feeling into which all different kinds of things you do can feed, and if you reach that stage, it doesn't matter what it is that triggers it. It's sitting there in the brain; evolved to be there because it serves a purpose and that purpose somehow could be thought of in terms of what is needed for success of that species, not just the individual. This might mean that the happiness another kind of animal feels may be very different from the kind of happiness humans feel. I was trying to separate it as a brain process, rather than a social process or a psychological process or a personal reward that is influenced by your actions in your life. My point is that you may be born with a strongly developed happiness potential or without it. Just as a person can be born and influenced toward a tendency to depression, the same may be true with happiness, the tendency to have energy or non-energy. Many of what we call psychiatric diseases are related to chemical and organizational functions of the brain.

Think of happiness as a disease. I don't mean it's good or bad. I use the word *disease* on purpose. It has a negative connotation, but we talk about a disease as a state of non-health often caused by an infection or by an inherent degree of damage to the body. This is to say that there is a characteristic state that is usually beyond the control of the individual and has happened to the individual. Maybe happiness is like that. Maybe it happens to you and it is beyond your control. Maybe it's a chemical state, and the organization of your brain, like intelligence and the mix of what happens culturally, plays on that.

Many people are seeking happiness and many of them don't find it. They may feel inadequate. They may feel they have failed. They may feel they tried something and it didn't work because what they were doing had no influence whatsoever on what they were trying to influence.

I know that when I do a lot of hard physical exercise, I

get a feeling that I know is influenced by the chemistry of the exercise. That feeling is usually a good feeling. There is substantial evidence that the good feeling is the result of some kind of chemical or endorphins. Maybe some people have more and some people have less capability to produce certain kinds of chemicals or to receive them or have the level of appreciation of this state of mind.

Some people may be able to sense a much greater level of happiness than others in the way that you could say some people have a strong appreciation of music and others are tone deaf. Or some people have a good sense of smell and others don't. People certainly have great differences in physical ability.

So if there is a hereditary element of happiness which we don't usually recognize, but which determines the capability of an individual to experience this kind of thing, it might be predetermined to an 80 percent level. Then a person could influence 20 percent of individual happiness by what he or she does. If this were true and a person erroneously thought that only 10 percent is hereditary and expected that 90 percent could be influenced, when in fact only 20 percent could be, that person would be very frustrated. So if a major part of an individual's ability to be happy is hereditary, little can be done to influence it. People can try, but it's beyond their control.

For example, if you have a color television camera and recorder and you plug the color tapes it produces into your black and white television monitor, you're going to get a black and white picture. No matter what you do in terms of color or how good a camera you have, the thing that displays it, the TV monitor, is only black and white. If the brain has only the black and whiteness of ability to appreciate and perceive happiness, it's all you're going to get no matter what you do. If happiness is thought of as a talent, then perhaps it's a lot less influenced by immediate things than we tend to think.

I haven't thought about this subject of happiness in this way long enough to know. But I do think that it's likely the capacity will vary considerably from individual to individual. You might have a certain nature. I have a friend whose child has osteogenesis imperfecta, which is a horrible disease of the bones, horrible because children with this disease have very great malformation and they break all their bones. This child must have had fifty fractures by the time he was one year old. However, it is recognized that people with this disease have an incredibly happy nature. The kids are devastated in terms of the physical things that they can do. Yet they have a marvelously happy outlook about everything. It is a characteristic of this condition, which is genetic. It's really there and it affects their state of mind. It's as if it's set up to counterbalance all the suffering. It also has something to do with the metabolism and chemical abnormalities that occur with this disease.

We know that high intelligence does not always bring happiness. If we think of happiness as a condition that has become valuable within the brain to serve a function, not just for survival but for advancement, we start really thinking about it differently. Maybe there are certain ways in which it is not valuable to have happiness all the time. I mean it could be absolutely counterproductive to be happy all the time. The brain may have evolved to disallow it. If you were happy all the time and you were a scavenger, as humans used to be before they were farmers and hunters, you wouldn't have a motive to chase your food or do whatever was necessary to eat. A snake feels great after it's had a big meal and curls up for a week to digest a rabbit or a mouse. It may be a state of contentment and happiness for the snake to crawl off to a little safe place and be as happy as can be while it digests the meal. When the food is gone, the snake begins to be hungry. Then it may be in a totally different mental state, based on the biochemistry of its body and the brain's interaction, which says it's time to go on the prowl. It's going to feel anxiety and it's going to feel ungratified, so it needs to do something that will make it feel gratified.

If happiness is a gratification for humans and it's evolved in a way that is a part of an overall process, continued happiness could very well be absolutely contraindicated. The brain could be set up in such a way that a state of happiness is precluded for more than an hour a day. If we think of happiness as something that is only achievable day to day, month to month, and year to year, we're totally fooling ourselves.

I think semantically the word is all wrong. I think happiness really means general success and fulfillment in life. It is often confused with something that could be a feeling of goodness. We all know when we are really happy and how good that feels. The idea that it could be projected to an ongoing level is unrealistic.

I am trying to look at ways of thinking about happiness that are more in line with understanding the brain processes rather than with understanding what is culturally glamorous in terms of seeking this "happiness" thing. The things I would emphasize are, first of all, that you don't control happiness as much as you might like. Second, people are probably looking for the wrong thing and they don't understand it—and I don't particularly understand it either. And third, acceptance of the impossibility of all the gratification you want may lead to a type of comfort and peace that cannot be achieved if you're always chasing happiness. That might be as satisfying a goal to people: recognition of the reality of what they are and where they are and how they fit in, as opposed to trying to make themselves be happy.

Ongoing, everyday, continual happiness, when you think about it, is grossly fraudulent. I really think that that concept is one of the worst frauds that's ever been put across.

If I took myself ten years ago and dropped me into my own shoes now, I'd be delirious. Probably the reason I'm not delirious is that the brain is not made that way. Good things have happened to me that were way beyond what I could have expected. At that time I was being rejected by medical schools, and I remember vividly the great rush of fantastic feeling I had when I was finally accepted. Everybody had told me I was no good. Now everyone's going in the opposite direction, which is untrue too, saying I've accomplished so much. If I had thought ten years ago that I would be in a position where people thought that I had done something significant for humanity, I would have said, "Gee, what a satisfaction that must be."

I probably have done something positive for some people. But many people have saved a few lives directly by their work. It's common. It's terrific. I'm sure it makes people feel good. But the level of public recognition for those few lives that have been saved so far is just overwhelmingly out of proportion. My work happens to be very powerfully symbolic, and because of that symbolism, it's been noticed. It's flashy. It isn't fundamentally better than saving a life by pulling someone out of a burning car wreck. The rewards and recognition I have received are pretty nice. It feels pretty good, but it doesn't make me happy in the way I might have imagined it would ten years ago.

I feel calmer than I used to feel. I feel more secure than I used to feel. I feel more mature, but that would have happened anyway. I have more opportunity but, fundamentally, I do not go around in a state of ecstasy and prolonged happiness. I still get down. I still have good times and bad times, just as I did before. I'm still basically the same person I was. That's because my brain is still what it was before. I think my happiness is as much a function of the type of animal that I am and the type of chemistry that I have. The kind of animal that I am as a human being and what I have inherited in my specific brain and my degree of seriousness or looseness about life is 98 percent of it. The 2 percent on top is all the work that I've accomplished over the last ten years. I think there's a fundamental nature of an individual and a fundamental nature of a culture and a fundamental nature of the human race. That has a hell of a lot more to do with happiness. Ninety-eight percent is probably the wrong number. Maybe it's 80/20—or even 50/50.

We learn about happiness as children. Through our parents and families we are taught many lessons about love, relationships, touching, fun, honesty, problem solving, and attitudes about life and people. Our happiness as adults is directly related to our happy or unhappy childhoods. Often we spend many of our adult years unlearning the wrong messages and lessons of the past. *Was I a happy child? Am I a happy adult? What are the lessons of my past that need changing?*

Dr. Martha Friedman suggests, "Parental and societal messages often cause guilt. We feel we're not worthwhile and we're not entitled to have anything good happen to us."

Martha Friedman, Ed.D., is a psychotherapist in private practice in New York City. A member of the American Psychological Association and the Association of Marriage and Family Therapists, Martha is the author of Overcoming the Fear of Success.

Martha Friedman, Ed.D.

My parents were married very young. They were part of the twenties and wild: my mother was a painted lady who used cosmetics and smoked cigarettes, and my father gambled. They drank too much, as did all their friends. I grew up in that strange milieu. They'd have people over for parties and I would hear them say, "Oh, we're not inviting her next week. She's a crapehanger." I'd ask, "What is a crapehanger?" They'd explain that years ago when someone died they put up crape in mourning. "Anyone who is depressed, who looks sad, we're not inviting." At the age of four or five I heard this—that you could get thrown out of the family if you didn't look happy. "They're not inviting people; they're dropping people," I'd say to myself. I would go out of my way to hear jokes so I could come home and tell them in order to be in good standing in the family. There was no such thing as coming home and crying, because my mother would say, "We're not listening to that," and my father would say, "Your face is going to get set that way." Crying was not permitted. The message was "You'd better be happy because that's what we want. We want happiness; we don't want anybody around who is depressed."

We get all kinds of messages about happiness from our

parents as we grow up. We learn about happiness in the family. If you come from a family of depressed parents there's a good likelihood that you'll be depressed. It runs parallel with alcoholism. Many young children think, "If I had been really good my parents wouldn't drink." The same thing is true about happiness. "If I had been a good kid my parents wouldn't be so sad." The truth of the matter is that the parents' depression has absolutely nothing to do with a child's behavior.

Heavy guilt trips are often placed on children. Parents say to kids, "If it hadn't been for you I could have written a book." The parents didn't write the book because they didn't know how to write a book, not because of the children. Many of my students tell me their mothers talk about giving birth. They say, "Oh, it took me three days to have you and I had such pain." The message is if that's how you came into the world you certainly don't deserve to feel good. Some parents say, "You were an accident," which means you're not even supposed to be here. Kids who are suicidal have gotten that message—"You were an accident." Penelope Mortimer wrote in *The New Yorker* that her birth racked her mother's womb. Some mothers have said, "I've never been the same since your birth." This is saying, "You've destroyed your mother, so how do you expect to be entitled to have anything good happen to you?"

The struggle for women in the recent past was "If I become independent I won't find a man. I'll be abandoned unless I appear dependent and helpless." They got that message from Mama and Papa's saying "What I want for you, my daughter, is that you find a good man to take care of you." Their message is "You're going to be happy when you find a good man to take care of you." Part of that message is "There is something wrong with you. You can't take care of yourself. A man has to do it for you." Many of the women who opted for careers, not marriage, think they should have listened, because now the message in our society has suddenly changed to "If you want to be happy, have a baby."

Some people have a fear of happiness, which they often

learned from parents. A student told me that his mother would say, "If you sing before breakfast, you'll cry before dinner." "Sing" means if you're "happy" in the morning, then you'll pay for it at night. We're also taught as we grow up that life is hard. You don't get anything for nothing, which is not true. You can get things for nothing. Parents say to kids, "Do whatever you want to do, I just want you to be happy." That's a confused message. That was a big message for the last twenty years. The kids would say, "You want me to be happy? Well, I'd like to go around the United States." Then the parents say, "Well, don't you think you'd better go to school first?" So it's not an unqualified "Be happy, do whatever you want to do." It's what makes the parent happy. "You be happy, but it will make me happy if you go to medical school and not on a camping trip around the country." In adult relationships, we say, "I want you to be happy." Really often what we want is to control the other person to make us happy. If people do what we want them to do, we think it's going to make us happy.

Sometimes there are family messages like "Who said you should be happy?" "Happiness can lead to misfortune." "If things go too well then the gods will look down and something bad will happen to you." "You can't have the succession of good days." We are supposed to believe that if we suffer it will make us good people. If we deny ourselves pleasure and postpone gratification, then we're entitled to things. Suffering is paying our dues and that makes us worthwhile. We feel slightly more deserving of happiness because we've suffered.

We all have to learn to postpone gratification. But some people learn to postpone it permanently. They fear gratification. People who have a pleasure inhibition are people who feel guilty about any of their impulses, probably sexual impulses primarily. They deny that they feel. They cleanse themselves by working hard. We glorify the workaholic in our society. The workaholic, if you examine him or her, is someone who doesn't eroticize pleasure but eroticizes work. Workaholics get all their kicks out of work and complain, "I work too hard" and "I just do it for the family," but there's no way they would come home early and be part of the family. They don't like to go to parties, but if they do they find a kindred spirit with whom they can talk shop or talk about the economy. They're not going to talk about fun and games. We're all inhibited—and we need certain inhibitions—but some of us are overly inhibited. We've learned a great deal about sexual dysfunction and the loss of sexual desire. It comes out of guilt. There are people who have absolutely no sexual desire and it's associated with depression. One of the symptoms of depression is the loss of sexual desire. It's interesting that a thing which makes people feel good, sexual release, is a thing they deny themselves. Happiness in part is having really gratifying sexual experiences.

If you listen to yourself talk you'll hear your parents talking to you. As you get to know yourself and appreciate yourself more you can begin to say "That message is not true about me." You begin to erase some of the messages as you begin to grow stronger, whether it's through therapy, through learning a new skill and building self-confidence, or through having someone who loves you make you feel better about yourself. You can begin to erase some of the messages that contribute to low self-esteem and unhappiness.

Any good business takes a yearly inventory of profits and losses, assets and liabilities, what is working and what isn't. Every once in a while, it is important for us to spend some quiet time to review our lives. The only person we can change is ourself, and we can move to new levels of growth and happiness only by a careful examination of who we are, where we are, why we are, and where we are going. An inventory might include an honest look at the quality of our personal relationships. Personality defects such as selfishness, pride, procrastination, fear, intolerance, and dishonesty should be held up to the light. The Ten Commandments and the seven deadly sins are good jumping off-points for looking at problem areas of lust, cheating, anger, envy, and our responsibilities to our-

selves, our families, our jobs, our community, and God.
The inventory does not have to be a laundry list of what
is wrong with us. We should examine our strengths, assets, uniqueness, and progress as well. Through an inventory we can sometimes see a repeating problem which
once discarded can bring us greater happiness. *Could taking an honest look at my life help me achieve greater happiness? Am I willing to take a personal inventory?*

Richard Simmons inventories his own life and says, ''My
mission is to bring happiness into this world, to make
people learn and laugh, and to make them healthy.''

*Richard Simmons has revolutionized dieting, exercise, and
nutrition through his sense of humor. In the 1970s he
opened a health food restaurant, Ruffage, and an adjoin-
ing exercise studio, the Anatomy Asylum. There are now
seventy studios across the country. His television program,*
The Richard Simmons Show, *in national syndication and
now seen on the Lifetime cable network, has garnered four
Emmy Awards. In addition to producing best-selling books
and records, Richard is a national spokesperson for spina
bifida, a degenerative spinal disorder. His Reach Foundation addresses itself to the health and fitness needs of
people with a wide range of disabilities.*

Richard Simmons

We live in the most visual country in the world. People
are judged by how they look. America totally discrimi-
nates against the overweight woman. She is the bambino
machino. She has children, her body goes through
changes, and that woman gains weight. She has an unsupportive husband and an unsupportive world.

America certainly didn't create junk food or plastic
food, but we improved on it. We made it easier and
quicker. We made it smell better, look better, and we
added jingles. Food is a billion-dollar industry; it's nothing that anyone can fix overnight. If a man is unhappy
because of weight, he has his macho image and he can get

away with it. The women of America have a difficult time. We are told on television by children with no pimples on their faces and by women who are all size 3s to take diet pills and at the same time to make a cake you don't have to frost. We live in a paradoxical society because we tell people to do one thing; when they gain weight, we tell them that they're slobs. America looks on people who are overweight as being less than they are. I have spent my time letting people know that if you judge somebody by reading the scale, you're a dork.

I'm a compulsive eater, so I totally understand the overweight human being. Because society paints such an unflattering picture of the overweight, overweight people have a grim existence. We're always going to have the big beautiful women who say that fat is beautiful. I say to them, "Give me a plate of five pounds of fat. Let's put it on the table and see if anyone whistles at it." Fat is not beautiful. I can go in any direction and in two minutes find junk food and fast food and convenience food and grease and cholesterol, but it's never going to be taken off the market. It will never change unless the consumer changes. In magazines like *Redbook, Ladies' Home Journal,* and *Woman's Day,* 90 percent of the pages are devoted to food ads because 50 percent of all Americans have something to do with food. They either make it, serve it, box it, or grow it. One half of all careers involve food, whether it's the man bagging groceries at Safeway or the woman making candy at home.

Overweight means being ten pounds or less over your desired weight, and obese means twenty-five pounds or more. Twenty-five percent of America's children are said to be overweight, and the true figure is probably much higher. I have lectured about nutrition and exercise in 175 high schools and elementary schools. Probably 40 percent of children are overweight; 30 to 40 percent of adult males and females are overweight too. Over 20 million women wear larger than size 16 dresses. They don't walk around the streets all day. When I was overweight I didn't spend my time saying, "Hey, I think I'll walk around and see if people make fun of me and point at me and call me names and put me down!'' There are 50 million reasons for being unhappy, just as there are 50 million reasons to be happy. If you are overweight it's very difficult to find happiness in America.

We are all preconditioned on how to talk to overweight people, how to cook for them, and how to influence them to lose weight. Our society makes it very, very miserable, which leads to unhappiness for the overweight. People say, ''Fat people are jolly people.'' That's not really true. As a child growing up, if you are overweight you're in a different category. Overweight children are ridiculed in school. Mother cooks and wants them to finish what's on their plates. Schools don't teach physical education, they have sports. Those children aren't chosen for sports so they sit on the sidelines. Those children have to make a decision, to say ''I'm either going to be a wallflower and let everyone step on me and make fun of me or I'm going to be funny or I'm going to be crazy or I'm going to be intelligent.'' Whatever it is, they take it on and make it work for them so they don't have to deal with the weight. Do you think fat people like to deal with their fat? We know how to go on a diet. I did a nutrition interview with 175,000 women. Most of them got A's and B's, but most of them were overweight.

Society's sending the message, ''Hey, go shopping, buy, buy, buy, make the quick rolls, stop and get hamburgers.'' Then society says, ''Ah, you're fat, this is horrible; how did you possibly get this way?'' How did I get this way? I turn on the television, the radio, I look in the newspaper, I go out for dinner, that's how I got this way. The overweight person in America today has a very difficult time, and it's not going to get any easier. We have to persuade the food companies to offer better food and we have to educate people. We don't educate people. In grammar school they're not educated. They have a nutrition book that was written in the fifties by someone who's dead and put everything in four food groups. We don't educate people when they're going through puberty. We don't educate people when they have a baby, and we don't educate senior citizens. I sat down with twelve hundred senior citizens in

Florida, and they all asked questions to which they should have known the answers. Why didn't they know? In spite of all our schools and PTAs, we're a very uneducated society in nutrition. We push chemistry and we take insidious courses like Latin, but we don't take any courses on how to live life and how to make it better.

Ninety percent of most people's self-esteem is tied up with their bodies. Ten percent we can fake. An overweight person can fake being happy. "Here's a present, everything's wonderful," but there are a lot of tears inside. There's a difference between being a big-boned girl and being an obese, sloppy person. The 90 percent of your self-esteem and self-respect disappears because all the doors are closed. There are closed doors romantically, sexually, in friendship, and in careers, all because you're overweight. When people keep on saying no, that slowly chisels at your self-esteem and your self-respect. Overweight people can build themselves up by saying, "I'm going to start on a good food program and nutrition." Slowly, as the weight comes off, their self-esteem and self-respect builds. Overweight people are not any less sensitive, any less smart; we just happen to have a problem.

I still see myself as an overweight person, not an obese person. If I could only let people know that just because you lose weight, it really doesn't mean that the emotional scars go away. If you're 100 pounds overweight, you're really 200 pounds overweight. You're 100 pounds overweight in your head. I guess I'm still fat in the head. I'm almost forty years old and I've never worn a bathing suit. I don't go to the beach. I have a nice body. I have a nice, sleek thirty-inch waistline. I have pectorals similar to Rambo's, but they don't give me whiplash when I turn. I have a great tushy; I have super legs because I work on them; but the scars are there. Every time I see an overweight person there's a Polaroid flashback on my life. Losing weight in the stomach is easy, but losing weight in the head is difficult.

I am a compulsive eater. If I'm sitting on a couch and I find an M&M, it's history. It's in my mouth. I can't have food around me; I will automatically eat it. I have to keep my refrigerator stocked a certain way. I try not to go out to eat anymore, I don't eat after a certain hour, and I lead a very regimented life. I now coordinate my food with my lifestyle, where previously I coordinated it with my desires, and that's the difference. I could eat a little Japanese sushi and twenty minutes later I could eat a cake without blinking my eye. Then in half an hour I could go out and eat a whole chicken and mashed potatoes and gravy.

Food to me means love, food to me means caring, food to me means happiness. Unfortunately it's not true. Food does not mean happiness, food does not mean security, food will not solve my problems. When I was a kid and I got a D in chemistry my mother and father screamed and yelled, but the cookies on the plate remained calm. They were my friends. When we don't want to deal with something we can always deal with fettuccine or pizza. Food doesn't really take thought.

I came from a show business family, which was the happy part. It was made up of a very strict father, a very Auntie Mame mother, a very perfect brother, and me. I made my own world. School was hard because I was the shortest and the fattest and the homeliest. As a child I really developed my sense of humor so I could laugh rather than cry. People say, "I'm fat because of an unhappy childhood"; you're fat because you put food in your mouth. Let's get down to the basics here. Maybe you came from a divorced family. Did the food make your parents get back together? Maybe your father was a semi-bum and could never keep a job, maybe he beat your mother, maybe you got bad grades in school. Let's get down to the nitty-gritty. Why are we unhappy? It's so easy to hang our unhappiness on fat. We all do it. It's a Catch-22: I'm very unhappy. Why are you unhappy? Because I'm fat. Why are you fat? Because I'm unhappy. It keeps going on and on.

One women said, "God's punishing me." We don't have that kind of a God. We don't have a God who says, "You messed around on your husband so when you go to Food Town I'm having the food fairy shove two pumpkin pies down your throat." It's easier to say "God's punishing me'' than ''I'm screwing up, I'm not thinking.'' People who overeat don't think and don't work through the problem and get to the solution. I've just been to a funeral home that featured a salad bar. Everything is surrounded by food. We love food. We love it, we love it, we love it.

My real name is Milton Tegal Simmons, so my initials are M.T. When I was growing up kids called me ''Empty'' Simmons because they related fat people to stupid people. They called me any name they could think of that described a little fat kid—Blimpo, Chunky, Walking Grocery Store, Candy Breath, Tubbo, and Pig. Kids can be very cruel. Those cruel kids learn it from television and from their cruel parents. As a child I would say, ''Well, they're calling me this name because I'm heavy, but they're not seeing anything else, so let's show them something else. Maybe they won't see the fat.'' So I created Richard Simmons. I created a very positive, a very funny, a very sensitive human being. I created this person from all the people I had known. As a child I was never around children except for the hours I spent at school. I lived totally in an adult world. When I had my tenth birthday there was no one under thirty-five at my party. Even I created that. I made friends with adults because then I could learn everything that I didn't know. They would give me ammunition so that I could start concentrating on what I wanted to do for the rest of my life rather than sit around and feel sorry for myself because I loved a few peanut butter and jelly sandwiches instead of one. I created who I am, and I was able to deal with the obesity because I put my emphasis on other things.

I was very religious. All the statues in the Catholic church were a little chunky. I went to church seven days a week. Religion was very important to me. You weren't judged by being fat. I was in a seminary for a while.

I went to Europe. I was very funny. I was very different from anybody they'd ever seen, and they took advantage of this and I made lots of television commercials and movies. That's when I got the note. That was my first slap in the face. A week before I got the note the elevator in my flat broke down. I lived in the penthouse. I had to sleep in the hotel next door until they fixed the elevator, because at 268 pounds I couldn't walk up the stairs. I was in a very down mood. I was making a lot of money, I could buy anything I wanted. I had three cars and two live-in helpers. I used to sit and see if I could tuck my bottom belly between my legs and make it disappear. If you've never been overweight it's very hard to understand it, because with all the hurt you go through in your life you choose to build a wall of fat around you so you don't get hurt again. In essence it just causes more hurt. I was feeling very bad and I was offered $200,000 to do a commercial. I was a freak, but they thought I was cute. It was no different from being in school except that now I rode in a Rolls-Royce.

I went to do a commercial and it was very funny and everyone laughed and had a good time. Afterward I found a note on the limo that just said, "Dear Richard, You're very funny but fat people die young. Please don't die." That was really my turning point as far as not wanting to be fat. I starved. I lost weight and ended up in a hospital, then began studying nutrition and exercise and that's how it all began.

The exercise gurus of the world were very serious and I said, "Hey, you had fun putting weight on, might as well have a little fun taking the weight off." I've had the exercise studio, the Anatomy Asylum, and the restaurant, Ruffage, for twelve years now.

I have a lot of responsibilities today, but I'll never let them get me to the point where I'm going to be the kind of person who will lose my childhood. That's what keeps me together—being silly, being humorous, being a little crazy. Most people are unhappy because they grew up. I was the class clown, I spent six months out of every year being punished because I was so crazy. My father would do horrible things to me. When I was being punished he'd take the refrigerator out of my bedroom. I'm a true American dream because I came from a family of broken careers who never really got what they wanted.

I am very attuned to people's unhappiness because we are a combination of different kinds of unhappiness. We have sexual unhappiness, physical unhappiness, emotional unhappiness, spiritual unhappiness, and mental unhappiness. The more you dote on being unhappy, the more unhappy you will be. My whole life has been based on a Broadway show. When the alarm goes off, the curtain goes up, and that's my show for that day. I could be hit by a Sara Lee truck tomorrow, but today this is my show. People are unhappy because they think about their unhappiness too much. People are unhappy because they compare themselves to what other people's happinesses are. People are unhappy today because there is so much unhappiness around us. Unhappy people pick up a newspaper and read about the unhappiness. They turn on the television news and see the unhappiness. They visit friends and talk about their unhappiness. We are surrounded by unhappiness.

People say to me, "I'm very unhappy, I'm fat." I say, "Hold it. Let's just say you're very unhappy. Let's put the fat over here for a second, take a sheet of paper out, and I'm going to ask you to comment on your life." We break it down: "How is your job?" "My job stinks." "How is your home life?" "I'm divorced." "Are you dating anybody?" "Nobody wants me." "How are your children?" "One's hyper and gets D's." "How is your love life?" "I just told you, none." You have to sit down with somebody and say, "If you're happy, tell me the reasons you're happy, and if you're unhappy, tell me the reasons you're unhappy, and let's see if we can mix and match." It's like the woman who says that she's overweight. She cries, "I just ate twenty cookies." Don't cry over the cookies; get up and work your tush off. Exercise and move those cookies around.

The question that people have to ask themselves is "Am I a happy person or am I an unhappy person?" If you're not happy, I suggest you take an inventory of your life as I did when I was very unhappy and watching everyone else play ball but me. I wish I could do something to make this world a happier place. I take it personally when someone overeats. I take it personally when someone won't quit smoking. I take it personally when someone won't go out and find a job. I take it personally when someone has wrecked his or her life in the name of love.

I haven't really changed. I still think the same way I did as a child. I wish I were Santa Claus; maybe then I could make the world happier. If people had a better sense of humor, if they allowed themselves to laugh and be vulnerable, it sure would help. My philosophy is if I'm unhappy, I really enjoy five minutes of being totally unhappy. I don't talk to anybody, I don't want to hear Annie sing, "Tomorrow." I want to be unhappy, but I want to be unhappy for only five minutes. Then I snap out of it and try to cure it. Unhappiness is something that you draw on for your life.

We are all the artists of our lives. Sometimes we paint a very unhappy life for ourselves. If people aren't working and they're unhappy, they paint someone sitting on a couch watching television, not getting a job. They make pictures for themselves. Maybe they're unhappy with their relationship and they paint a picture of their unhappy marriage— of a husband coming home late or a wife being stuck in the house all day with the children, making beds and watching soap operas. They paint their lives. We're all portrait artists and we all work on our own portrait. It's like Dorian Gray. Go up in the attic and check on your picture. If it's getting grumpy-looking and gooey-looking, you painted that. We're all our own portrait artists and if we live in an unhappy state it's because we choose to do that in certain ways. Unhappy, overweight people paint meals, paint beef stroganoff, and paint key lime pies. They don't paint brewer's yeast and sliced carrots.

We all paint our own picture. I've painted my own picture, but I've had to redo the smile a few times. It's a picture of an aerobic Puck. I live a life much different from the one people think I do. I am reclusive. I am celibate. I live more like a seminarian than I did when I was a seminarian. I have great purpose in my life because I know that if I do what I'm doing now I'll have a Jacuzzi in heaven, and that would be very nice for me.

People who continually try to achieve their goals always have a little temporary unhappiness. But it's not really unhappiness, it's peaks and valleys. Anyone who is always on the journey has very few unhappiness pebbles. If an overweight woman exercises, she feels better about herself. If two people who are married and having fights sit down and talk, they feel better about themselves. If a man who is drinking goes to an AA meeting and gets his act together, he is on the road to happiness, even if there are little pebbles of unhappiness. You can have all the money in the world, you can have your picture in every magazine, but unless you like yourself, none of it really matters.

What makes me happy is that I can touch people's lives and change them for the better. What makes me happy is when a woman says to me, "My baby died and I watched your show and you made me live again." It's that simple. When a man says to me, "The first time I saw you on TV I thought you were a dancing fruitcake, but you care. I lost forty pounds, and I got into a bowling league, Dick. Thanks." I've taken all the years when I felt so inadequate because everyone put me down for the way I looked and acted and I've tripled them and I've taken each day and tried my best to make sure that all those things don't bother anybody else.

When you're in an unhappy state you create unhappiness, not just for yourself, but for everyone around you. Like yourself. It's a whole different world, a really good one and a really happy one.

So get that brush in your hand and sit down with your canvas. This is your life. Ralph Edwards is not going to walk out and give you a charm bracelet and party at the Waldorf-Astoria. You must paint a good picture of your life. You must use positive brush strokes and happy colors and make it work for you. Challenge yourself. No one else does it for you.

It can be shouted from the rooftops, but we still don't get it: happiness is on the inside, not on the outside. Happiness involves a positive concept of self-worth and a positive vision of the world and the events of life as they unfold. People can enhance our happiness, of course, but people cannot make us happy. Events and accomplishments can add to our happiness, but they cannot make us happy either. What we need to work on is changing the inside, not the outside. We change the inside by listening to our feelings, changing our thinking, and changing our behavior. *Do I really understand that happiness has to do with my attitude toward myself and the way I see life?*

Dr. Wayne Dyer explains, "By giving children lots of affection, you can help fill them with love and acceptance of themselves. Then that's what they will have to give away."

Wayne Dyer, Ph.D., is a nationally known psychotherapist, author, and lecturer. His book Your Erroneous Zones *was the top-selling book of the 1970–1980 decade according to the New York Times, and his later books,* Pulling Your Own Strings, The Sky's the Limit, *and* Gifts from Eykis, *have all been best sellers. Wayne has appeared on more than five thousand television and radio broadcasts, has run a minumum of eight miles a day for the past nine years, and has published his eighth book,* What Do You Really Want for Your Children?

Wayne Dyer, Ph.D.

In Eastern thought, "Happiness is the way." It's something they've learned, especially the higher-level thinkers. These are people who understand that you don't find happiness. It's not anything you'll ever get. It's what you are. If you are happiness and you carry it with you everywhere you go, then you bring it to all the activities of your life. You bring it to your breakfast in the morning, and you bring it to your travels. It is you and you are it and there's no distinction made.

In Western culture, we have a different notion, which is that you are not happiness. In fact, you are, if anything, unhappiness. What you have to do is work for it, find it. If you do all kinds of things, then you will be happy. If you get into the right marriage, if you get the right job, if you make a certain amount of money, if you pay your bills, if you work hard, then happiness is something that will be yours. We have a concept of a psychology of striving versus a psychology of arriving. The psychology of striving is a psychological dead end. If you're looking for happiness in anything, then you will always suffer from a disease called "more."

The disease called more works like this. "I will be happy if I can get a hundred thousand dollars in the bank, or if I can get my kids into the right college." Your life becomes a striving for that. So you spend a year or two years working for the hundred thousand in the bank, or struggling to pay your mortgage, or trying to get your kids into the right school. It's a principle of "If I set goals and achieve them, I'll be happy." Then you get there. The whole period of time is spent between point A and point B, A being, "I'm operating from lack"; that is, "I don't have what it takes for me to be happy. B is the point at which I will, if I get those things, have happiness." When you finally get to B, then all you have known all of that time is striving. That's what your life has been. So when you get to B, that's what you will begin doing again. You will say, "Well, I'd better get two hundred thousand in the bank" or "I'd better make sure I have enough to get those kids through graduate school." You'll upgrade that goal. You'll spend another hunk of your life striving for it.

Wendell Johnson called it the IFD syndrome, which is what all of us in the West seem to be stuck in. It's a circle. At the top of the circle is *I,* which stands for Idealizing. You idealize about what it's going to be like next Friday when you go out on your date. Then you work in a circle and you come around a third until you get to *F,* which is Frustration. You're always doomed to be frustrated when you're idealizing about the future because happiness is now. Now is being avoided when you're idealizing about what it's going to be like in the future. So frustration is the only payoff you can have for spending your life setting goals and idealizing. The only way out of frustration is to be Demoralized. That's the result of frustration. That's the

D. You're down, you're depressed two-thirds around the circle. The only way out of that depression, or that downness, is to idealize again. Then you come full circle. The essence of escaping it is now.

The now is the working unit of your life. Everything that happens, happens now, happens in this moment. The past is gone and the future is promised to none of us. So all you get are present moments. What you have are people who are looking for the things they think will give them happiness instead of simply being happiness, living it, experiencing it, where happiness becomes as much a part of you as your pancreatic juices. It becomes as much a part of you as the air you breathe. It's what Abraham Maslow called a psychology of being rather than a psychology of becoming, or a psychology of trying to get there. When you have that inside you, then you always have it, even when things are really bad. It's there even when you're having an argument with your wife or boss. What you understand is that an obstacle is an opportunity for a breakthrough.

An obstacle is really something to celebrate; it is not something to wallow in neurotically, but to experience. Instead of looking to fix it, saying, "I'm motivated to get there by repairing all the deficiencies in my life," you operate by a motivation that Maslow called growth motivation, which says, "Wherever I am is fine. If I've got a cold I've going to celebrate it. I'm going to get in touch with it. I'm going to find out why I have created this kind of dissonance, or dis-ease in my body. If I've got a problem in my relationship, I'm going to really look at that. What is there in it for me? How can I grow? What's the opportunity in this?" You're bringing this thing called happiness to this thing we call a problem. When you're doing that constantly, then you're not saying, "I am deficient, there is something wrong with me," in terms of having a problem, but "I am terrific. I am choosing to be in this relationship in this way, or I'm choosing to relate to my spouse in this way and as terrific as I am about it, it still isn't working for me. But I can still be happy."

Happiness is a condition. It just is. It's what I've got

going for me. I have found that people go into a relationship believing that if they have a problem, that means something is wrong. Then your problem is who is going to help you solve the problem in this relationship. You've got only you and the other person. The only person you can call on to solve this problem in the relationship is a disabled person, because you've already admitted that there's something wrong. If you're admitting that there's something wrong, this problem means that you've got a disability. So you've got a disabled person to deal with the problem right away. Whatever is going on, you have to operate from lack. There's something wrong with you or there's something wrong with the other person. You're heading toward "Happiness" by trying to have two disabled people solve a problem.

The opposite of this is to say "All relationships have problems." That's a condition of being in a relationship with a human being. There are differences. Two human beings think and behave and act in different ways; you have different goals and perceptions of the way the world is. That's the way it's supposed to be. Now, instead of a disabled person to solve the problem, you have an able person who says, "Hey, there's nothing wrong with me and there's nothing wrong with you. We just have this challenge." Now you have two able-bodied people who say this is what they have to do. They can approach it from a solution-oriented approach to life instead of a problem-oriented one.

A problem is something that begs for two approaches. One is to continue to make it a problem. That's "problem thinking." That's a happiness-is-something-I-will-get-to kind of thinking versus there's-a-solution thinking. The solution is in you. It has nothing to do with your happiness. These are things that you have to learn how to bring to everything in your life and the obstacles that come into your life. The problems that come up in your life are just simply opportunities or breakthroughs, opportunities for you to break through into tremendous new territory. This is a challenge. This is what you have to do with virtually everything that faces you. Instead of seeing it as a problem, see it as a challenge. If you don't meet the challenge, then it tells you something about you. Something terrific about you.

You're often in conflict. It's what life is. It's what it means to be alive. To be in conflict with the forces that are out there that are different from you is terrific. When there's a conflict, it's something you can get hold of. That's what makes it meaty and that's what makes life exciting.

Happiness is something that I just am determined is me. I am it. I have lots of it inside of me and that's what I give away. In the service of others you'll find your happiness and your fulfillment. It means stop the whining and the complaining and looking at life with a poor-me kind of attitude. Have you ever noticed that there are some people who never have enough, and there are some people who always have enough? Loving people or happy people live in a happy world. This is the only world we get. Unhappy people live in an unhappy world and they see unhappiness everywhere. It's the same world. Unhappy people look out on the sunny day and say, "It's so cold, it's windy, this is the fourth day this month like this." They're looking for all the bad. They read the papers from the perspective of what is wrong and how bad things are. Their conversations are about all the tragedies in life and who's dying. They're looking for that. They're trapped in that business that they're not happiness, happiness is something that eludes them. They don't understand that in order to have it, all they have to do is just decide to be that way. Just be happiness. You practice it just like everything else.

The purest form of sanity that you can get to is nowness. Total, complete, present-moment nowness. The more you can get to that point, the more you see yourself as a part of the unity of all of this. All this stuff that's going on "out there" isn't something that is separate from you. Say, "I am it." See yourself as part of it all, the unifying part of it all. Start from a premise that the universe is perfect and it makes no mistakes. There are no mistakes in a perfect universe. You are as much a part of the universe as is the moon and Pluto and all the billions of other galaxies. Everything works. The universe doesn't ever say,

"Oh, I just don't know what to do with these problems. I think I'll have a nervous breakdown and get some Valium." It works. It's a never-ending process, and each one of us is a part of it. Now look out at that and see yourself as a part of the universe. You're starting from your own perfection. Most people you talk to believe nobody's perfect. Perfect doesn't mean flawless. Perfect just means you are a perfect creation in this universe and you are here for a reason. The reason that you're here, in my estimation, is love, to give it away. It's the glue that holds the whole system together. It's harmony and cooperation and love.

Take a microscope and focus in on the tiniest cell of your body. What makes that cell work? Harmony and cooperation. I think each person is a cell in our whole universe. That's the metaphor I use. When you are filled with harmony and cooperation, you cooperate with all the rest of us and love. You give that away, and that's what will come back. That's the karmic principle of what goes around, comes around. You send happiness out, it's going to come back. You send misery out, misery's going to come back to you. When you've got misery in your life, instead of asking, "Why is the universe doing this to me?" you ask, "What is it about me that I'm putting this stuff out, because that's what I'm getting back?" In another part of the world, a couple of billion people believe that you get back what you put out into the world. It's people in the Western culture who believe that somebody else did it to us and that it had nothing to do with us. In the working unit of your life, the "now," change from being somebody who believes that these things are happening to you to "I am a creator of these things in my life."

I'm talking about being motivated from the position of growth. Look at the sky. I ask you, "Is the sky perfect?" You say, "Well, it's the only sky we have, and it's what we get." The sky has to be perfect, it's what God gave us. That's it. Now, look at the sky an hour from now, and ask the question "Is the sky different?" "Yes." "Is it still perfect?" Can we be changing and perfect is the question that we have to ask ourselves in this concept of perfection. Can we be growing and still be perfect? We grow through meeting the challenges of life. Perfection has nothing to do with not growing. It doesn't mean that you can't grow. Nobody can reject you any more than you can walk around and say, "You know, there was no moon last night; it rejected me." I ask, "How could the moon reject you?" You'd say, "I was expecting it to be out and it didn't come out." And I say, "Well, that's crazy." That's what we do in our relationships, and all the other things that bring us unhappiness.

When things change, which they're always doing, and when people are growing and changing, we treat that as rejection instead of saying, "Well, that's where they are. That's where they are in the journey. That's where the world is. That's how they see their world. They can no more reject me, unless I choose to feel rejected, than the moon can reject me because it didn't come out when I wanted it to come out."

One of the key things in happiness is to allow life to unfold without taking it personally, without judging it, and without saying, "If only it were different." The question to ask yourself is "Am I a person who can be happy independent of what's going on outside of me?" What's going on outside you doesn't care about you at all. It isn't going to change because you want it to. The only thing you can take responsibility for is you and your own karma. How people treat you is their karma. How you react to how they treat you is yours. That's really important information. People have a right to behave toward the universe any way they want to, depending on where they are on the path. That's all they can do. The evidence is that that's what they did. That's all the evidence you need. They did it. How you react to it is up to you. If you react to someone sending you rejecting messages with anger, despair, frustration, hurt, and pain, and that's what you are sending out, that's what you're going to get back. When someone sends you hate and you react with hate, that's your karma. You're sending out hate, and you're going to get back hate.

The highest place you can get to, which is what Christ, Buddha, Mohammed, and all the other great religious teachers have tried to teach us, is when somebody sends you hate, you send back love. Because that's what's inside. Squeeze an orange as hard as you can and what comes out? Orange juice. Why? Because that's what's inside. It doesn't make any difference who put the pressure on. The same thing is true of a human being. If someone puts pressure on you and tells you that your marriage isn't going to work, or that you are fired, or "I don't love you anymore," it all depends on how you react. If what comes out of you is anger, hatred, despair, stress, and pain, it's because that's what you have inside. Otherwise it couldn't come out.

The only way that anything can get inside of you is through the way you think. Your thinking process puts everything inside. Emotions don't happen to you. Emotions are the result of thinking. Your rational mind controls your emotions. What puts emotions there is your evaluation of the world, your judgments of it, and your beliefs. When you tell yourself, "This shouldn't be happening," that sentence is what is causing the despair to come out of you. You tell yourself that people have no right to treat you that way instead of saying they are treating you this way and this is how you're going to react to it. Instead what you do, neurotically and self-defeatingly, is say, "They shouldn't be doing that." What you're really saying at that moment is "If only you were more like me, I wouldn't have to be so unhappy right now." If you want to change that around, you can say, "You're never going to be like me, because you're who you are. You're unique and I'm unique, and I'm going to try to love you and accept you because that's what I have inside. I have acceptance for you. I have love for you. I have kindness for you, even when you treat me in ways that I find abominable. What I have inside of me to give away is love, and that comes from having only loving thoughts."

Your feelings come from your thoughts; therefore, you can control your feelings. You manage your emotions by looking at the thinking system that supports these neurotic, unhappy reactions. How did that depression get there? It comes from the way you think. You're thinking depressing thoughts. "If only this person hadn't left me."

"If only you were different." "If only you weren't dying on me right now." "If only the tax bill were not here." "If only the dog hadn't chewed up the carpet." Depression or stress or anxiety—or unhappiness—is not the result of the way the world is; it's a perfect system. It all works. The whole thing works perfectly, and you're part of it. You are unhappy because you tell yourself it should be something different from what it is. The only way to get out of that is to stop telling yourself the things that got you there in the first place. You didn't just inherit unhappiness, you simply learned it through the process of choice making and thinking. It's now habitual. As long as you keep believing the old way, you're trapped.

If you're looking for explanations in the subconscious to explain why you're happy or unhappy, you can find them. They make a lot of sense. The fact is, if you're not happy, you're the only one who's living with that. Nobody else is living with it. If you don't like what you have been choosing all this time in your life, then what you say is "All of that is gone, it's over. I can't be looking back at what I did or didn't have. I am going to start making some new choices today." Of course, a miserable childhood can affect a person later in life. But so what? It's gone. It's over. You can't get it back. You can't redo it. So what you say is, "All right, those things happened." The neurotic says, "They shouldn't have and I'm so unhappy." The no-limit person says, "They happened and that's a great opportunity for me."

If you are unhappy, the question you should ask yourself is *"Why am I choosing not to be happy?"* not "Why is the world in such a state that I can't be happy?" The world is presented to us. It's perfect. Everything on our planet that was given to us is. All unhappiness comes from thinking. "Why do I believe that happiness is something that is external to me, instead of understanding that I am happiness?" Why not start seeing yourself as an example of what happiness is. In other words say, "I'm going to be happiness." Thoreau said, "When you are advancing confidently in the direction of your own dreams, and you're endeavoring to live the life which you have imagined, then you will meet with a success unexpected in common hours.'' I don't ever tell myself I'm not happy. I don't do that. That's a death sentence.

Here is the parable of the kitten. A little kitten is chasing his tail and an old cat comes up to him and says, ''What are you doing?'' The little kitten says, ''Well, I'm chasing my tail. I've just been to cat philosophy school and I've learned two things: one is that happiness is the most important thing in the world for a cat, and two, that happiness is located in my tail. That's what they taught us in school. So I've got it all figured out. If I chase it, and I get hold of it, and get a good bite on it, then I will have an eternal lock on happiness, and I will have solved the riddle.'' The old alley cat says, ''You know, I never got to go to school. I've been in the alleys all my life, and I'm thirteen years old. I've scrounged around for everything. But it's funny, in the alleys I learned the same thing that you learned in school: that happiness is the most important thing in the world for a cat and that it's located in my tail.'' Then the old cat says, ''The only difference between you and me as far as I can see is that I have found if I go about my business and lead my life the way I choose to, it follows after me wherever I go.''

Contributors' Comments

Dr. Pierre Mornell on Success

The most successful people I have treated have had at least one parent who has been a demon—a perfectionist, critical or silent. Successful people were not given praise as children, and they're driven to succeed.

You see people working eighteen hours a day and having lots of people around them saying, ''Terrific, wonderful, sensational.'' Does that produce success? Sure. Happiness? Some. But what do they go home to?

You have to pay high dues for public success. You have to let down somewhere, and often that's done in private life. The successful person may go home to somebody who says, ''Yeah, but wait a minute. What about Johnny over there? He hasn't seen his dad for all this time, and

Mary's having trouble in school, and we haven't had sex for three weeks, and you seem increasingly distant.'' Highly successful people have often been short-changed in the personal apprenticeship of life: how to talk; how to express feelings; how to get angry; how to show affection; how to be sexual.

Successful people have very few outlets for expressing anger or frustration. Perhaps a lawyer can do it in a courtroom. In my day surgeons could throw scalpels across the operating room. In show business the star can throw a temper tantrum. But in most cases, people who have a need to please—that's the reason for their success—cannot be cranky or irritable and turn people off. They cannot express frustration. Their success is, in large part, based on an ability to get along with people. They swallow a lot of frustration, a lot of irritation, a lot of anger. They wear a mask; they smile a lot; they're charming; they're cheerful; they're reasonable; they're responsible; they're respectable. There's no place to take that mask off and not smile; not be charming; not be cheerful; not be reasonable; not be responsible; not be respectable.

If you do that for days, weeks, months, years at a time, then things are adding up, adding up, adding up, and repressed anger can often lead to depression, it can lead to ulcers, it can lead to migraines, it can lead to a lot of physical problems.

Dr. Ashley Montagu on Despair
Stand on any street corner and watch people's faces. Many people have lost the struggle. Many of them have given up, and their faces show despair and failure. The real tragedy for human beings lies in the difference between what they were capable of becoming and what they've been caused to become by the false values by which they live.

11   Change

The greatest cause of unhappiness is self-pity. It totally immobilizes us from any action that may bring us happiness. To wallow in self-pity is to play the victim. Sometimes friends and family disappoint us, people don't love us the way we think they "should," or events and plans don't go the way we expect. These things can threaten our sense of security or self-worth. The real truth is, we don't control life—and if we feel *personally* rejected we should remember: people do things because of them, not because of us. *Am I playing the victim? What is the payoff? If my circumstances are negative, what am I doing to change them?*

Father Vaughan Quinn challenges us to get out and do something for somebody else.

The Reverend Vaughan Quinn, O.M.I., is the executive director of Sacred Heart Rehabilitation Center, an alcohol treatment facility in Detroit and Memphis, Michigan. An avid sailor and runner, Father Quinn plays goalie for the Flying Fathers, a hockey team made up of Canadian priests who raise money for charity throughout the United States and Canada.

The Reverend Vaughan Quinn, O.M.I.

The single greatest barrier to happiness is self-preoccupation. People get so preoccupied with their own little world they live in a world of one. That's narcissism. My definition of a narcissist is a person who is having a great big love affair with himself but can't stand the object of his affections. That is hell. Until a person is able to break out of that, through unconditional love that is given to him by other people, he stays very much alone and feels very strange. The thing that triggers self-preoccupation is self-importance.

The laws of maturity are to love yourself, to accept yourself, and to forget about yourself. To love youself means to accept yourself exactly as you are because that's how God created you and that's the way he wants you. To accept yourself means never to try to be anybody else because when you mimic others you're going to copy the wrong things. To forget about yourself means you really are not that important, so get on with the business of living.

Anger, resentment, worry, self-pity, fear, and guilt get people thinking about themselves. They compare themselves with other people. They are envious of other people's possessions. They want to be like somebody else. They are unable to appreciate themselves. They are not aware of their own gifts. Some people get locked into these negative emotions and stay there because they are happy with that. They cry, "I'm a sewer, I'm a sewer, I'm a great big sewer." "Nobody has seen the trouble I've seen. Woe is me!" Being miserable is an attention-seeking device. These unhappy people think they're the only ones in the world who are suffering pain.

There is pain in life. We all have to take bumps in life. We all go through pain. However, most of the pain we suffer is not channeled in a proper life-giving way. What we should be able to do is stop and ask, "Why am I angry? Why am I lonely? Why am I resentful? Why am I envious?" Pain can be a great learning experience. Learn how to handle it and grow.

What keeps us unhappy is that we blame our misery on others. "If Charlie would only change, if Judy would only change, then I would be happy." Maybe Charlie or Judy is never going to change. If they don't the unhappy person can stay miserable and keep blaming Charlie and Judy.

The payoff, which keeps this person immobilized, is martyrdom. If you want happiness, rather than engaging in introspective navel gazing, look outside yourself.

The only way to get positive feelings about yourself is to take positive actions. Man does not live as he thinks, he thinks as he lives. If he starts doing things for other people, and puts a smile on his face, he's going to get positive feedback. He's going to start feeling better about himself because other people will be saying, "You are doing good things."

The greatest power we all have in our lives is the power to love. Love is a decision we make in our lives that says others are as important as we are and we will make a commitment to their happiness, development, and security, to the same level as we would do for ourselves.

There are a lot of people with low self-esteem. They are that way because of the messages they have been receiving: "Why don't you keep your room clean? Why don't you pass all your exams? Why don't you come in on time? Why aren't you like your brother? Why can't you be like somebody else? Why aren't you self-sufficient?" If you dig a hole in front of people, the only thing they can do is crawl into the hole. If you put a pedestal in front of people and give them encouragement, they will eventually get up on the pedestal and feel good about themselves. If at twenty, thirty, and forty years of age the negative tapes are the same, how can a person feel good about himself and be happy?

The only way people can get out of that hole is through unconditional love, and they will start experiencing it from the people around them as soon as they start to take positive action. In unconditional love there is no pan scale. The minute we ask, "What's in it for me?" we become losers.

Put a smile on your face and help somebody with a suitcase. Write a letter. Visit a hospital. Do something nice for your spouse. The reason relationships break up, the reason marriages fail, is that we take the other person for granted. One of the most important laws of human relations is "Appreciate somebody and that person will become more to you; belittle somebody and that person will become less to you." We take for granted the people who love us and say, "Well, it's my due." People in the midst of a most heated family argument should stop and ask themselves this question: What is the kind and loving thing for me to do right now concerning this other person? If we let that direct us, we would learn by coming out of ourselves. We must cure ourselves of selfishness or it will kill us.

There are some very practical ways to get out of depression, which is usually anger turned inward. Depression immobilizes us. The first thing is to do something for your body. Get out and do a little exercise. It might be just brisk walking. It might be swimming. It might be riding a stationary bike. It might be running. Get out and get the adrenaline going. It's very important. "Two men look through bars. One sees mud. One sees stars." If our vision is negative, all we are going to see is negative. The coffee is always going to be too cold. The eggs are always going to be greasy. The mountains are always going to block the view. We have to do something to change that within ourselves. The first way to feel better about ourselves is to go out and get some exercise.

The second thing is to pursue the joy of discovery. We all have many gifts within us, and there are many gifts around us. People get locked into the same type of routine living and they get bored. Boredom is the inability to make any sense out of the present with regard to the past and with less with regard to the future. Do something different. Open up new vistas. If you have never been to an art museum, go to an art museum. If you have never been to a concert, go to a concert. If you have never gone out and appreciated the flowers, take the time to do that. Pursue discovery. There is a world out there that's speaking to us all the time. Some of us close it off; we don't see the beauty around us.

The third thing is to avoid materialism. A lot of people who start to feel bad want to buy something to change the way they feel. They buy a new hat, a new coat, or a new dress, or a brand-new car, and that's supposed to change the way they feel inside. It doesn't. They are still very depressed and resentful about people, and they get mad at the things they buy. The buying backfires. Our attitudes are the fathers of our actions. The challenge is to change the attitudes within ourselves. Don't go out and buy an external thing to change the way you feel. There's no magic. It's similar in the world of addictions. Don't put something into your mouth, such as alcohol, pot, pills, or any mood-altering chemicals, to change the way you feel.

Number four is to develop your potential. We all have things we can do and want to do, but because we're afraid to make a mistake we don't. Try. Men who make a million dollars playing baseball are missing seven out of every ten times they go to bat, and they are our heroes. They're only hitting .300. Lots of people won't take risks. Unless they can play the guitar or the piano perfectly or do whatever their potential is, they say, "No I can't do it, but I'd like to be able to do it." Everybody has potential. Everybody has gifts. It's through assessing ourselves and looking at those gifts that we have the chance to develop them. That takes discipline. It takes stick-to-itiveness. Immaturity means we want everything to happen in a hurry. If we practice for an hour we think we should have the thing down pat. Good pianists practice eight hours every day. Figure skaters are on their skates six hours every day. We want to be able to do things well without going through all the discipline and the work. There is no such thing as a free lunch. The only things that are available to us in life are the things we have earned by the sweat of our brow. There are no freebies.

Number five is to work on relationships. If you want to know where you are in life, examine your relationships with the people who love you as well as the people who refuse to love you. That will tell you a great deal about yourself and how you are responding to situations. If you are trying to control people or manipulate them, if you want everybody to love you all the time, that is totally unreal and you will be very unhappy. In our relationships we must accept others as they are. Spirituality means changing the inner hostility into hospitality, by developing enough solitude within ourselves and changing our own visions. We should accept the stranger as the bearer of gifts. Relationships cannot be predicated on expectations. Examine your relationships: How do I feel when I am with that person? Does that person bring out the very best in me? Am I saying, "I really love you because when I'm with you I really feel good about myself."

Number six is to play. Play a little. Everybody in this world needs diversification. You cannot spend twenty-four hours a day asking the question, "Is being better than nonbeing?" We all have problems and plenty of responsibilities. The sense of play is the life of Walter Mitty. While you are playing you know it has no connection with what your world is at home, at work, or even at leisure. You are totally involved in it. You're involved physically, emotionally, and intellectually, whether you're skiing or just goofing off. You do that so you can get your batteries charged in order that when you come back to do the responsible things in life, you can do them with less effort. A real pro is effortless. If you're a hockey fan you know that Wayne Gretzky makes it look very, very easy. At the ballet, Mikhail Baryshnikov makes it look easy. When people are depressed everything becomes an effort. To get out of bed is a big effort. To go grocery shopping is too much of an effort. On the other hand, when they're hitting the bull's-eye and doing things properly, it's almost effortless. It's joyful. Play helps make that happen.

Number seven is to look redeemed. If you are having a good time, inform your face. Change the perennial funeral in your heart into a sense of celebration. Realize the gifts you have. Celebrate the wonders and joys of life. Realize that the gift you have is the gift of life. A tree can be a sense of celebration. Music can be celebrated. Open yourself up to those things. Celebrate what you are able to do. Celebrate other people. If you want to see the real creative works of God and God's presence on the face of this earth, don't look to north or south or to heaven; look into the eyes of people. See them change

and see them grow and see them live and laugh and cry
and love and be happy.

Turn your head off and your heart on. The secret of life
is opening up the eye of the heart. We don't live our lives
by giving intellectual assent to doctrine, dogma, and definition. Life is a response to the situations in which we
find ourselves.

People think as they live. If you want good feelings
about yourself, do something for somebody. I'm not talking about the great big things that are going to make the
headlines or the TV news shows. It's smiling at people,
telling them they look good or saying, "It's nice to see
you" and "Thank you very much for calling." If you
want to be liked by people, go out and do some good
things.   •

Circumstances and people in our lives may be the cause
of our unhappiness. Our personal behavior may be causing
us trouble. Many times we may not be the direct cause of
our unhappiness, yet we are still responsible. Subconscious motivations may be guiding our actions, which lead
us into situations that make us unhappy. It is our feelings
that cause our unhappiness. These negative situations are
opportunities for us to reach deep within ourselves for new
answers and actions. The ability to change is predicated
on desire, willingness, and effort. *What is really causing
my unhappiness? Am I willing to go to any length to
change?*

Dr. Robert Schuller believes that change requires decision.

*Dr. Robert Schuller is the founder and senior minister of
the Crystal Cathedral in Garden Grove, California. He is
well known for* The Hour of Power *television series and
the twenty books he has written. His newest book is* The
Be (Happy) Attitudes.

Dr. Robert Schuller

The biggest obstacle to happiness is a lack of self-esteem. People who lack an internal sense of self-value, self-respect, and self-worth become very egocentric. A lack of inner security always produces a very destructive ego. If you know that you are a wonderful human being, then you don't have to have your way all the time. The destructive ego produces all kinds of dishonest defense mechanisms, and before you know it, you're caught in a spiritual spider web from which there is no extrication.

I think we are born insecure. We are born not trusting. When we speak of self-esteem or self-respect it's the same as having faith in our ability to make decisions. It's internal security. It's self-confidence that we can acquire the wisdom to make the right decisions. Every human being is born without faith. Faith comes only through the process of making decisions to change before we can be sure it's the right move.

Sin is lacking faith. It's our unwillingness to believe in ourselves and our unwillingness to believe in other people. It produces cynicism and it produces suspicion. It's our unwillingness to believe in God. Our negative behavior demands proof before we will make any commitment, demands answers to all the questions before we will say yes, and demands assurances and guarantees before we will take any risks. The Bible says that without faith, it is impossible to please God.

Faith has to be caught more than taught. I think it has to come through personal experience. As we are growing up a lot depends on the kind of parents we have. Overprotective parents are very destructive. In our family, we've had a rule with our five children that, when each one graduates from high school, he or she has to get out of the house. They all have to pack a suitcase and say good-bye. We give them the freedom to pick college or the freedom not to pick college, but after they graduate from high school they have to be far enough away from home so they can't get into the car and come running back to Dad and Mom. That's to teach them faith in themselves. The eagle stirs up the nest that the young may learn to fly.

Most people don't have problems, they face decisions. For example, unemployed people don't have a problem; they have to make a decision to learn a new trade or a new skill or even to move to a new town. It may mean that they have to move away from their family and relatives and the place where they grew up. People say, "I can't. I have to live here. I was born and raised here." Well, I was born and raised in Iowa and love my brothers, and my wife loves her brothers and sisters, but I packed up and came to California because this is where I had to be to make a contribution. It was a decision, not a problem.

A woman whose husband is an alcoholic has to ask, "How am I going to respond to this?" Her decision should be to go to Al-Anon and seek counsel, saying, "I need help, I can't do it alone. Tell me, how do I deal with this?" It is not a new problem and they are experts. They can tell her, "Here's the right way and here's the wrong way for intervention." Even for people who live life in a wheelchair, I think the biggest problem is *seeing* it as a problem. If they can't get to where they want to go, maybe they can make a decision to encourage people to put in a ramp.

We must develop the faith that things will be okay or if they are not okay, so what? If things do not work out, what's the big deal? Don't be afraid if things don't work out; all you have to do is make another decision.

When I say people don't have problems, they face decisions, what I am suggesting is not to surrender leadership to a human situation or a human condition. What I am really defining is the doctrine of the human being as a person who has the capacity to be a leader. Leadership is deciding how you are going to respond, how you are going to react, what are you going to do when faced with a challenge, a difficulty, or a presumed obstacle.

When I am faced with a frustration or an enormous challenge, my biggest problem is to practice what I preach, and that is to choose the positive reaction to situations over which I have no control. Even my response to a situation over which I have no control is a decision.

I can choose to be happy. When I am faced with an upsetting experience, I do not face a problem. What I face is a decision, and the decision I have to make is how I am going to react to what is happening to me.

In the final analysis, integrity of personhood comes into the realm of decision making. Decision making is easy if there are no contradictions in your value system. If living is primarily decision making, then you have to make darn sure you make the best decisions. In difficult situations I don't make decisions without consulting other people.

Why is decision making so difficult for people? When people are miserable, why are they so afraid to make a change? You'd think that if they are miserable, they would gladly welcome a change, but that's not true. When life is miserable, why is change so difficult? It's because of the fear that they may jump from the frying pan into the fire. Decisions take courage more than anything else. To change is to decide and to decide is risky. The bottom line is fear of failure.

Don't be afraid of failure, but do be afraid of not trying to change, to improve. If you try, it is impossible to be a total failure, because you have not failed in the face of fear, you had the nerve to try, you had the courage to take a chance. It is possible to be a total failure if you don't even dare to try. You have failed to have enough nerve to take a shot at it. The fear of failure holds people back more than anything else. It's impossible to be a total failure if you are just willing to try to change.

Sometimes with difficult situations and major decisions we must reach out. If you are too proud or too afraid to admit you are hurting, don't be surprised that nobody seems to care. That's pride in the destructive sense. Pride can be both constructive and destructive. Pride in the destructive sense is a form of insecurity, which is a lack of self-confidence, which is a lack of self-esteem, which is a lack of faith. Pride keeps people from reaching out because they fear that they will be exposed as imperfect persons. Don't fear imperfection; it only means you are a member of the human race. Join the human race.

You don't get to vote on the ways things are in your life, you already have. Whatever actions you have been taking have gotten you where you are today. You're getting what you're getting because you're doing what you're doing. If you don't like what you're getting, change what you're doing. To blame others, the world, or life as the reason we are where we are is to negate our own responsibility for our lives. The only thing we can control is our own actions, and our actions today will determine where we are tomorrow. *Do I like my life? Am I happy? What are the things I want to change?*

Carole Bayer Sager put in the effort that brought about a dramatic change in her life. She says, ''When I find I'm spending too much time on myself, helping someone else feel better makes me feel better.''

Carole Bayer Sager is half of one of the world's most successful songwriting teams. ''That's What Friends Are For,'' which she wrote with her husband, Burt Bacharach, was the number one song in the United States on three different record charts simultaneously. Recording stars Frank Sinatra, Dolly Parton, Barbra Streisand, Neil Diamond, Michael Jackson, Ray Charles, and Carly Simon, among many others, have recorded her songs. In addition to her work as a lyricist, for which she has received various Grammy and Oscar nominations and an Academy Award, Carole has recorded three albums of her own songs.

Carole Bayer Sager

I did not start out in life happy. My childhood recollections are just disastrous. I am happy now. None of us walks around smiling all the time, but it is an attitude. It is something that you work at and you earn the right to be happy. I had to exorcise a lot of stuff about who I thought I was. We inherit certain things from our parents whether we want them or not. We don't realize until we've done some work on ourselves that these things aren't necessarily ours. The anxiety I had used to make me twitch; maybe it was never mine. Maybe I just put it on the way I put on a dress because it was my mother's and it was hanging in her closet. Even if I have a bad day, I snap out of it. Is the glass half empty or half full? Until about ten years ago, I definitely thought the glass was half empty a lot of the time. It didn't just change for no reason. It took years of therapy.

One thing I did was to get out of New York. I was surrounded by a life there that I had lived from childhood, and I felt trapped within that life. I was anxious and nervous, and if I did feel happy, I'd get worried that it would be taken away. I often felt that I was the female equivalent of Woody Allen. I didn't perceive myself as pretty. I was short. I didn't see myself as sexy, because I wasn't big-chested. I was insecure.

I had success in my work early on. The songs were hits, but I didn't enjoy the success. It was almost as if I made some kind of deal: "Okay, give me the hits and I won't enjoy them." I worried about the bomb dropping until I got my own anger released and realized that the bomb was inside of me. I worried about dying. I thought I was going to die very young. I was always hypochondriacal. When I was living in New York I would go to a therapist wearing a fall—fake hair—and over the fall I wore a hat. That's how covered up I was at one point in my life.

If I'm ever feeling not happy, all I have to do is think about how my life was ten years ago, fifteen years ago, twenty years ago, and I get real happy. I feel so grateful that I've changed, that there were choices and I said, "I'm going for it." I worked hard on myself. First of all, I've got a real understanding of where all my craziness came from. That's important only to a point. It's not an answer because if you know where it came from and just stay in it, where are you? I do think it's important to go back, look at it all, and figure it out.

I remember the Golden Globe Awards in California in 1978. "Nobody Does It Better" was nominated for best song. I thought, "I won't get to the stage. My lip will twitch and I'll probably pass out, so it's better just not to win. Don't humiliate yourself with a lousy statue." Now when one of my songs is nominated, I go there and think, "Let me win that thing. Let me up on that stage."

It's all changed in the last ten years. I think Burt made a big difference in my life. Things happen when we're ready for them, and I was ready for Burt. I had been married once before, in New York. It was a debilitating relationship for me. Though my husband was a lovely man, he encouraged me to remain infantile; he would take care of me. I realized when I met Burt that you don't win any points with him for being infantile. It's not his thing. There was no reward for staying in bed and not feeling good. He didn't come in with presents. There was no reward for baby talk. It didn't turn him on. So I was forced to be an adult if I wanted to hang out with Burt, at least as adult as he is. We're both on the border line. We play together. It's good. You have to; you can't lose the child in you. It's important to keep the healthy child and get rid of the helpless child. I had a lot of the helpless child but I don't have it anymore.

I think happiness has to do with functioning. It has to do with doing and being. It's a balance. It's really about balance, not acquisition. It's not about having the most beautiful dress. It's not about external things. I thought it was at one time and worked hard to get those things and got them early enough to find out that they weren't it. It kills me when I read an article about me that says she has everything and she's this and she's that. I think, "Yeah, but I haven't had it for long. Give me a break. I only just started."

I had a volatile mother and I never knew what to expect. She had her bout with alcoholism, but she's been sober for more than twelve years. Our relationship has changed dramatically since she took responsibility for changing her life. I really like her now. I loved her even in the bad times, but I didn't like her. Her love was so inconsistent because she didn't like herself half the time. When she didn't like herself, she couldn't nurture me much. My father died of heart disease after ten years of illness. He was twenty years older than my mother. When I came along, my mother went into direct competition with me as to who was going to get Daddy, because she was a kid herself. It never had anything to do with me, but I personalized it all.

Before you can be happy, you've got to let go of the things that are preventing you from being happy. I walked around with rage, but it was turned inward. I was passive. I wanted people to like me: "Step on my head, it's okay." I had to let go of a lot of these labels that I had put on myself before I could put on the happy label. I had to give up all those other ways I perceived myself: insecure, unattractive, frightened, angry. It's all just kind of started to happen. I had to forgive my mother. I had to stop making my father into Saint Francis. I had to grow up. That's the big one. The payoff in being unhappy is that you're not a fully realized adult and you can blame others. You can say, "Well, I'd be happy if . . ." I decided to take responsibility for my life. I was in therapy, on and off, from the age of twenty-one to thirty-five. It's amazing to me that I'm not in therapy now.

My work is important to me. I need some creative outlet. If someone said to me, "You can't write," I'd have a hard time remaining what I perceive to be as happy because that's very essential to who I am. It's the freedom to create. Burt has made a tremendous impact on my being happy—not that we are continuously happy—but it's such a good relationship. I had never before felt that I could say whatever I was feeling in a relationship. The minute you can't do that you're suppressed, and the minute you're suppressed you can't be happy. We have revolutions because people have to be free. The minute you're editing yourself, you are not fully anything. I would tell Burt, "Oh, Burt, I was so miserable. I was such an unhappy person." He met me at a point in my life where I was already on my way to happy, so he didn't believe me. He still doesn't.

I love people. I love the interchange of being with people. I love to laugh. Even in the times when I wasn't happy, I could still have a good laugh. I find that it's important to try to have supportive people around, people whom you support and who support you, and I don't mean professionally. I mean they support your growth. They support your desire to be all that you can be and on the most personal level, Burt supports that in me and I support him. That's another reason it's such a good relationship.

We're all entitled to be happy. I think it's God's birthright to us, but I don't think I felt deserving of it for a long time. Now I feel it's okay to be okay. I don't think happiness just happens to you, I think you have to feel you deserve it. I'm definitely happy.

Sometimes life is very painful. We are filled with negative feelings and there is a sense of hopelessness and despair. We try to deal with hurt. Many of us resort to killing our pain with such substances as alcohol, drugs, pills, or food. Our self-image may be so low that we form unhealthy dependencies not on substances that temporarily make us feel better, but on people who we believe will make our hurt go away. However, the pain becomes greater, and sooner or later we have to take an honest look at the mess we have made of our lives. When we are sick and tired of being sick and tired, we are often motivated to change. Human beings are capable of dramatic change; out of the greatest pain frequently comes the greatest change. The quality of life after a remarkable turnabout is amazing. *Am I trying to solve my inner problems with something outside myself? Am I ready and willing to change? Will I work for it?*

Og Mandino tells his powerful story and says with gratitude, "I'm just so lucky to be here."

Og Mandino is one of the most successful motivational speakers and writers in America. His books The Greatest

Salesman in the World *and* The Greatest Miracle in the World *are classics, and his anthology of selected motivational writing by other experts in the field,* The University of Success, *is one of the most important books of its genre. His newest book is* Mission: Success!

Og Mandino

I was very blessed. I had a spunky, red-haired Irish mother with a freckled face and green eyes. She had a dream. Where she got this dream I don't know. I never had a chance to talk with her about this, as it turned out.

Long before I ever went to school, she kept telling me over and over that someday I would be a writer. She had me reading grown-ups' books before I ever went to school. She had me writing compositions and short stories when the other kids were struggling with Dick and Jane. I bought the dream. I liked the idea. I was reading two books a week when I was five years old. We kept the dream all through school. My last year in high school, I was editor of the school paper in Natick, Massachusetts. We were all set. I was going to go to the University of Missouri. We had figured, after looking at many catalogues, that it offered the best journalism school. The year was 1940. I graduated in June. A month after I graduated, while she was making lunch for me, my mother dropped dead in the kitchen. That was the end of the dream.

I couldn't wait to get away. I joined the Army Air Force and became a bombardier. I flew thirty combat missions over Germany and got back alive and in one piece. I moved to New York. I rented a cold-water flat on West Forty-fourth Street, bought a secondhand typewriter, and started to write. In one year I collected I don't know how many rejection slips. I tried everything, even poetry, and couldn't sell a word. I went back to New England, where I'd come from, and I married my childhood sweetheart.

The next ten years were hell—hell for my wife. I got a job selling life insurance, and I was the world's worst. We bought a little home, but I was always only one jump ahead of the bill collector, driving an old automobile and working seven days a week. I'd call on a prospect anywhere, Sunday, ten o'clock at night, it didn't matter. I was bustin' myself trying to make it. Each week we used to make a list on a legal pad and decide whom we'd pay and whom we couldn't pay. I began to do what so many do. On the way home from work I would stop at a local tavern for a drink. After all, I deserved it. I'd had a long, tough day. One drink soon became two, and two became four, and four drinks became six. I became a miserable husband and a terrible father. God had blessed us with a lovely little daughter in the meantime, but I was boozing. I'd come home drunk, or my wife would go down and bail me out of the drunk tank.

Finally, I came home one Sunday afternoon from an insurance convention that was held in Bretton Woods, New Hampshire. I found a note on the kitchen table saying, "So long." Those two had had all they could take from the miserable male in their life. Then I really went down the drain. I drank more. I lost my job. I couldn't keep up the payments on the house and lost it. I threw my clothes into my old Ford and hit the road. I was a bum. I drove a truck. I worked on a construction crew. I went across the country, just bumming. I spent several nights in drunk tanks. I was about as low as anybody could get.

One morning in Cleveland, it was pouring rain and I had no topcoat. I was leaning against a pawn shop window and I saw a little handgun—$29 was the price on a little yellow tag. I can still draw the shape of that tag today. I had three wet $10 bills in my pocket; that's all I had. Hair down to my shoulders, a beard, bloodshot eyes. A bum. A real derelict, thirty-five years old. I thought, "There's the answer to all my problems. I'll go in and buy that thing and I'll get a couple of bullets. I'll go back to that mangy room where I'm staying and I'll load the gun, put it to my head, and pull the trigger. I'll never have to face that miserable failure in the mirror again."

I've been asked the question a thousand times: "What happened? Why didn't you buy the gun?" I wish I had an

exotic answer, that I heard a voice which said, "Don't."
I joke about it now and say, "I didn't buy the gun because
I don't think I had enough guts even to do that." I just
wandered up the street and went into the public library.
There I stumbled on a lovely gold mine that's in every
library—a row of books on success and how to achieve it.
The Maxwell Maltzes, W. Clement Stones, and Napoleon
Hills of the world. I began to read. I spent a lot of time
in libraries. I was enthralled by W. Clement Stone's philosophy on success through a positive mental attitude. He
wasn't offering any pie in the sky. He was saying, "Baby,
you want it, you can have it. But you've got to pay a price
for it." I was so intrigued by the whole concept; it was
new to me.

I went looking for Stone's insurance company, and I
found it in Boston. While I was looking I met a girl who
had a hell of a lot more faith in me than I ever had in
myself. Stone's company hired me and I married the girl;
we've been together a lot of years. Stone's training was
fantastic. The first insurance company I worked for spent
a day and a half training new employees, gave them a rate
book and a map, and said, "Go get 'em." This company
really spent time on them and also motivated them. So I
went out and in a year I was a sales manager. My territory
was northern Maine. You can't get any tougher than that.
It's about forty below zero from November to May. I hired
potato farmers and young kids right off the farm, and sent
them down to Boston to train them. Then I worked with
them in the field. In six months, we had the top crew in
the country—average sales per week per man. We were
leading the country.

The dream of writing had never really left me. I took a
week off and rented a typewriter, and I sat down and wrote
a sales manual on how to apply Stone's positive mental
attitude philosophy to selling insurance in rural areas. I
typed it up pretty and sent it to the home office in Chicago,
just praying somebody back there would recognize what a
talent they had buried up in northern Maine. I got a letter
from the sales promotion manager. I went to Chicago for
an interview. The next thing I knew, Betty and I and our

new son, Dana, were moving to Chicago. All we had in
the world was in or on top of our car. I went to work in
Chicago writing sales promotion material for $9000 a year.
I was so thrilled because after all these years I was writing. I loved it.

About a year later, the editorship of *Success Unlimited*
opened up and I applied for the job, although I didn't
know a damn thing about editing a magazine. Stone picked
me, and I'll never forget my first meeting with him. He
said, "Og, I'm going to get out of your way. This has just
been a house organ up to now. I'm going to give you a
blank check. I want you to take this magazine and make
it something national." We took it from a circulation of
two thousand to over a quarter of a million by the time I
left.

Nine months after running the magazine, I had not written one single piece. There hadn't been time. I was trying
to keep eighteen balls in the air and learn what I was
doing. We came up one article short for an issue and there
was nothing on file I could use. I went home that night
and wrote an article on Ben Hogan, the great golfer, and
his comeback from a terrible automobile accident. He had
been told he would never walk again. But he did and he
won the U.S. Open. I ran the piece in the next issue of
the magazine.

A publisher in Long Island got a toothache and went to
his dentist's office. The publisher was a golf nut. While
he was waiting he picked up *Success Unlimited* and read
my article. When he got to his office that afternoon he
wrote me a letter saying, "You've got talent. If you ever
want to do a book, get in touch with me." Eighteen
months later we published a small book called *The Greatest Salesman in the World*. The idea in the book is that
you really are a miracle, you don't know how good you
are, that you're only using 10 percent of your potential
and that you can accomplish great things with your life.
The book took off like a rocket, with one edition after
another after another, all selling through word of mouth.
There was no promotion, no advertising, no book tour.
Nobody knew me. It just went.

On his way to London to celebrate Christmas, old man Stone, at his wife's urging, read the book. He timed his cablegram to me so that I got it on Christmas morning. It said, "Your book is the most marvelous thing I've read since *Magnificent Obsession*. See me soon as I return." When he returned, I made an appointment and went to see him. He said, "Og, I want you to call your publisher and tell him that I want to buy ten thousand copies. I want to distribute one to every shareholder and to every employee in the whole country."

When sales reached 350,000 copies in hard cover, Bantam was interested in buying the paperback rights. Frederick Fell, my publisher, said he wanted a buck a book, or $350,000, for paperback rights. It was going to be the highest price ever paid for that kind of book up to that time, but before Bantam would buy the book they wanted to talk to me. Nowadays, it doesn't matter what kind of a book you write; unless you can go on the road and talk about it, it's not going to go. I was petrified.

I flew to New York. My salary at that time was $12,000. My whole life was in the balance. I'll never forget that board room. It was monstrous. I walked in and saw thirty-four people around a long oval table. They fired questions at me for about an hour and a half. Finally, Oscar Distel, who was chairman of the board of Bantam, stood up and walked over to me. He put out his hand and said, "Og, we bought your book." I couldn't wait to get back to the New York Hilton from 666 Fifth Avenue to call Betty. I was about half a block from the office when the skies opened up. It was a horrendous thunderstorm, so I dove into the first doorway. It was a small church on Fifth Avenue. Nobody was in the church. Somebody was playing an organ in the basement. I could hear the rain smashing on the roof. I walked up to the altar, fell down on my knees, and began to cry. All I could think was, "Hey, Mum, wherever you are, we finally made it." I was forty-four years old. It had taken a long time. Unbelievable.

I never used to talk much about myself in my speeches. People would say, "It's easy for you to lay out all these

wonderful principles, but you don't know what it's like."
I thought, "They've got to be made to know that I know
what it is to lie on that concrete. I know what it is to come
back from that." Another thing they'd say is, "Well, it's
too late for me." I'd say, "How old are you?" and they'd
reply, "I'm thirty-six" and I'd say, "Oh, poor baby. At
thirty-six I was still groveling in the gutter. I didn't write
my first book till I was forty-four. Stop sucking your
thumb, for God's sake."

I don't frustrate myself by trying to convert everybody
and trying to change everybody from being a failure to a
success. A much better man than I tried to do something
like that two thousand years ago, and he didn't get them
all either. There's a certain group that have settled into
mediocrity and they're going to stay there. You can shake
them, they can read books, and it doesn't mean a damn
thing to them. They'll just read them and put them aside
and that's the end of it.

I remember doing a show in Houston with Steve Edwards, who was holding my latest book. He said, "Og,
what'll this book do for me?" I'd never heard that question
put quite like that before. I remember saying, "Steve, it
won't do a damn thing for you. It's just some pulp and
some glue and some ink. If you take it home and you read
it tonight and you think your whole world is going to
change tomorrow morning, you might as well take the
nine bucks and buy a few martinis with it. You'll be better
off." You've got to say to yourself, "Hey, my way has not
been going so well and I think I'm ready for a change and
I'm willing to give it a shot. Let me give it a fair shot. I
can try. Maybe I can change." One common denominator
among people who have the capacity to change is that
they've had a horrible event or crisis happen in their lives
and they say, "From here on I've got nothing to lose. Let
me try." Being down there scared the hell out of me, and
I'm still alive.

So many of us spend half our lives, or all of our lives,
trying to fulfill the prophecy made about us by our parents or by a teacher who said, "You'll never make it."
What Stone's book did for me was turn on the light. I

realized, "I don't have to be this way. I've been as low as I can get, so it's going to be better from here on." The most essential ingredient, I think, was learning to deal with each day, to roll with the setbacks, and realize that tomorrow will be another day. It'll be completely different. I also learned not to strain so hard, to go with the flow—just kind of ease back and let it happen and don't push so hard.

One of the major causes of unhappiness is resentment. Our anger is directed toward some person who didn't do what we wanted or expected that person to do. Brutal honesty will reveal that the real problem is ours, and if there is a finger of blame to be pointed, it points right back at us. Many times we have a hidden agenda with others, and we are really trying to manipulate them for our own gain to shore up our self-worth. Rather than look at the truth in ourselves we focus on the behavior of others. Our own unreasonable expectations and selfishness are often at the root of our resentment. Anger turned inward causes depression and self-pity and diminishes our sense of self-worth. The next time we are angry, it would be in our own interest to really examine the resentment and try to discover what we did wrong. Surprisingly, the antidote for resentment is honesty and the miracle of apology. *Do I hold any resentment? Can I apologize? Would I rather be right than happy?*

Jack Gregory suggests, "If you don't accept that you're okay, then you're never going to get that thing called happiness."

Jack Gregory, M.A., is a family therapist and counselor at the Personal and Family Adjustment Center in Birmingham, Michigan. He is also a consulting therapist at Guest House in Lake Orion, Michigan.

Happiness to me means to be coping adequately or well with the problems we encounter and having occasional peaks of joy and heightened pleasure. Great stress or anxiety would have to be absent, and they are absent if we're using adequate coping mechanisms. Life is going to be good, bad, and so-so, and that's going to include a lot of tragedies. The longer we live, the greater the number of tragedies. The only way we can have peace of mind, contentment, and "happiness" is to be able to cope with whatever is presented us each day.

A big problem with people's unhappiness is their failure to accept the way life is. In every twenty-four hours you can find something that could meet the definition of good, bad, and so-so. On the other hand, if you go a month you'll find a greater range, if you go a year you'll find a greater range still, and if you go ten years you'll find an ever greater range. The longer you live, the greater the chance that you will experience something that somebody defines as tragedy. Losing your license to practice a profession would be regarded by some as tragedy, going to bankruptcy from a millionaire status would be defined as tragedy, and certainly losing someone you love or losing good health would be a tragedy in practically everybody's mind. Even so, by using certain coping mechanisms, you can maintain a satisfactory life even when confronted with tragedy.

I'm a low-handicap golfer, and if I three-putt a green, which I've been known to do of late, that's a minor tragedy. I've lost a seven-year-old daughter who was run over by a car and killed; that is a major tragedy. Each one, however, requires, from my psychological perspective, the same way of coping. It involves applying some psychological principles to cut our losses. These coping mechanisms are attitudinal. Some of the ideas I've been using in my work as a therapist have turned out to be quite suitable, and I still use them for myself every day. It would have been nice if I could have known these many, many years ago, but unfortunately it takes a long time to learn them or a good teacher to present them and convince us to employ them.

The most useful idea I know in psychology is "Everything that has happened should have happened." I used this coping mechanism when my daughter died as a way to cut my losses and to allow grief to arrive, which is nature's way to deal with loss. By believing that she should have died when she was run over by a very heavy car, I cut my loss somewhat. The reason this idea is so valuable is that if you don't figure out some way to eliminate the anger and resentment and self-pity that goes along with something unpleasant in life, then the chance of cutting losses is poor and grief does not get a chance to get in and do its natural work. The reason this principle is so important is because two of the biggest bugaboos that interfere with happiness are resentment and anger. Behind all resentment and anger lies the irrational belief that something shouldn't have happened. If that belief can be reversed, then the resentment and anger can become moderated to the extent where it goes away. You can't both hold the belief that "everything that has happened should have happened" and stay angry and resentful. That's why I push this principle ad nauseam.

Another useful thought involves a person's value system. From my view, until the system of values is such that it's close enough to the behavior that the person is living, that person is not going to be content or happy. In making choices when we are young, we begin by using a system of values which early on was imposed on us by the big people in charge, often called parents. As we get older and wiser and more educated, a percentage of us start to have our own input instead of using only what other people have told us is their system of values. The principle to be examined is "Your system of values should be pretty close to the way you're living." If you believe in "Thou shalt not kill," you obviously ought not to be in the murdering business. If you believe very, very scrupulously, "Thou shalt not steal," the chance of your being a thief is going to be that much slighter. If, on the other hand, you believe in the double standard, that you are entitled to extramarital alliances without consulting your spouse then, of course, the number of symptoms that are going to affect happiness are essentially zero. The symptoms would be guilt, shame, remorse, usually anger, and sometimes depression. In all three cases the system of values and the behavior are in agreement, which contributes to happiness.

Most of my work as a psychologist has to do with relationships. Relationships contribute most to happiness. If you have a good relationship then you are going to be described as a happy person. If you have a poor relationship then you're frequently going to be describing yourself as not so happy. If your system of values and your selection of behavior are such that you want to opt out of the relationship business, you can be quite content. But if you say, "I want a relationship intently," and you don't have one or you have one that's one-sided, then of course your happiness quotient is going to be reduced. There are, naturally, a few laws of relationships that pop into my mind.

Number one is—and I am an optimist, not a pessimist— "At any given time most relationships are one-sided." When two people are first dating, the chance of their relationship appearing to be a fifty-fifty one is very good. The attraction is there, the chemistry is there, and for a time it looks as though it's hunky-dory. Then the relentless law, "at any given time most relationships are one-sided," starts to work on the relationship. Somebody needs a little more interest than the other is willing to provide. If you happen to have the good fortune of a giver meeting a taker, and if the giver contributes 60 percent to the relationship and the taker 40 percent, that'll work pretty well for an indefinite period of time. But if both are takers, then you're going to have clashes from the word *go,* and these relationships don't last long.

Here's where the coping mechanisms and the system of values come into play. How far apart they are, what degree of giving one partner is capable of, and what is the quality of taking in the other partner are also involved. Somewhere along the line, if the giving and taking are within reason, then the relationship sails along in pretty good shape. A few relationships result in what I call the grand prize—mutual love with societal approval, forever. I see evidence of it here and there. Those kinds of things are priceless. Anything that is priceless has a tendency to be rare. However, the probability of each person remaining in precisely the same relationship with another person a lifetime is pretty rare. People grow at different rates. They have different interests at different times. They have different health problems at different times. There are many reasons.

Individuals who are coming off a broken romance wonder if it was worth it. I like to snatch out of the air the figure 58 million as the number of perfect mates, not to mention a goodly number who are not bad, sprinkled all over the world for each of us in case we move. When you consider the billions of people on earth, that's entirely possible. There are lots of people who report that they've had relationships later in life which were extraordinary and mutually delightful. At one time in their lives, after the end of a relationship, they didn't think they were likely to find such a thing again. We can hold out to anybody who is in the relationship rat race that there are any number of folks who, with a little luck or skill, can be found and related to. Keeping in mind the system of values and some coping mechanisms, two could have a pretty good time with a relationship and be "happy" for a long period of time. It could even be for a lifetime.

Now I'm forever saying, "We don't need romantic love." Other people often make hay out of that statement and say, "We do need love." I have a problem as a psychologist. What if I happen to be working with a string of people, one right after the other, who don't have any romantic love in their lives because of a variety of circumstances, including appearance, system of values, or choice. We have to hold out to them some hope of ability to adjust and have a fine life even though they aren't going to participate in this thing called romantic love. I urge people to believe that romantic love is nice, but it's unnecessary. While many people opt to look for it, even seeking the grand prize—mutual love with societal approval—some people are denied this opportunity. For example, if they are in a marriage where their system of values says, "Till death do us part," so they can't conceive of ever ending the union, and there is no more romantic love, that underlines the point that it's nice but unnecessary.

"We are not responsible for our feelings" is another psychological dictum. As certainly as love could come and Cupid could shoot his arrow into the left buttock, we also find love departing willy-nilly, sometimes for no accountable reason. We've all heard the expression "There's no accounting for tastes." This is true. And there's no accounting for the departure of love, it once having been present. In my work as a marriage and family therapist, this is one of the most perplexing things in the world to deal with. People are constantly putting themselves down, saying, "I'm not doing enough to keep his—or her—love." The truth is that we are not responsible for our feelings, and feelings can come and go regardless of behavior. I try to train dejected people not to be so down on themselves because this phenomenon has occurred. I'm often asked, "What should you do when bad things happen and you're angry and resentful? What do you suggest?" I say, "The muttering of darn and shucks is a very good idea."

If the atmosphere is reasonable, then the chances of love arriving or staying are better. It's not guaranteed. This is what perplexes people. "I do everything for her," they say, "and still the love dies." We start then to use some of the other coping ideas we've already looked at. Looking back to the start of the relationship, I ask the question, "Should the person have fallen in love?" The answer, of course, is "Yes." The person did, and "everything that has happened should have happened." I then ask the question, "Should this person have fallen out of love?" The answer, of course, using the yardstick "everything that has happened should have happened," is if she did, she should have. It's applicable whether you're coming or going. "We are not responsible for our feelings" is ever present. Of course, "We *are* responsible for our behavior" is also present, and what we work on is the willingness to take the consequences of our chosen behavior.

People who think that everything ought to go their way and that there shouldn't be bad things or unpleasant relationships in their life are programmed to a greater degree of misery when the good, bad, and so-so unfold. Also, any number of people are decidedly unhappy because what they insisted on occurring did not unfold. They're so locked into expecting a certain outcome that they're unable to adapt and behave if some other occurrence develops.

By the selection of this philosophy and these principles, you can create an atmosphere in which the feelings we describe as negative will depart and you will experience greater happiness.

One sign of maturity is knowing when to ask for help. Women seem to be better at asking for help than men, who often believe they must go it alone and solve their own problems. We see asking for help as a humbling experience, and we hate to be human. Pride often gets in the way. If we have car problems we quickly take the car to a garage and ask for help. If we want to play a musical instrument or learn computers, we feel comfortable in taking lessons or a course. However, if we are hurting on the inside, we very often do nothing. For many of us asking for help is an exciting first step forward on the road to greater happiness. Sometimes we need professional help. *Am I so unhappy that I need help? Am I willing to ask for help?*

Dr. Joan Harvey comments on those who never got the help they needed. "One of the saddest things I see is elderly people who are bitter and depressed because they feel they have done all the wrong things and have missed their chance at life."

Joan C. Harvey, Ph.D., a clinical associate in the Department of Psychiatry at the University of Pennsylvania, is affiliated with Associated Psychiatric Services in Newark, Delaware. Joan is a clinical psychologist in private practice in Philadelphia, Pennsylvania, and author of the book If I'm So Successful, Why Do I Feel Like a Fake?

Joan C. Harvey, Ph.D.

A lot of people go through life saying, "If only I had chosen a different career." "If only I hadn't married her my life would be different." "If only I had gone to college when I had the chance." If you are "if onlying," you're spending a large part of your time suffering for something that might have been but isn't. If you recognize that the "if onlys" are a habit and you can name ten things that you could do now that might become an "if only" ten years from now, you have the opportunity to change. The solution is to do the things you want to do—now.

You, what you do, and the people you're involved with are the three parts of life. Ask yourself these three questions:

1. Do I think I'm a pretty good person?
2. Do I like my work?
3. Am I satisfied in my personal relations?

A big part of happiness is contentment. If you feel satisfied with life and you don't feel you're missing anything essential, you're probably happy. If you think you're a terrible person, you're probably not very happy. If you think you're better than everybody else, you're probably not very happy either, because others don't live up to your expectations. If who you are, what you do, and who you are involved with are okay and you still said, "I'm not happy," the questions to ask are "Why?" and "What do I feel is missing?" Frustration might be a part of it. If you have idealized expectations of anything, they're not going to be met. What do you expect out of life? Are you making assumptions that are not based on reality? Who says life is happy or the goal of life is happiness? There's no law. All you can do is to try to make life work for you the best it can.

We have to establish expectations, but then we have to ask ourselves, "Are my expectations realistic? Am I going to be unhappy if things are not perfect?" Happiness isn't perfect. Nothing about life is perfect.

If you don't like your work or your relationships the questions to ask are "What can I change? Do I want to change? What is my motivation for being where I am? How did I get here? Why did I get here? Why are these parts of my life unhappy? I must have done something wrong, or I must be doing something wrong. What are my alternatives now? Should I just go on being miserable and unhappy? Why would I choose that?" You have to decide: "What do I want to change? What am I able to change? Where do I begin?"

If all areas of your life are bad, it's not going to be an easy process, but you have to begin someplace. Sometimes people say, "I hate every part of my life and I'm going to change it and it's going to happen tomorrow." That doesn't happen of course. That's part of wanting perfection, to think things are suddenly going to turn around. Some people talk about having revealing moments when they know exactly what to do, but that's rare. For most people it's a step-by-step process in which they have to take credit for every little step they make along the way. Be patient and see it as a growth process and realize that it will not happen overnight and there will be setbacks. It's going to take some time to turn things around.

Step one is to focus on yourself: "Who am I? What do I like? What are my strengths? What are my weaknesses? How can I maximize my strengths? What makes me happy?" Step two is to look at your job: "Do I like my job? Why not? What kind of work will bring me satisfaction at the end of the day? What would I like to do? What kind of work can I think of where the hours wouldn't drag? What kind of work can I do in which I would not be worrying all the time?" Step three is to examine your relationships. This is tough, especially if a very important relationship isn't working. "Do I want to try to work it out? Do I want to go to marriage counseling? Do I want to preserve this relationship? How important is this relationship to the other person? Can we work on it together?"

A lot of people in therapy often say they don't know how to decide whether a particular relationship is worth the effort or not. The bottom-line question is "Do I love this person?" If you can't answer, you're in trouble. If the answer is yes, then it's usually worth a try to work something out. Both parties may be able to compromise in some way so both are allowed to keep some neuroses and give up on other things. Everybody has flaws. Nobody is married to the perfect person. It comes down to the ultimate question, "Are the positive things that my partner offers me so worthwhile that I can put up with the flaws and accept him or her?" Certain things are going to be the way they are forever. You should really be willing to say to yourself, "I cannot change my partner. Is this particular relationship important enough to me that I can compromise?"

If you see your relationship as extremely destructive, then you really have to ask, "Am I a scapegoat for this person? Is he or she going to change? Have we tried? How long have we tried? Do the same patterns repeat themselves over and over again? Is something I'm doing making it the way it is or contributing to it?" It's harder to leave a long-time relationship because it's so familiar. In a lot of marriages pseudomasochistic power struggles go on all the time to the exclusion of any kind of enjoyment or happiness whatsoever. If it's primarily the other person who is doing the using or blaming, that's hard to live with. Guilt-prone people question and doubt themselves and accept the blame. They think they should be more responsible for the happiness of their relationship. A very bad relationship might be worth giving up.

Part of grandiosity is thinking, "I can do it all myself." In life, you sometimes need help. Nobody has the universal knowledge of how to do everything. Nobody's really objective about herself or himself. It's very hard to be both the actor and the observer in your life. People often need a partnership in which they have input and feedback from an objective person who has nothing to gain from whatever decisions are made. Psychologists, psychiatrists, counselors, family therapists, the various "anonymous" self-help groups, and career counselors are good at helping you to find yourself and to find your own way. If you want to change and feel you need help, seek it out.

Contributors' Comments

Life doesn't change, we change. Life doesn't get better, we get better. Many of the contributors have learned some lessons along the way that make their lives easier, and they offer them to you.

Marva Collins on the Right to Happiness
You can be so busy serving up everybody else's happiness on the proverbial platter that you don't get your own. I do not feel guilty about my happiness. I have earned it. I am taking it.

Eda LeShan on Depression
Depression occurs when you are not being yourself. You're probably doing things that you don't want to do. You may be doing things for other people that you don't think you should be doing. When you feel the demands on you are absolutely impossible, that's when you drink or when you eat. The depression leaves the minute you come back to "Who the hell am I? What am I doing?" You can be responsible and you can do the things you have to do for other people, but you don't have to do it by killing yourself. That destroys you. Depression is really saying, "I'm hating myself. I'm not giving myself the things I need to love myself."

Pat Carroll on Personal Responsibility
I find most of my resentments are with my kids, because I want them to do what I say instead of what they must

do. What is frightening is that I really believe I'm right. Then I think of my mother and my dad, who is gone, and say, "What would have happened to me if I had done things the way they wanted me to?" The only thing they wanted me to do was get my college degree. I couldn't have used that degree. I can't even use it now. It has not been necessary to my life. I am better educated without it, as a matter of fact. If I had followed their wishes I would have missed some tremendous life experiences. I would have missed the beginnings of my career. The way I did it was best for me. I resent my kids because they don't do what I tell them to do, yet I know they have to do it themselves.

You have to whistle your own tune. You have to walk along the track yourself. Nobody else can lead you. Nobody else can really help you. Once you get the feeling that it is your responsibility, it is the most freeing thing in the world.

Carole Bayer Sager on Choice

Burt and I did a concert and afterward went to dinner in a small restaurant. Two couples were arguing with each other. They were so loud that we ended up listening to them. The women were talking about women's lib. One woman worked and the other didn't. By dessert, the woman who didn't work had come over to our table and was crying. She said, "I'm just so unhappy. I'm just miserable. My life is over. I don't know what to do with my life. I'm trapped." I said, "How can you be trapped? How is anybody trapped? You can change."

"It's sad," she said. "In the sixties I had my life in front of me. I was on my way to Canada when I met him. He was going to be a lawyer. He was a trial lawyer, but he's gone into wills now. He does wills and I hate it, I wish he'd go back to trial law." She said, "It's easy for you to say 'change.' You can do anything. You're successful and you're rich, but what can I do? It's him and the three kids." It was an unforgettable scene and I really felt for her. I said, "You have to stop blaming him, just as a start. You just can't blame him for your whole life; you have to take responsibility. You were a partner in this choice and you still have a choice.''

Every single one of us has a choice all the time. Sometimes we don't have a choice about things that happen to us, but we have a choice about how we deal with them. This woman saw herself as having no choices. If you have no choices, you're pretty unhappy. If you can see yourself always as having a choice, it's a lot easier. Happiness is a choice and happiness is having a choice.

Jimmy Coco on Anger

I used to make a list of the twenty-five things that really made me boil, really made me aggravated. I promised myself I would cross off one every day, just one. I'd start at the bottom and say, ''Why am I still angry at this? This happened twenty years ago. Get rid of it!'' I'd cross it off and never think about it again. Or I'd say, ''I'm really irritated at this person. How stupid, it's just jealousy. Forget about it.'' And I'd cross it off. I'd look at the next one. ''I don't have to still feel sorry about this.'' And I'd cross it off. It would narrow itself down to maybe three or four things that I was still struggling with, but that's so much better than twenty-five.

People should realize that there are many things that they can never change, some that happened years ago. Stop it already, it's enough. Stop tormenting yourself with all that garbage. There's nothing you can do about it. A lot of these things are so unimportant, and they're such a waste of time.

Dr. Joyce Brothers on Adjustment

The adjustments my husband and I have made have all happened so gradually that we weren't aware of them. The only time we became conscious of our adjustments was when we went on a trip with another couple. When we wanted to go walking, they wanted to sleep; when they wanted to sleep, we wanted to go to a movie. What surprised us was that we as a couple were in total agreement about what we wanted to do, and we were at loggerheads with the other couple.

All these adjustments got us to the point in life where if he says, "Let's go to the movies," I'm up for it, even though I know it's a movie I don't really want to see. This has been the nature of our lives and our adjustments. I have never really thought of them as we've been doing them. They've just been done.

John Naisbitt on Optimism
I get accused of being an optimist as if it were a grave crime. But it's the optimists who get things done in the world, not the cynics or the pessimists.

Carole Bayer Sager on Envy and Jealousy
Some people think being happy is just about success and about acquisition. It's not "Whoever has the most toys at the end of life wins." People who look at Hollywood lives on *Entertainment Tonight* think, "Wow, that's the life." But I know miserable people who attend the big events shown on television. They're perceived as happy by the public at large. They're not happy because they're owned by what they think they're supposed to be. They're not free. They're not in touch. They're not even aware. They're just going through the motions. Their talent keeps them successful, so it gives them the appearance of happiness.

Marva Collins on Love
People need nurturing all the time. Everybody feels better with a hug. Everybody feels better when they hear "I love you." For some reason we stop saying, "I love you," in relationships and marriages. It's the flowers, it's the candy, it's the perfume. We think of love as something that's given only to young children. We think of love as something that's given only in a new relationship. It's like a new car. When it's new, we wash it and keep it clean. As it gets older, we let it go. Love has to be kept up constantly.

Shelley Duvall on Negative People

It's not very pleasant to be around people who are negative and unenthusiastic. I don't have a whole lot of respect for people who don't have a curiosity about life. I have empathy for them, feel sorry for them, but I don't necessarily want to be around them.

Pat Carroll on Communication

We all have some guilt, a feeling that we are doing something wrong when we are doing something for ourselves. I'm not a person who functions because of guilt, nor can I function with guilt. If I feel it, I deal with it immediately. I call the person whom I feel guilty about and say, "I'm feeling lousy. Was I wrong about this? Did I do something to hurt you? Did I do something that was untoward?— because I'm really feeling lousy."

It is pain that goads me into an action that will help me. My children have been the ones who have taught me to open up more on this level, particularly my older daughter, who is a natural psychologist. I used to not talk when I was upset. I'd freeze up. My daughter was the one who finally said, "I can't take this anymore. I'm not going to live with twenty-four hours of silence from you. Now, what the hell is in your craw? Let's sit down right this minute and don't get on the phone and don't go out, because we are going to settle this right now." Don't harbor resentment, rancor, guilt, whatever the hell it is. Get it out. Don't have little hickeys all over your face and your body. Get them out of the bloody system. The pipes get clogged and really back up. You're not going to have a plumber's helper in your hand all the time. My kids have helped me to open up more.

Ken Kragen on Pain

My first wife left me at a point in my life when parts of our marriage were less than perfect. Yet, overall, it wasn't bad. She was a good friend and a good person. I got bronchial pneumonia and I got depressed. The depression probably came first. I was depressed because I hadn't found a meaningful relationship. I'd had a lot of fun, but

I was missing sharing certain things. I got turned off women. I got to where I didn't want to date and didn't seek to date anybody. It lasted about four months. I got lonely. I forced my own loneliness. I created it. I got lonely to the point of pain, physical pain. I suddenly recognized that loneliness could be a physical pain, and you could feel it, and it hurt. Then I thought, "Here I am, single and well-off financially. What about an eighty-year-old woman who's lost her husband, who's on welfare, who's got nothing in her life and most of her friends have died? What about that kind of loneliness? I know there's a solution to this." I turned the thing around.

One of the best things that ever happened to me was to go through that terribly depressed, lonely period, because it gave me a tremendous appreciation for what it was like. I'd never had a period like that in my life before. Even with something as severe as that, I turned it around and viewed it as something I was really thankful for. When I got through that period, I felt that I would never be uncomfortable being alone again. I learned, during that time, how to live with myself and be happy by myself, if necessary.

Burt Bacharach on Faith
I believe in God. It's an invented religion. I had no religious upbringing, so I kind of just constructed my own. It's a hope. It's important for me to say my prayers every night. I don't ever miss.

Helen Thomas on Self-esteem
Maybe some people are born with more self-esteem than others. When you have an inferiority complex, and probably the majority do, self-esteem is often a long time in coming. As you grow in stature you realize that you have to make sharper judgments and you have to be willing to rely on yourself a lot more. You really toughen your own value judgments of others and how you want to be treated and how you treat others. We learn by growth and development and by living itself.

You have to learn to say no. Yet you don't have to say

it unkindly. You can't be all things to all people. If you think that being liked or being loved is the most important thing, you may try to be ingratiating, but you may sell a bit of your soul. As you get older, you find that it's less necessary. You let the chips fall where they may. You have more a sense of being yourself. It isn't that you don't care what others think—far from it—but you all went through that. Now you have more of the ideal of what you think of yourself.

John Naisbitt on Being Right

One day, a long time ago, I realized how powerful it was not to have to be right. If you have to be right, then that's what is really running you rather than you just being you. Not having to be right makes you very open. You say, "Oh well, maybe I'm wrong about that. What do you think?" If you have to be right, you're in there arguing your position, and you're closed down. You hunker down on it. The real secret is knowing how powerful it is not to have to be right. Not many people know that.

Dr. Ashley Montagu on Attitude

Large numbers of people find themselves in circumstances in which it is impossible to be happy or even to imagine being happy. However, even under conditions that some people find impossible, there are people who can be happy.

I recall two young men whom I met shortly after the end of World War II who had spent two years in Auschwitz. At one time they lived in Vienna in a cellar where they'd been kept by some Christian friends of their family, all of whom had been exterminated because they were Jews. At the end of the war they walked all the way from Vienna to Berlin, where they thought they had relatives. They didn't find their relatives, but they were picked up by an American Jewish soldier who brought them to America. Both of them wanted to be doctors, and that's where I came into the act. I was teaching medical school and my friend, who had brought them to this country, asked me whether I could do anything for them.

I interviewed them and asked how it was that they happened to be such cheerful characters? They didn't exhibit any of the scars that one might have expected from their unhappy existence. They said, "A group of us decided that no matter what happened it wouldn't get us down and we would survive." They did this by attempting to be as cheerful under those circumstances as they could, never yielding for a moment to the idea that they were in any way inferior to their captors and their guards.

So, depending on your temperament, it's possible to overcome the most untoward circumstances. These two people were quite healthy human beings. If you have positive qualities, you can find happiness in the face of unhappiness.

Jack Anderson on Resentments

I have had many people approach me with what I am sure are legitimate grievances. Somebody didn't get a promotion that he was entitled to because a falsehood was told about him. Or someone got shafted by his boss, who blamed him for something that someone else had done. Or someone didn't get the inheritance that he was entitled to or the pension that was owed to him. So many of them are obsessed by the injustice that was done to them that it has ruined their lives. The obsession has become much bigger than the injustice. Don't dwell or brood on any injustice. If it's an injustice, accept the Mormon philosophy, which says that out there somewhere is a perfect law of justice. You will get compensation for every injury done to you, and you will pay for every wrong you do to others, if not in this life, in another one. Brooding about an injustice that has been done to you will compound the problem. There is something to be said for being able to close the door on these things.

Shelley Duvall on Self-pity

You cannot count on other people for your happiness. You have to count on yourself. There are too many wonderful things in this world to ever say "I'm bored" or "My life is horrible."

Margo Howard on Self-acceptance

I have great acceptance of my shortcomings. If something is loose in my head, I say, "Okay, that's me, and I don't do that very well." I'm sure that there are people close to me who think that I'm too accepting of my own shortcomings, but it offers me comfort. The acceptance may be the key to why I feel good most of the time.

Marva Collins on Risk

There's no such thing as a "happily ever after" situation. The man on the white horse doesn't come and whisk you away. That just doesn't happen. There isn't a castle that doesn't leak, or lawns that don't have to be mowed, or flowers that don't have to be tended.

I've had people ask me, "If you're such a good person, why do bad things happen to you?" Bad things are no respecter of person. The more you do, the more you're subject to bad things happening to you. The more you step out of line, the more you're going to have problems. You're susceptible because you're not playing it safe. When you play it safe, nobody punches you. If you don't reach out, you're never going to get rejected.

Everybody's looking for that perfect situation. Everything has a price. Success has a price. Failure has a price.

Ted Shackelford on Change

If you don't like something about yourself, change it. If you can't change it, then accept it.

Carole Bayer Sager on Balance

I don't think fun is the same as happy, but you have to have some fun if you're going to be happy. You can't just work on yourself. When you're driven, you're so busy pursuing happiness that you're a mess. Let me do my yoga, let me do my exercise workout, let me eat right, let me do my work. All those things have some connection to a holistic kind of approach to happiness.

Og Mandino on Appreciation

On a TV show I did in Los Angeles, one of the guests was a famous author of romance novels. She was complaining about her two teenage boys. They were driving her *bonkers*—that was the word she used. Their rooms were always a mess and they both had stereos tuned up very loud to different stations. I had just gone through seeing my youngest off to college. I said to her, "The day's going to come when you're going to walk down that hall, past two very quiet rooms. You're going to ask yourself, 'Where did they go?' " I told the audience, "Go home and hug your kids."

May Sarton on Pets

Animals are great givers of happiness. I think as one grows older it's absolutely essential to have animals. It forces people to take care of something. What gets me up at five o'clock is my cat, Tamis. He wants to get up. I'm often asleep and I don't want to get up, but then I'm delighted because I really want to get started on the day. Tamis does that for me.

Margo Howard on Action

Activity is a great antidote for sitting around and worrying.

Jimmy Coco on Being Positive

I try never to be negative. I am most definitely a positive person. I can't stand it when I see negative people. I say, "Why are you doing that to yourself?" You've got to be positive. Be positive about everything. If people are ill, don't bury them, be positive. That miracle can happen.

I was once in a situation that was absolutely death, with a stark raving maniac, and I could have been murdered. It was dreadful, but maybe because I'm an actor I turned it around. The man was a chauffeur who'd gone berserk. He was driving a limo I'd hired from a rental agency, and he was going to kill me. I was trapped in the car, and I said to myself, "It won't happen. I just know it won't happen. I won't let it happen." I became very calm. He had locked all the doors. I just kept talking and talking and convinced him to stop at a certain corner so I could make a phone call. I got away from that person. I never for one moment doubted that I would. I think that's because I'm so positive, I wouldn't let it happen.

Dr. Joyce Brothers on Self-discovery

In each of us are places where we have never gone, which is very surprising. You'd think that you would know yourself after having lived with yourself for a lifetime. There are places in me that I didn't know existed. Only by pressing the limits do you ever find them.

I'm a city person, born and raised in New York. When I was a kid I was told that cows slept on their backs at night so the cream would be on top in the morning, and I believed it. I had no contact with the country. It was just not part of my life, and it was of zilch interest to me.

My husband decided we ought to have a farm. I dragged my toes along the sidewalk for a bit, hoping he would get over his enthusiasm. Finally we bought a farm, and I started to put things in the ground. I discovered in myself a love for growing things that I did not know existed.

I think that the places inside ourselves that we don't know are there are sources of happiness that can be explored if only we're willing to try something new.

Dr. Joe Arends on Self-improvement

One of my heroes is Abraham Lincoln. Of all his admirable qualities, the one Lincoln treasured most was that every year he was able to say to himself, ''I get better every year.'' I try to achieve so that every year I get a little better. I get a little better in my emotional well-being. I get a little better when I can communicate my ideas and my thoughts. I even get a little more effective with my family. I become a little better at control of my life. I can do a lot of little things every year and get a little bit better all the time. I'm never going to be perfect, but I'm always going to get a little better.

Rabbi Harold S. Kushner on Helping Others
The more I feel sorry for myself, the more I go into a downward spiral. My home remedy for depression and self-pity is to find somebody to help. Going out of my way to be nice to somebody lifts me up. When I feel frustrated by what I haven't been able to accomplish, I think of all the people I have helped get through crises in their lives. When I feel really down on myself, one of the things I do is visit people in the hospital. It's not because I want to be reminded that some people are worse off than I; that's cruel. People are not sick in order to make me feel lucky. However, the experience of giving to somebody pulls me out of my self-pity.

Jack Anderson on Self-importance
I look at the universe and I know there's an architect. A universe that runs with such precision did not just happen. I think we live in the most exciting time in history. Not since Columbus has there been anything like it. That must have been an exciting time, an adventurous time to live. Every generation needs a dream to inspire it, an adventure to ennoble it, and I don't know of any adventure in the history of mankind as exciting as the challenge of space. We are just on the shores of outer space, beginning to learn the lessons that are out there, beginning to explore the planets. The more you see of the universe, the better you understand it. One of the astronauts told me that when he was in orbit an astronomer was among those on the shuttle. The astronomer, with great excitement, spotted a galaxy two million light years away, and he called the others around him to show them his great discovery. Then he said, "I wonder if it's still there." They were seeing ancient, ancient, ancient history. When you think in those terms, it's preposterous, it's incredible, it's unbelievable to suggest that we're the only formal life in all of this vast mosaic.

Tom Peters on Self-respect
For the sake of sanity, pleasure, and relationships, I developed a set of rules that I stick to with very, very rare

exceptions. I do nothing on weekends. I don't do things out of the Bay area of California on Mondays and Fridays. I do my national travel on Tuesdays, Wednesdays, and Thursdays. I haven't tried to use the notoriety that's come along to get involved in the social side of things. I don't go to the "right" parties.

I get a fair number of invitations, and because I believe that I have an obligation to participate, I will give, say, $500 for a dinner to honor some scientist. But I damn well won't go to it. I really try to protect a substantial hunk of my soul from the greedy who would consume me if I wanted to be consumed. I do what I do and I try to do it as best I can. I try to keep myself intellectually retooled and save my spare time for watching the grapes grow, spending time with Kate and her kids, and reading.

I speak to many groups. Each one wants you to come in the night before to have dinner with the chairman. "If you can't come the night before, can you come in and have breakfast with the chairman at seven o'clock?" It would be nice to do, and I'm sure they're all lovely human beings, but that's one of my clearest cut-off points. Learning to say no is difficult for everybody. I know that it's been hard for me to learn to do it.

I've also learned to be a complete tyrant in demanding the best equipment, for example, in audiovideo materials and the right kind of microphone. I say, "I want a cordless, lapel, clip-on microphone or I ain't coming. What I'm trying to tell you is, in the end, you're going to be happy that I'm being a real jerk right now."

Kate and I bought a farm in Vermont about a year ago. That was a dream. We work hard with our rules to make sure I do a certain number of things on the East Coast so we can spend four- and five-day weekends in Vermont a half dozen times a year. The ability to be able to carve out space, whether it's a dream like Vermont or building enough self-confidence to say "I'm not coming to dinner," has come very, very slowly. The ability to say that has been, in a lot of respects, my personal accomplishment of the last couple of years.

Og Mandino on Giving Love

If you want to bring more sunshine into your life, start treating all those with whom you come in contact—family, friends, customers, even enemies—as if you knew a very deep, dark secret about them. The deep, dark secret is that they are going to be dead by midnight.

Carole Bayer Sager on Happiness

I read a famous story about a man who was miserable all his life. He pretended to be happy, but it was just pretend. In fact, he became what he pretended to be. When he died, he was a happy person.

Rabbi Harold S. Kushner on Life

If I were seventy-five and looking back on my life, I suspect the question that would bother me most would not be "How much longer do I have to live?" but "Have I used my time well?" I would think the scariest thing for elderly people is not the fear of dying, but the sense that maybe they didn't live the way they were supposed to—that they had one chance to be alive and they blew it.

Max Cleland on Reaching Out

I have a friend who is an expert on stress. He studied the subject for fifteen years, and he gives a thumbnail sketch of the difference between a victim and a survivor. A victim says, "I can't do it because look what's happened to me." A survivor says, "I *can* do it because look what's happened to me." It is possible to overcome things by the grace of God and with the help of friends. I went on my own strength for a long time, and I realized that I could be broken.

Life breaks us all. There's not a one of us who can stand up to life by ourselves. If we try, we're going to continue to stumble. What I've realized is that the valleys of life are an opportunity to learn. One of the things we learn is that we can't do this thing called life on our own. We have to want to move forward, but moving forward out of the valley may teach us that we have to accept the grace of God and the help of friends in the process. Then we get strong at the broken places and are able to move through the valley. When we get to the other side of the valley, we have a greater sense of happiness and enjoyment and pleasure and appreciation than before we went through the valley.

The Lord didn't set us up to fail. We're winners. Not that we're going to win everything and achieve everything. We're supposed to be successful in life. We're supposed to move forward through our valleys. We're built that way. We're supposed to have a sense of overcoming, a sense of being content and happy, a sense of serenity. When the valleys come, and that's usually the most difficult time for us—it's when it's most difficult for me—it's not a bad thing to know to keep on moving.

Pat Carroll on Being Nice

The magazines for the young women have all the secrets for becoming Miss Congeniality. Everybody forgets the basic thing: people are not going to love you unless you love them. It has to start with you. You can't wait for others to love you. You have to love them first. By God, it pays off. If you feel ''those bums'' are out there, they are going to be there the minute you walk out the door. All the bums are going to be there waiting to poke you in the jaw. On the other hand if you smile and say, ''Good morning'' to those same people, almost without exception they'll be startled. But then they'll relax and say, ''Oh, good morning.''

Four of us went to Ashland, Oregon, to attend a Shakespeare festival. I had never been there before. We saw six shows in five days. Beautiful. There's an outdoor Shakespearean stage and an indoor seven-hundred-seat theater. It was wonderful. Everyplace we walked, in every store, every Bed and Breakfast, every restaurant, people looked at us and smiled and said, ''How are you?'' They really wanted to know how we were. We wouldn't have dared tell them we were ''lousy.'' We were in a small town whose citizens knew it was wonderful. People opened doors for other people—it didn't make any difference for whom. Women opened doors for men. Humans together.

They smiled. They shook hands. They said, "How are you? Are you enjoying the show?"

We walked out of the Elizabethan theater one night. The costuming, the lighting, the acting, had been wonderful. I suddenly became very aware of something. I thought, "What is this?" There was no shoving. There was no pushing. There was no yelling. There were no high-pitched voices. People were talking. Very pleasant. There were no policemen. We were all walking out like human beings who respected each other. I realized, "We're acting civilized. We're acting as if we have regard for each other. We aren't pushing our bodies. We aren't offending our sense of hearing. We aren't taking advantage of one another's spaces. We are regarding each other." I thought, "I like this place. Why can't we act like this in New York and Chicago? Why can't we do that?" It made things so pleasant for each of us. It was that marvelous thing of being nice to one another. Nice is a dull word. *Nice?* What is that? Seventeenth century? I say we could use a bit more of it. I want a dollop of nice every hour. It is so easy to make life more pleasant for one another. We don't have to take out our credit cards for a smile.

12   Action

Action is the name of the happiness game. Unhappy people sit and dwell on their apparent misfortunes and contemplate how bad their lives are. Isolation and loneliness compound the unhappiness. The answer to solving the problem of unhappiness is often to get out of the house, get out of ourselves, and get with other people. Happy people know that their happiness is their choice and a direct result of their positive actions. They are not afraid. They are curious about life and how it works, and their interest in things outside themselves motivates them to action. *Am I curious about life? Am I actively seeking my own happiness?*

Jack Anderson talks about his willingness to get involved. "I am constantly being spurred to take on new challenges."

Jack Anderson is considered to be the "most trusted and best-read newspaper reporter" according to a nationwide survey conducted by President Ronald Reagan's private pollster, Richard Wirthlin. Jack's political column appears in more than a thousand newspapers throughout American and abroad. A winner of the Pulitzer Prize for national journalism, Jack Anderson is the epitome of an investigative reporter.

Jack Anderson

I was the oldest son of rather stern Mormon parents. They expected me to live a righteous and virtuous life. They expected me to attend church and tend to my duties. Frankly, it never occurred to me to do otherwise. It was not only something they preached, it was how they lived.

One of my more graphic memories is of a father who met one of my friends on a bitter cold wintry evening. My father was lugging a Christmas tree that he had purchased two blocks up the street. He had stopped for his first rest when my friend confronted him. He said hello. My father was muttering. My friend said, "What's the matter?" My father said, "I just bought this doggone Christmas tree and I just counted my change. That fellow gave me twenty-five cents too much. Now I have to go all the way back." It didn't occur to my father not to return the quarter. He was very annoyed because he had to go back to return the money he had been overpaid.

At a later time my father was traveling in England and came down with a slight malady, but it was serious enough that he was taken to a hospital. At the end of his stay he asked for the bill, but since his medical care was provided through the national health plan, there was no bill. He was outraged; he wanted to pay for the services. He was told that it couldn't be done. So he estimated the cost of the services, went out, bought gifts equaling the amount he thought the services were worth, and came back and distributed the gifts to the doctors and nurses who had taken care of him. This was a father who was poor. He never had money.

I remember getting five dollars from him a while ago. This five dollars, which was a good piece of change for him, was in repayment for something that he apparently felt he owed me. I have no idea what it was, but I knew better than to return it. His pride and independence are worth far more than five dollars.

Mother had equal integrity. Father had an explosive temperament, but Mother never got excited. My daughter told me that when she took her fiancé to meet her grand-

parents, my father immediately started on a tactless dia-
tribe that suited his mood of the moment. In the middle
of it he stopped abruptly and addressed my mother, saying, "Agnes, stop kicking me under the table." My
mother is calm, cool, reserved, unmoved by his volcanic
moods and unaffected by them.

Most Mormon young people are called for two years of
service in which the missionaries work with the people,
assisting them both practically and spiritually. I had my
two years. During that period my parents had to support
me because the church does not pay the way. My parents
were always poor. So my mother got a job driving a taxi
for the sole purpose of sending me the money so that I
could live and do my missionary work.

When Dad would ask us to do something, we would
ignore him until he reached a certain decibel level. We
knew he really didn't mean it until he was yelling at the
top of his lungs. Mother would just speak in her normal
voice and if she said to sit, we wouldn't even turn around
to see if there was a chair. We would sit. I don't know
why I felt I had to obey Mother but that I didn't have to
worry about Dad.

My two younger brothers and I had a happy childhood.
I was very conscious of being poor. My parents moved to
an affluent section of the Salt Lake valley because the
schools and the environment were better. But they were
over their heads. They bought a house that was more expensive than they could afford. We wound up having to
live in the basement and renting out the upper stories.
Because there was no bathroom in the basement, they built
an outhouse. We had to use a laundry tub, the only sink
in the basement, for baths. All my friends were the children of wealthy parents. However, I never felt inferior to
them. In fact, I was the student body president of our
junior high and later of our high school. These very kids
were the ones who elected me. But there *was* a certain
humiliation in having my affluent friends who lived in fine
homes come to visit me in the basement and have to go
outside to use the bathroom.

One of the great values of the Mormon church is its

belief in freedom and free agency. Mormons believe the eternal struggle is not just between good and evil, but also between freedom and force. Wherever you find force, that is evil. True development comes from freedom of choice. Every man and woman among us has the right to make the wrong choices, but happiness comes from making the right choices. True happiness comes not from pleasure but from achievement. Real joy does not come from inheriting money or finding money; rather, it comes from earning it. It is better to climb mountains than to sit on your fanny and slide down them. This is my own version, of course; you wouldn't find quite that wording in the doctrine. You gain strength and experience from overcoming obstacles. The strength and the experience are what's worthwhile. If you have no obstacles to overcome, you have somehow been deprived.

A disinterested observer commenting on my career would say that I have a successful one. But like so many people who have had a successful career, I find a certain insecurity. We are a little afraid that down underneath it all people will discover how inadequate we really are. In my hair-down talks with celebrities and successful men and women, I have detected this underlying apprehension, and I think I have it as well. I think I have been more successful than I deserve to be and that I have not been as successful as I would like to be and should be. The newspaper column is the most successful political column in the United States, but instead of settling down and enjoying that, I have accepted new challenges.

I have taken on the Young Astronaut Program, which is calculated to stimulate the younger generation into preparing for the twenty-first century. It's going to be the technological age, the space age, the information age, and our children are not ready for it. We must broaden our base. The object of the Young Astronaut Program is to familiarize our kids with the technological tools that will be everyday equipment in the future.

I have become co-chairman with Peter Grace of the Campaign to Reduce Waste in Government. I have watched the way the bureaucrats and special interests operate in Washington for over thirty-eight years. Through their champions on Capitol Hill, they collect all the taxes they can get and they spend all that they collect, plus as much more as they can get away with. When the public gets alarmed or when there is a budget crunch, they immediately call for more taxes. They never offer to cut their excessive spending. In my years here, the income of the median family of four has increased seven and a half times, but the amount of taxes that family pays on its income has increased 246 times. The problem has been not too much taxation or too little taxation, but too much spending, and the way to cut back, in my opinion, is to cut out the waste. We have our work cut out for us, but if we don't do it I think we could spend ourselves into chaos. Five million people have signed up with us in the battle against government waste. I get satisfaction from that, but not contentment because there's still too much more to do.

I have never looked on myself as an alienated critic, but rather as part of the process. I believe our country is strong enough to be criticized, and it is essential that we criticize. I look upon what I do as similar to what a doctor does. If you were told you had cancer that would be terrible news. It's not something you would want to hear, but the doctor would be doing you a great service by telling you that you had the disease. Then you could receive treatment for it and perhaps be cured. If it were incurable, you would still be better off knowing it; then you could adjust to it and make preparations. Our government is strong. I am in the business of pointing out the cancer with the hope that I am pointing it out in time so we can cut it out and treat it.

I am by nature an amiable person who does not like to upset people, but I upset people probably as much as anyone in the United States does. It's a peculiar job for someone of my temperament to have. I do it because I believe that it is an important job. Most people would rather lose an arm or a leg than their good names and their good reputations. Yet I assail the reputations of public figures. I do it because they are public officers of public trust.

Those who abuse that trust have to be exposed, and so I expose them, for the good of the rest of us. I can't say that I enjoy it. I create very powerful enemies in the process.

The struggle for power is much more intense than the struggle for money. People will do for power what they would not do for money. The things I write about affect the power struggle. Those whom I deprive of power, those whose power is threatened by my column, do remarkable things to stop me. I have tried to be fair. I have tried to be accurate. Politicians, when they hit back, don't try to be fair. They have accused me of being a traitor, called me a Communist, called me a crook. In cavalier moments I act as if they don't bother me, but in fact they do. They would bother anyone.

Richard Nixon and Jimmy Carter would have liked to destroy me. They looked for ways to discredit me. Both of them believed that I played an important role in depriving them of power. I hope they're right, because they did not deserve the power they held. One was venal and the other was incompetent. Neither of them deserved to be president of the United States. If I played a role in keeping them from continuing in the office, then I did something worthwhile.

I am a very careful reporter, not a reckless one. I am extremely concerned about the individuals I write about, even the Jimmy Carters and the Richard Nixons. I understand and sympathize with their human reactions. I tell my reporters how important it is to be fair. So, being that kind of person, I can say, "Yes, I'm fair." When somebody accuses me of something I know is wrong, yes, I fret a little about it. But it's nothing I brood about or worry about too much because there is nothing I can do about it. I never have figured that I should spend too much time worrying about something I can't change. I don't worry about the weather. I have never learned how to change it. I just try to adapt to it. There are other things that I cannot change, so I do my best to adjust.

One thing I can't change is the past. People have condemned me for my past actions. Sometimes they are

absolutely justified, but they go on and on. I have made
some bad decisions in the past. I have done things that
I would do differently if I had them to do over. When
people assail me, I listen to the diatribes about the mistakes I have made. I finally end it by saying, "All right,
you have made your point. Let's go back and do it over
again."

I made an unforgivable mistake about Senator Tom Eagleton, which was just bad reporting, in a story about
drunken driving. It was at the time when Eagleton was
losing his place on the Democratic ticket with George Mc-
Govern. I went to Eagleton's office and apologized to him.
He called in the press and I went out, looked into the
television camera with him standing beside me, and I said,
"I made a mistake and I want to apologize for it." Change
what you can. What you absolutely can't change, adjust
to. That's the best key to happiness.

I'm not as bold and brave as I am curious. I have been in
many dangerous situations as a correspondent. I was in Vietnam. I was in Beruit when Israeli bombs were falling all
around me. I was a war correspondent in World War II. I
took chances, not because I was foolhardy, not because I
was brave. I took chances because I was curious. I feel I have
a passion as well. But that passion keeps me dissatisfied, and
there is always a gnawing in the pit of my stomach because
I'm never quite satisfied. I never feel I have done quite as
well as I should have, or know as much as I want to. That
does not weigh heavily, but it does spur me into new action.
I have happiness, but I am not content.

My family warms the cockles of my heart. When I
drive home of an evening and see the car of one of my
kids parked outside, particularly if some of my grandchildren may be visiting, it's uplifting. I look forward to
getting inside the door. With the love of my family and
friends I could survive very easily if I didn't achieve anything more.

As we grow older the days seem to go by more slowly,
but the years go by more quickly. When we were children

next month's summer vacation seemed ten million light years away. As adults we are not happy with the thought that another birthday is here already. In evaluating our lives we should be able to look back with justifiable pride on our accomplishments and look forward to the things we still want to do. It is wonderful to say to ourselves, "I have used my time well," still anticipating with enthusiasm and optimism that the best is yet to come. *What have I accomplished? What are ten things I want to do?*

Cleveland Amory derives his happiness from making a contribution. He says, "You can give of your talent, you can give of your possessions, or you can give of yourself. For God's sake, give something."

Cleveland Amory is well known to American readers as a social critic and author of such books as The Proper Bostonians, Who Killed Society? *and* Man Kind: Our Incredible War on Wildlife. *He has written regularly for such magazines as* TV Guide, This Week, *and* Saturday Review *and currently writes profile pieces for* Parade *magazine. He is the founder and unpaid president of the Fund for Animals, which has over two hundred thousand members and is regarded as one of the most effective anticruelty societies in the world.*

Cleveland Amory

Happiness is not a subject that a Bostonian who wants to go back to Boston would care to discuss. Happiness in Boston, when I grew up, was a word for children. If you were no longer a child, that is, over thirty, you should not want to think of such childish things as happiness. You should want to put it aside. A man who was told he was a happy person was not suitable for the family firm. Although a Bostonian did not like to contemplate the possibility of a Bostonian having mental aberrations, a happy person was considered to have a serious defect.

The Puritan inheritance in the proper Boston I grew up

in literally made happiness unacceptable as an option. You had an option to compete with your brothers and others within and without your family. You also had an option to make something of yourself, and you had the option of making a lot of money while you were doing it. As an uncle of mine once said, "If I can do a good deed and at the same time make money, I feel all of my powers moving in harmonious cooperation."

My brother was a very fine student. He got five A's his freshman year, was elected to Phi Beta Kappa, and received his degree magna cum laude, going through college in three years. He was on the *Harvard Law Review* as well. That made it impossible for me to compete scholastically, so it left two other fields, athletics and extracurricular activities. Athletics were difficult because the New York Yankees at that time had stolen Babe Ruth from the Boston Red Sox, which left a sour taste for baseball in all good proper Bostonians. I was not quite fast enough anyway. I could hit a baseball pretty well and played pretty fair tennis, but I was not good enough to make a go of it. Instead I went out for the school paper, the *Milton Academy Orange and Blue*, got to be head of that, and then at Harvard became editor of the *Harvard Crimson*. That launched me on a writing career.

People ask me from time to time if I like to write. I know if they ask that, they are (a) a little bit off their rockers or (b) not very good writers. There's no such thing as enjoying writing. You're not even allowed to enjoy something nice that somebody may have said about your writing. That leaves a pretty bleak future. However, the Boston character has always sympathized with the downtrodden so that helps.

I had really espoused no cause of any kind until I saw a bullfight when I was working for my first newspaper, the *Arizona Daily Star*. Bullfights were held across the way in Nogales, Mexico. Working in Nogales, Arizona, I was sent to Mexico to write something nice about our sister-city relationship, as it was called. I was a little nervous about the bullfight, but the promoter had told me not to worry. He said it really was a wonderful end for the bull, compared to dying in a slaughterhouse. After the bullfight his meat was given to the poor people, so that was good. I shouldn't worry about the picadors' horses, I was told; the padding covered them completely. If the bull was very brave, he told me, he would be pardoned and go to some field where he'd have the cows of his choice for the rest of his life. It was the most dangerous sport in the world and matadors dropped by the hundreds in the ring, he assured me.

At the end of the first two fights, even the promoter was absolutely appalled by what we were seeing. The horses were blindfolded on the side the bull charges from, and their vocal cords were cut so they couldn't scream when the bull was coming at them. Of course, the bull's horns got under the padding, so the horses were really unprotected. Even Hemingway admitted that when the picador got through, the bull had no fight in him at all because he had no neck muscles. He can't do anything with his head but go up and down. That's why the matador can do all that fancy-pancy stuff beside him. As far as the moment of truth goes, there wasn't one clean kill that day. Most of the time the bull was mournfully going along the sidelines, trying to find a place to die quietly. I just got madder and madder.

It was a damp day and the cushions that came with the seats were real soggy. I went down toward the front with my cushion. One time when the matador came around with the two ears of the bull I let the cushion fly and hit him right back of the ear with it. We Bostonians never said we weren't good pitchers. We thought Babe Ruth was a pitcher. I got the matador good, and he went down like a stone. It was one of the best feelings I ever had in my whole life. I felt so good about it. Actually, there was a hush in the place and I yelled, "I know none of you are going to do anything about it because you'd have to be a coward to like something like this," which endeared me to the Mexicans, I'm sure.

When I got back I went to a library, where there were eighteen books about bullfighting on the shelves. Every one of them told how wonderful bullfighting was. Anybody who went to that library would think there was nothing wrong with it. Here was something that was against the law of almost every civilized country in the world. Even countries that didn't have any other laws about animals had laws banning fights of that sort. So I started writing about that, and I joined just about every organization that came along. I got as far as honorary vice president of the National Catholic Society for Animal Welfare, which is surely as far as any Boston Episcopalian can go. I was jeopardizing my future, but I joined them all.

In 1967 I formed the Fund for Animals, dedicated to making a go out of what I saw as damn hard fights ahead. I said at that time we were going to put cleats on the little old ladies in tennis shoes. Nowadays, of course, you couldn't say anything like that, but you could then. I meant no putdown of their size or their age or their footwear, but I did envision tough times ahead and I think the fund has more than justified my hopes for it. The rescue of the burros in the Grand Canyon, the rescue of the dolphins at Iki, Japan, stopping the painting and clubbing of baby seals off the ice floes of Canada, and the ramming off the coast of Portugal of the pirate whaling ship *Sierra*, whose crew was killing every kind of whale, have been important successes.

Since the fund has consumed so much of my time, I have tried to find a way of supporting myself, because I don't like to take money from it. I try to find some way of writing that will make money in a short time. The magazine I work for, *Parade*, certainly has the largest circulation in the country. It pays well and I enjoy the work. I still feel in my conscience that I should be working on books too. That's where the rub comes, because I don't really have much extra time for that. When I go back to the office and there are fourteen telephone messages about abnormal problems in various parts of the country and world, there's a lot of things to attend to.

If you come from my kind of background, you're probably happiest when you don't know it—when you're so busy and there's so much going on that you just enjoy the doing. However, I think my problem, and the problem of many Puritans brought up in my era, is that we don't really stop to enjoy anything. I would think at my age it is high time to be thinking not of what I'm going to do but of what I want to "have done." If I could decide what I want to "have done," knowing what to do would become a hell of a lot easier.

Some people are too young to understand about the "have done" thing, but I think the earlier one can focus on that the better. We really wouldn't do many things, if we knew we were going to have enough to eat and to support the people we love. Why do it for just money? Why do anything for any reason except to "have done" it or in our work to feel we've become better at a particular craft.

I keep thinking, like all people who have led the kind of hectic life that I have, that someday I'll slow down. I will get to smell the roses or travel to Bangkok. Marion Probst, who has worked with me for twenty-seven years, says, "I know you won't do it and if you do it, you'll do it because you get a free lecture tour on a ship." I sigh and respond, "A Bostonian must get it free."

Our happiness is directly related to the roles we play in the lives of others. We all have specific skills and aptitudes. Each of us is unique. When we can use our specialness in cooperation with others for the benefit of others it makes life worth living. *Am I excited about the contribution I am making to the lives of others? What is uniquely me that I can give to others?*

Carol Channing bubbles as she describes her work in the theater. "The thrill of the theater is teamwork. It's harmony. We are all working together in one direction."

Carol Channing's rise to international stardom began with Lend an Ear *and* Gentlemen Prefer Blondes. *She lost count after her three thousandth performance in the role of Dolly Gallagher Levi in* Hello, Dolly! *on Broadway, on tour, and in London. Carol has won Tonys (stage), Emmys (television), Grammys (records), and an Oscar nomination for the film* Thoroughly Modern Millie. *Most recently Carol and Mary Martin co-starred in* Legends.

Carol Channing

Triumph over something makes me happy. Licking the challenge. It seems to me all of life is overcoming. What's the problem here? What's this? Face it. Figure it out. It's just that life isn't rehearsed enough. There's no such thing as luck. There's never going to be a time in life that you don't have sinking challenges. I guess that, just as in childbirth, nothing good comes easily. It seems to be a part of nature. I just dog it. I'm not good at solving problems. It's just that I want things so badly.

I have noticed that the happy people are the ones who have a banner; they believe in it and they dedicate their lives to it. There is nothing they won't do to get to carry that banner. They believe in a cause, a cause they will die for. They give all their energies to it. Every function of their body, their entire metabolism is used in the effort of the job. No matter what's in the way, it's just got to be overcome. I got this from my father. If I needed a leg up, by golly he was there. "Okay, what's the problem?" I'd dump it and then he'd say, "Okay, you do this and don't let anything stop you."

When I was in high school we had a talent contest. I found out from one teacher that I had won, but the other teachers changed the ballot so that a girl who was studying opera with her mother would win because they wanted culture to be the most important thing in school. I was doing comedy. I came home and said to my father, "My gosh, I understand that I really won that contest but they changed the vote and the students don't know anything about it. They made the winner this girl who simply knows how to form her upper epiglottis. They feel that's culture." So my dad said, "All right, are you going to mope about it and carry on like a little baby or are you going straight to the principal and tell him exactly what happened? Don't tell him who told you, just tell him how it happened. Ask him, 'How do you expect us to play fair in life? What kind of rules are these? If we don't find out here in school what makes us win, we never will. We'll go through life thinking, well, the thing to do is take lessons and form your upper epiglottis.' That's not what makes you win in life, that's not it at all.'' My father said, ''You can whine around me or you can handle this situation.''

At school the next morning, I was doing another show, playing an old lady. The drama teacher was making me up for the play, so my hair was full of powder and I had a barber's cape over me. I was sitting there boiling and I thought, ''I can't stand it another minute; I'm going down to Mr. Stevens's office and I'm going to tell him all about it.'' So I went to the principal's office and told him the whole story. I went to the vice principal and told him the story. I was flying through the halls, wearing the cape with my hair all white yelling at the top of my lungs. I went from teacher to teacher, asking, ''How do you expect us to know what wins in life if you don't prove it right here? We've got to know. It's for the fellow students as well as me. You can't twist things like that and have us think that's the way life works. It doesn't work that way.'' My father was a Christian Science lecturer, and I made a Christian Science lecture out of the whole episode. I stood there and hollered and by golly they all bowed down and said, ''You're absolutely right.'' They were wonderful to me. When I graduated, I won the drama award.

I'm so dogged on one goal. From the time I was born I wanted to do just what I'm doing. Naturally, you can enjoy all kinds of things in life, but what's the thing you'll die for and that never leaves you? The happy people are the ones who are carrying a banner and believe in a cause. It doesn't matter what the cause is. They have a banner and they cannot let it down. They have to hand it to the next one if they go down, but they have to keep that banner going. Those are the happy people because then the vicissitudes of life are merely mosquito bites. They don't stop you from the goal.

If I'm late for a show, I have to get there. Doing the show is my way of helping people. I remember talking to Julie Andrews about this. We were making the movie *Thoroughly Modern Millie* and she asked, "What sent you into theater?" Julie is so curious, she wants to know everything. We agreed—but we wouldn't tell anybody else—that we're little Florence Nightingales. We are uplifting the human race for whoever wants to come to see our little production. We honestly believe that. Some people know how to bind up a wound, but to us, our way of being helpful is a world of ideas, a world of emotion. We can create a world that is beyond the table and chair, the mundane. It's the theater. "When I face facts," she said, "I suddenly realize that we think we're little nurses nursing the audience, lifting their lives."

When you see a work of art it opens a new portal for you. Oh, the happiness of having created something that your fellow man considers worth paying to see and which enhances their lives. That's different from sitting there and not trying. I have to try. That's what keeps me after the goal.

People used to say to me before I could get a job in the theater, "Carol, you are impossible to be around. You think that if you get a job in the theater it's going to solve everything." It did for me. Once I got a little bitty job in the theater—in Mark Blitzstein's *No for an Answer*—it solved my whole life. I became the sweetest person to be around, just a doll. I had time to be kind and love people and help them.

It all goes back to the fourth grade, the first time I was on the stage. I was running for class secretary. I did impersonations of people in the school, and the waves of laughter came. They recognized those I was doing and laughed. We were all laughing together. We were all on each other's side. To me it was incredible! I made up my mind right then and there. This is it. Here's my banner, and I won't let it down. I'm going to hang on to it. I don't care what I have to go through. I'm dedicated to it.

False pride, ego, selfishness, and self-importance can lead us to believe that the sun rises and sets just for us. That kind of thinking will get us in trouble. However, there is some truth to the idea that we are the center of our universe. It is an amazing thought to contemplate that the world was created for us and that everything which exists—all the people, places, and things—are available for us to experience and enjoy. It is as if we are children who have been offered a free visit to the candy store. It is only we who limit ourselves, and more often than not, the usual cause of our inability to experience what life and the world have to offer is our self-centered fears. Happy people take risks. They know that sometimes they may fail or not even like the things they try. But they try and they do. They participate in life as an adventure, which continually opens new doors that bring them greater happiness. *Am I meeting new people? Am I trying new experiences?*

Malcolm Forbes states his philosophy in three words: *"While alive, live.* I don't recommend a hedonistic approach. But we'd have been left in the womb if we weren't meant to become people."

Malcomb Forbes is the editor in chief and chairman of the business publication Forbes *magazine. In World War II he was awarded the Bronze Star and Purple Heart. An internationally known balloonist, he was the first person in history to successfully fly coast to coast across America in one hot air balloon. Malcolm has received thirty-four honorary degrees and a variety of awards, including the Order of Merit, the highest civilian honor bestowed by the French government, and Publisher of the Year from the Magazine Publishers Association.*

Malcolm Forbes

People often ask me, "How do I become successful?" I say, "Whatever you like to do, just find a way to do it."

The biggest mistake people make in life is not trying to make a living at doing what they most enjoy. There's no job that's all joy. But to work at a job you hate is probably the biggest waste in life. If you don't care about it or you can get by with it and if you're not really consumed to do anything else, fine. But that's a waste. We're all responsive to something and we do our best when we're doing something that has a turn-on to it. There is no other way to go.

Doing what you like to do is the only way you can be a success. You may have a reputation as the best Christmas tree decorator or the best woodwork polisher. If you love it, you get good at it, and even though it's the furthest thought from your mind, success snowballs. For example, if a guy can repair a car, knows foreign cars and loves them, and is good, he has more business than he can handle. Success follows doing what you want to do. There is no other way to be successful.

The short cut in the arithmetic of money—and people discover this too late—is, of course, to pick parents who have money so you can inherit it. It's a much quicker way to the top than an M.B.A., but it's very hard to do it retrospectively. What you have to do is become the parent and then be sure that your children have a leg up.

Through utter good fortune—and I'm deadly serious—and quite a little inheritance, my business has grown, and I'm making more money than I could ever have contemplated. And there's fun in it, I can tell you. Building a new boat or seeing a motorcycle and being able to buy it is great. However, if I were making $25,000 a year I'd still enjoy what I was doing. I wouldn't have twenty-five motorcycles, but I think that I would have one. I wouldn't have properties all around the world, but I probably would have a cabin on some acreage in the Rockies. People with their cabins can see just as much from their five acres as

I can see from my 250,000 or so acres. Only the scale
would be different. Instead of owning balloons, I'd probably have teamed up with other people to be around balloons. You help the guy who owns the balloon, and then
you get to ride. You crew for somebody. It's more fun to
commission balloons and own them and get into them and
just go, but if I didn't have all this and I were into bal-
looning, I'd find a way to participate. Most things are
achievable on a different scale. Money isn't the first req-
uisite. Everything's relative. People who don't have a lot
of money do go skiing. It's damned expensive because
they have to pay the lift fee, twenty-four bucks or whatever
it is, and then buy skis. But they can go to garage sales
and buy skis for $10 a pair and get the poles for nothing.
Within a modest framework, things are doable when you
want to do them enough.

In other words, money isn't the sole determinant of what
you can do. It has to do with the scale and the scope and
having the best of everything. You can enjoy a sports car
but not everybody can have a Lamborghini. Lots of people
end up souping up their own stock cars and giving them
a personality. That's where their money goes. That's where
their joy goes. If I had less money, instead of having many
pieces of art or many toy soldiers, I might have a few. I
doubt there are many things I'm into now that I wouldn't
be into on an infinitely smaller scale. I can't think of things
that I would have scrubbed, except when I got down to
making choices. If I wanted to make the monthly payment
for the five acres in the Colorado mountains, I'd have to
forgo getting the nifty print or the lithograph. I would
balance things and have much less. I'd have to make my
choice between the new tires for the motorcycle or going
for the ski weekend. Sometimes being forced to make the
choice also makes you relish it more than when you can
have the whole smorgasbord just for the wanting. There's
something to be said for that. The joy comes from having
to sweat a little and sacrifice to get something that is really
important to you.

I've not always had everything. I've never been over the
barrel, but when I was young I wanted a new bicycle. I

had to work all summer to get the money. I wasn't brought up lavishly or wantonly. It was during the Depression, so I couldn't have been even if my father had been so inclined, which he wasn't. People can look at me and say, "It's easy for you to talk like that." For many people, however, the holdback is that the yearning isn't strong enough. Nobody is unable to do something he or she is dedicated to doing. Whatever the adventure, if it's in the mind, if it's something you want enough, there is no reason it can't be done. Most people say, "Oh, I'd love to do that." They read cruise books and say, "Gee, I'd love to go on that cruise." Well, there aren't any working people alive who can't go on a cruise. Maybe they can't also buy a dishwasher or put snow tires on the car, but they can go on a cruise. I'm not talking about the bottom income rung; I'm talking about people with jobs. You have to sort out those eleven things you want. You have to have priorities. The one major reason a lot of people express desires as being unfulfillable is because they don't desire them enough.

No single desire in unfulfillable. People just can't have them all, so they sort them out. They want to have children more than they want to travel, or vice versa. They can't do both. One's going to cancel the other for twenty years, but they make choices all the time. Very often it isn't the fact that they can't afford something, it's the fact that they don't want it enough to afford it at the expense of other things.

Very often you don't have either the focus or the opportunity to do a lot of things that you hoped to do when you were young. I'm talking about sports, travel, and active pursuits. You put them aside because of a wife and children and home and job pressure and earning a living. Number one, that's a mistake. Squeeze them in if they're worth doing. It's a turn-on for kids. Going skiing with Papa is great for a kid. You don't have to turn off activity as early as most people do. To say that there's any age at which you shouldn't take a crack at something is foolish.

In your teens or in high school or college, if you can't play some sport, you're less inclined to try it. Kids tend to make excuses: "Oh, I hate to go horseback riding" or "I think skiing's stupid." What they can't do, they knock because of peer pressure. By the time you're forty-eight, say the hell with peer pressure. You don't care if you fall down while learning. The thing to do is to try when you get the chance. "Motorcycles. Who in their right mind . . . ?" It was only because I heard that reaction that I got on one. A young fellow who wanted to borrow the money to buy a bike gave me a ride, and I found that I enjoyed it. I bought a little trail bike to start. It was a whole new experience. I do a lot of motorcycle riding now to make up for all the wasted years.

Things are adventurous only if you don't do them. If you're doing them, they're fun. All those things open up new horizons. It's never too late to take up handball, tennis, or ice skating. Age doesn't preclude it until you get to where your bones are too brittle and you can't stand up. There will be plenty of time if you hang around long enough. You're apt to have later years when it's just out of the question. So while you are physically able, try snorkeling, try surfboarding. Try all these things that look to you like nonsense or dangerous. Instead of thinking it would be fun to try horseback riding, get on a horse. You may find that you like it. Your muscles may be sore so you have to rub them down, and then you may decide it's more trouble than it's worth. But that's okay too.

As you get older, there shouldn't be anything you won't try. You don't have to like it, but at least you can say, "I gave it a try and I think it's ridiculous." I tried playing golf. My father loved it. I tried for two summers, but for every shot I hit that made me feel good, I hit twenty that made me furious. I just cannot cope with the damn sport. Everybody else finds joy in it. At least I can say, "I can't do it." I don't have to say, "Oh, I think that's foolish." I don't think it's foolish, I just know I can't do it very well. It's no fun for me.

If you're down at the shore where there are surfboards for rent, try one. I don't care if you're sixty or thirty and you're afraid of looking foolish in front of your kids. Say

to them, "Come on, you can watch Daddy fall down."
You add a whole new dimension to your life, and your
friends will look at you astonished and say, "You do that!"
You just tell them, "You can do it too." It's the trying.
You get out of the habit.

The payoff is that you open up whole new avenues that
are fun. You open up a new dimension to your life. It is
fun to do something wholly new and different. It recharges
the batteries. It exposes you to a whole new interest in
life. Suddenly you start reading about it and you see it on
TV. You can see things on cable TV you never contemplated. Lawn bowls is the damnedest thing. I say, "Gee,
let's try it." "Let's try it" adds much more to your happiness than saying, "I don't know how."

It's a misinterpretation of life to live it in preparation
for the next one, if there is one. To subordinate the one
you've got to an indefinite next round is foolish. It's a
waste of this life not to live this life. Essentially every
religion takes the Golden Rule as its guide, and that's absolutely essential for this life. It's not a matter of being
punished if you're not good in this life. Very often those
things even out on this planet. What's next is anybody's
guess.

13   A Good Heart

Our bodies are the most complex pieces of machinery that exist. Our minds are the most remarkable computers that will ever be created. Our emotions are so deep and varied that we are capable of experiencing ecstasy, joy, grief, despair, love, and hate. We are all alike, yet each of us is unique. Each of us is an irrepeatable mystery. However, we are our own harshest critics. We have been conditioned to focus on what is wrong with us, what is lacking in us, our faults, our mistakes, and our failures, rather than to appreciate how special we are. We see only our shortcomings and are blind to our strengths. The beauty and wonder of life can be seen not only in the ocean, the mountains, and the flowers, but in the twinkle of an eye of a human being. *Does being me bring me happiness?*

Father Peter Fraile believes, "As humans, we're stuck with our smallness, but we should admire our greatness. Within human beings I see the amazing beauty of life."

The Reverend Peter A. Fraile, S.J., is the founder and executive director of the Divine and Human Institute. He holds master's degrees in theology, philosophy, psychology, and business management, was a missionary in China, and presently conducts the Divine and Human seminars in South Africa, South America, and Europe, as well as in the United States at the St. Francis-St. George Hospital, Cincinnati, Ohio.

The Reverend Peter A. Fraile, S.J.

I used to go to a jail in the Philippines twice a week, and I would bring cigarettes for the inmates. I found in the jail an inmate who was different. I tried to communicate with him but I couldn't. I gave him cigarettes as I did to everyone else. He never said anything, never thanked me, never gave any sign of appreciation at all. That went on for six months, and I challenged myself to find out what was inside that man. I couldn't get at it. One day, after six months, I came into the jail, and when I gave him two cigarettes, he smiled. That day I went home so happy because I saw a breakthrough. I had thought he was not human, but he was.

The next time I went to the jail he was standing in the narrow doorway that led to the cells. I had to pass through that door, but I couldn't because of him. I dared to touch him on the shoulder, and as I touched him I said, "How is good Julian today?" I'll never forget his reaction. He jumped back in a gesture of surprise and said, "Father, I'm no good." Those were the first words he addressed to me. I didn't know what to say, but I was happy because we were talking. To keep up the conversation I said, "What do you mean, Julian?" He opened up and began to speak. He said, "I'm a criminal. I have a sentence of twenty years. I probably will spend all my life in jail. I have no friends. My family doesn't want to visit me or to know anything about me. I have no lawyer, and I'm doomed."

Julian was a very strong man and all the inmates were afraid of him. He had a brutal appearance, with tattoos all over his body. I said, "I don't think you want to hurt me." Again he showed amazement. He looked at me and said, "No way will I hurt you, and while I am here in this jail, nobody's going to hurt you." Naturally that made me feel good, but I reacted in a way that surprised me afterward. Without realizing what I was saying, I pointed to him with my finger and said, "Therefore, Julian, at least toward me, you have a good heart." At that moment Julian opened his big eyes in awe. He was speechless. Because of his reaction I didn't know what to do. I was speechless too. So I turned around and I left him.

After that day something began to happen. He knew which days I came to the jail. There was a small window with four bars and I would notice a head looking out from behind those bars. As I arrived at the jail, Julian would be at the gates every time. The guards would open the gates for me, and Julian, without saying anything, would follow me throughout the jail. Julian had decided that he was not going to let anybody hurt me, so he became my bodyguard. After three or four weeks the guards asked me, "What did you do to Julian?" I said, "Nothing." Julian began to smile, and he had never smiled before. He began to talk with the other inmates, and as the weeks went by, not only was he my bodyguard, but he became my helper. He initiated conversations and asked me questions.

The culmination of this came a few months later. We had a breakfast for the inmates of the jail. I set up a table with sandwiches. I had brought six cases of Coke but forgotten a bottle opener. Julian was around me, helping. He asked, "What are you looking for?" I said, "Julian, I am looking for a bottle opener. I forgot to bring one. How in the world are we going to open these bottles?" He said, "Don't worry, Father. Look." He took a bottle in his teeth and he opened it. I said, "Julian, we have six cases." "Don't worry," he said, and he took one bottle in each hand and opened the bottles on all six cases with his teeth. It was easy for him. He was joyful. He was happy he could help.

I never understood the change in Julian's life until almost ten years later. What had happened with Julian was that for the first time in his life someone he respected had looked at him and said, "Julian, you have a good heart." Julian looked inside himself and saw that he really had a good heart. Before that, he would look inside himself and see that he was a criminal, that he was full of anger, that he had no friends, that his family didn't want to know anything about him, that he was doomed to be in jail the rest of his life. That day, he looked inside and in between all of the other stuff, which was real, Julian saw the good heart, and he became a goodhearted person.

The face of a criminal changed into the face of a helper, a protector, a friend, a normal person. It took just one moment, a lucky moment, for Julian to experience it, to see it, and to believe in it. His life changed completely. Did I put the good heart into Julian? No, it was already there, but it was buried by the painful and sad experiences of life. He was buried underneath all that trash. Someone, by luck, cut through it and pointed out that the good heart had always been there. The good feelings had always been there. But they didn't have an opportunity to come out because nobody was asking for them, nobody was seeing them, nobody was pointing them out. Julian never let go of the new image that he got of himself, and that changed his life. Looking inside himself he could see his good heart. He had a friend. He felt happy and that life was worthwhile. Everybody has a good heart, and it is bigger than people think it is. The art is to discover it and to share it.

Life in small letters leads us to LIFE in capital letters. Once we are in life we can't get out of it. Life is in us, and we are in life. We don't stop to enjoy it because we are afraid of it. The writer Tony De Mello tells a story of a little fish who is a dreamer. He wants to find out everything about life, so he begins to swim. He leaves his family of fish and begins to surge for the great life, for the ocean. He swims and swims, but he cannot find the ocean. He goes north and he goes south and he goes east and he goes west and he doesn't find the ocean. Finally he comes across a huge old fish who is just relaxing. The little fish approaches the big fish and says, "Old fish, wise fish, may I ask you a question?" The old fish says, "Yes." The little fish then says, "I'm sure you have traveled a lot in your life because you have lived many years and you have a lot of experience. Can you tell me how I can get to the ocean?" The big fish says peacefully, "You are in the ocean." And the little fish says, "But this is only water."

That is what happens to us. We are searching for life. We are searching for meaning. We are searching for God.

We are searching for whatever we can hope for, and we have it inside. We say, "But this is just life." It's a great life. The LIFE in capital letters. It's really in us and we are in it. If we'd just allow ourselves to perceive the beauty of it and the greatness of being in it and of being alive, that perspective would change us and we wouldn't need to fight life or fear it so much.

I received a letter from a sixteen-year-old girl who, in a beautiful, clear, literary style, told me about a problem she was having with a classmate: another girl was stealing her friend. She wrote about the jealousy, the anger, the frustration, and how she dealt with it. She went on to say that even though she now dislikes her, the friend is still as lovable and valuable as she is herself. When she was about to end the letter she said, "I was going to close off, but something hit me right now like a ton of bricks. I have seen my father's library, and he has many books that I want to read. I have lots of time ahead of me to read and to learn, but I just realized one thing. No matter how much I learn, no matter how much I experience, no matter how much I write, if I don't love, I don't know anything." She was telling me that love is the center of the meaning of life. It is not love in a selfish or emotional way or just a transaction of affection. It's love in the mystical way of recognizing and discovering the powerful unity and oneness that exists among all of us. If we reduce life to our physical experiences, it would not be enough to want to continue being here. If we take from people the invisible factors of their lives, they have no motivation, no hope, no desires. Their world would crumble. What keeps the whole thing together is the secret force of love.

We reduce life to buying and selling, to fear, to anxieties, to news, to cruises or vacations, but we cannot deny the spiritual forces of life. We know for sure that the reservoir is there. It is a reservoir of love, of compassion, of union, and of understanding. People like to love better than hate. We should let the goodness out instead of letting out defensiveness, rejection, fear, anxiety, using one another, stepping on one another, back stabbing.

We make life unbearable for ourselves because we take

ourselves at such a shallow level. It's more enjoyable to live with the positive realities, which we all have, than to live with the negative realities, which we affirm as being the only ones we have. That is wrong, that is an illusion, that is lack of vision. Through cultural conditioning, through training, through the need to survive, we build walls around ourselves to protect ourselves. Our learning process is very much conditioned to protect, to defend, and to distrust. If people would apply themselves to the task of discovering all the goodness that is in them, they would discover it because it's there. Many people fear that if they open up they will not discover any good, because what they have experienced of themselves is all bad.

The good qualities are there in all of us, and the deepest is love, or belonging. We are aware of belonging to a friend, belonging to a family, belonging to a company, belonging to a country, belonging to an age. Those are outside belongings. Underneath that, many people don't realize that they belong to mankind, they belong to spiritual forces, they belong to their God.

A common quality in everybody is hope. As with love, unfortunately, we reduce hope to little things. Many people hope for a new car, a new house, a new job, or a new vacation. Those are small hopes. Beneath them everybody hopes to be, everybody hopes for a union with the whole world, with the cosmos, with the universe. Everybody hopes for life eternal. Everybody hopes to be recognized and valued and admired. Everybody hopes, in one form or another, for a union with God.

I believe in a God who is a source of life. Without that source I would not be here. I'm not going to try to prove my belief in God because there is no need of proof. I just believe it and I experience it. The new perception of God in the future, I suspect, isn't going to be God up there or on the right hand or the left hand; it's going to be to realize that God is in us and we are in him. People won't have any need to reject God as an opposite, or as someone who is judging them, or controlling them, or making demands on them. It's the very essence of my being. The moment that I can perceive my oneness with my God, then I cannot help but feel a totally new joy and a new life. My life will become tremendously hopeful. I will have nothing to lose anymore. I will have achieved the goal of being. I will have gotten there, and the anxiety of not getting there or getting lost disappears. The fear of dying disappears. The courage to give, to love, to share arrives, and it's a whole new set of emotions, a new set of visions, and a new set of joys.

Common in everybody is a desire for respect, which is the recognition of value and of being. At the same time, even if many don't realize it, they desire to respect others. Living in a climate of respecting and being respected is a climate that makes existence sacred and comfortable. All people want to appreciate and be appreciated. They admire something beautiful, because inside themselves they all have beauty. When they see something beautiful outside, that is an echo of their own beauty. Everybody desires joy. The joyfulness in life is reduced sometimes to silly things. Joy is a manifestation of harmony. If I belong to a group, if I click with my job, it is called success. I sense a harmony with a team of people with whom I work, and that harmony makes me feel joyful.

Every person has a potential for love, hope, and faith. Every person has a tremendous potential to perceive the spiritual because the spiritual is in every person. The spiritual inside everyone is God. It's mystical, it's mysterious, it's manifested through goodness, it's manifested through attitudes, it's manifested through respect, through sacredness, through reverence, through beauty. It's a mystery which is very real and it's inside every person.

People don't take time to look at the wonder of themselves. They are scared to death of putting themselves in a situation where other people would wonder at them and want to get to know them and want to love them. Underneath they fear that if they open up and look at themselves they will see only bad things, because that is what they see in themselves. We're afraid of being loved. We think if we let people love us we are obliged to respond or reciprocate in some way and we're scared to death of not having anything to give back. We suspect that we have those virtues and those potentials. We know that we have a good heart, but the fear of letting others see it is in all of us.

Happiness is having the courage to share our inner selves. That would mean losing the fear of being and recognizing that probably all we ever wanted is already within us. It means letting people see it and sharing that with others. The movement of sharing is the opposite of the movement of selfishness. The selfish person is always unhappy, is always unsatisfied, is always unfulfilled. A generous person who shares and gives what he or she has inside to others is always happy, is always fulfilled. This is a paradox because the illusion is that when we get is when we are fulfilled. The reality is, when we give is when we're fulfilled. The problem is that we don't know what we have and therefore we don't know what to give. If we can discover the great potential of beauty and goodness that we have inside and allow ourselves to give it to others, that would be the essential element of happiness, of joy. There's nothing more enjoyable than sharing something with a friend. If you find the joy of being, your spiritual dimension, your goodness, your compassion, your beauty, your honesty, your truth, your God within yourself, the great joy is to call a friend and say, "I found it; I want to share it with you." It is sharing of values which are so beautiful and so deep that not even a million dollars can buy them.

As an act of compassion, sharing yourself with a friend who is in pain or sharing your joy with a friend is more valuable than sharing a meal or sharing a thousand dollars. What people want is to share themselves. These things that we have inside ourselves are priceless. We can share our listening ability, our compassion, our love, a smile. We look at attention getting or impressing other people as being happiness, but the beautiful example of people who fall in love is that they want to give themselves to another person. Saying "I want to *have* the other person" is not love; it is selfishness.

When people find that they're valuable, when people find that they themselves are lovable, when they find that there's no reason to have so many fears, they become enthusiastic about it and want to discover the same things in others. The motivation is the search for the positives. Once you find the positives, the motivation is not necessary. It's a question of discovery. The moment a person begins to use that capacity to share and to give, that person is happy.

Several years ago, during Easter week, it was my turn to preach at Mass. Self giving as an attitude, as opposed to selfishness, was the theme of my talk. This is what I said.

Americans are great practical people and I love it. I'm going to invent a parable. Don't be afraid; it's just my imagination. Imagine I have a big basket. Everybody is used to collections, so don't be afraid of the huge basket. I put the basket in the middle of the church and I say to you, "Put your hands into your pockets and take out all the change and loose bills that you have and throw that money into the basket." We have five hundred people giving an average of ten dollars per person, so we have five thousand dollars. Good? No. That's nothing. If I am going to ask something from you today, if I am going to talk about sharing, I want something more. If my God, who is much greater than I, is going to ask for something, he will ask for more than ten dollars. Five thousand dollars for my God is nothing. So put your hands into your pockets again and take your wallets, your checkbooks, your purses, and throw them into the basket. What's there? One credit card per person with a credit limit of a thousand dollars. We have five hundred people and five hundred credit cards. We're now talking about half a million dollars. A good basket? I say that's nothing. If I'm going to ask you for something for my God, what does he care about five hundred thousand dollars? Nothing. Go home and bring back the title to your house, the title to your car, your stocks, your savings, your jewelry, all your valuables, and put them into the basket. We have one hundred families and one hundred thousand dollars per family, so we now have ten million dollars. Ten million dollars is nothing. If I'm going to ask you for something today, I want more.

Go back into your lives from the day you were born and collect all the love you received from your parents, from your friends, from your loved ones. Collect your smiles, your joys, your hopes, your dreams, the times you have been wrong and you have been forgiven, and the good feeling of belonging to a group, or being with a friend. Put all these things that you cannot buy with money into the basket. We have five hundred people with an average of twenty years per person. That is ten thousand years of love, understanding, of caring for a baby, of helping a friend, of having a party, of enjoying something unique, of seeing a sunset or the falling of the leaves or flowers growing in your garden. We now have ten thousand years of invisible, priceless things that you cannot buy with money in the basket. Now that you have put all that into the basket, you've already forgotten about the ten million dollars. Never mind, this is still very little. I'm going to ask for more.

Look ahead of you. Each one of you has an average of twenty years ahead, which is another ten thousand years. Collect in these years all the joy that you can give and receive, all the forgiveness and compassion that you can give and receive, all the love that you can enjoy and are going to make other people enjoy. Collect what you will give to your children and your parents and your grandparents. Collect the dreams, the hopes, the peacefulness, the light of your life, the inner joy of being and everything you cannot buy with money and put it into the basket. Even this is so little, I'm going to ask you for more.

Imagine that this basket here in the church is a fountain or a tub, and the basket or fountain has five hundred faucets and you turn them on. When you open them, out of each of those five hundred faucets flows joy, hope, understanding, humanness, appreciation, wonder, amazement, life, respect, union, and sacredness. Open the faucets and leave them open. Through each of them flows the stuff that you have in your hearts. All of you have it, but your faucets are closed. Open your faucets and leave them open. That is what I am asking you to do. That is what my God, who is your God, is asking of you today. Let us all open the faucets and let out the good stuff, which is already in our hearts. God put it there. Let it flow out.

Can you imagine what would happen? If we had that fountain in the middle of the church with five hundred faucets open and flowing with the stuff that we cannot buy in the supermarket, the four television stations would be here to cover it for the news. The radio stations would be here, and the newspaper reporters would be here. Tomorrow the headlines of the paper would say, ''There's a place where there's a fountain and it flows with what everybody's looking for.'' You'd see planes and buses and pilgrims coming from all over the world. People would come here from every place on earth to drink from the water that they have been looking for all their lives.

Do you have the power to open the faucet? Of course you have it. What you have inside, give to others—Love, Forgiveness, Compassion, Understanding, and the Life of Light. We have them inside. They were given to us. What right in the world do we have to keep them hidden? Open the faucets and let them out. That sharing would begin the greatest revolution in the world.

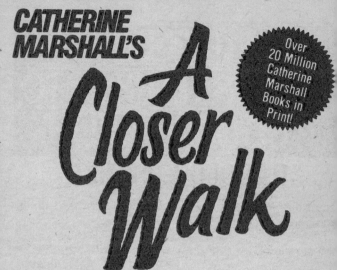